Brockworth
Community Project

Tutankhamun

THE ETERNAL SPLENDOR
OF THE BOY PHARAOH

T.G.H. JAMES

WHITE STAR PUBLISHERS

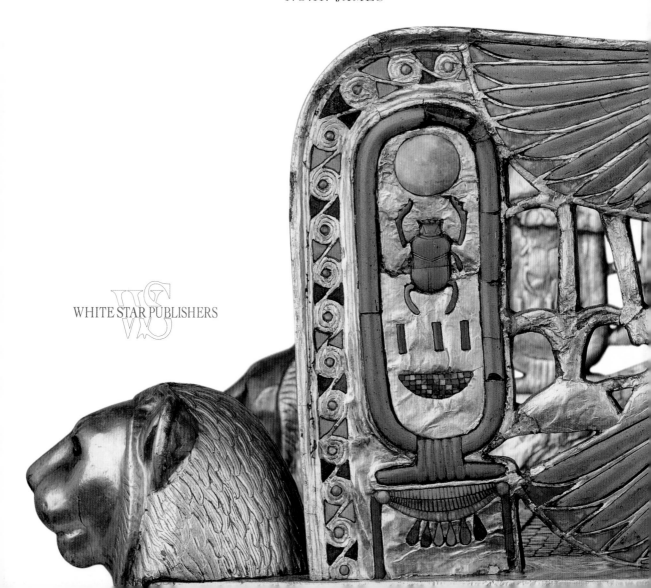

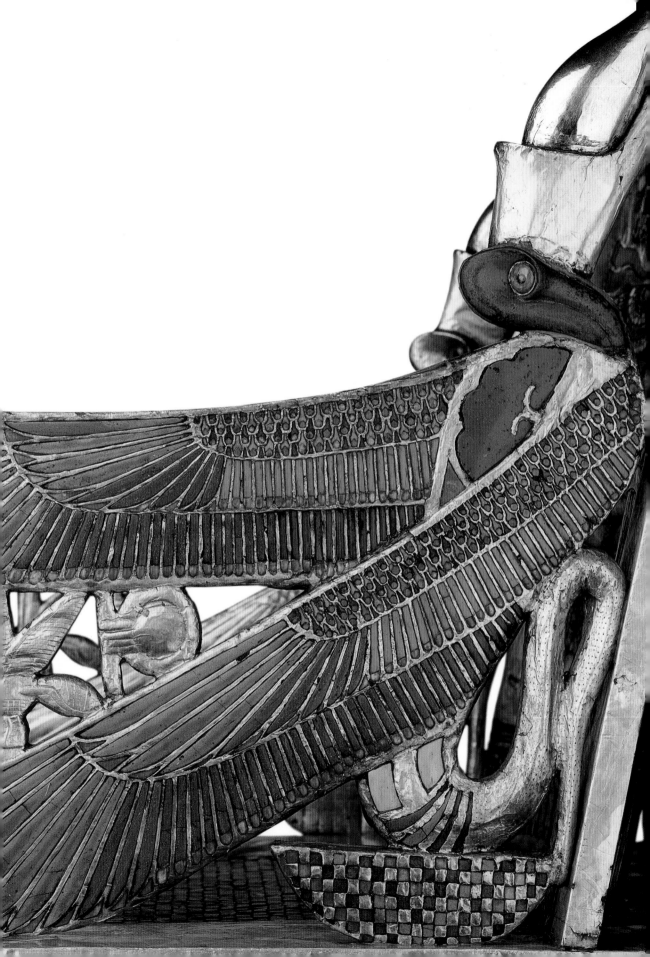

CONTENTS

TEXT BY
T.G.H. James

PHOTOGRAPHS BY
Araldo De Luca

DRAWINGS BY
Elisabetta Ferrero

EDITED BY
Valeria Manferto De Fabianis
Laura Accomazzo

GRAPHIC DESIGN
Patrizia Balocco Lovisetti

© 2000, 2007 White Star S.p.A.
Via Candido Sassone, 22/24
13100 Vercelli, Italy
www.whitestar.it

Revised Edition

ISBN 978-88-544-0354-3

Reprints:
1 2 3 4 5 6   11 10 09 08 07

Colour separation Fotomec, Turin
Printed in China

1 *Necklace with falcon pendant and heart-shaped
counterpoise from the mummy of Tutankhamun.*

2–3 *Detail of the side panel of the Golden Throne
with winged uraeus protecting the royal name.*

4–5 *Scene from the Golden Shrine. Tutankhamun
shoots wild fowl and Ankhesenamun hands him
his next arrow.*

6–7 *Pectoral found in the Anubis shrine in the Treasury,
showing the two goddesses Nephthys and Isis kneeling
in support of a large scarab representing Khepri,
the sun-god at dawn.*

8–9 *The back of Tutankhamun's Golden Mask: the texts,
from the Book of the Dead, protect the mask.*

Preface

The superlatives applied to Howard Carter and the momentous discovery of the tomb of Tutankhamun, piled up and reiterated over the years since 1922, should have dulled the responses of most people. In fact, interest in the tomb is perhaps greater today than at any time since the early years of the discovery.

When the tomb was found in November 1922, the news broke with unexpected force on a world public which seemed to be only too ready to enjoy the thrill and drama of what was happening in distant Luxor. It was not as if there had been no archaeological discoveries of importance in the few years since the First World War; but nothing could compete with the tantalizing revelation of a tomb entrance, blocked and sealed with the promise of untold treasure beyond. Carter himself was not at all sanguine: he had received disappointments in the past, when expected success turned to naught.

Now to discover a new tomb in the Valley of the Kings was in itself a dramatic achievement; to discover one which was still furnished with a huge quantity of remarkable objects, and an intact coffin and burial, was almost too much to expect.

The representatives of the world press descended on Luxor like vultures on a dying prey. Every stage in the clearance of the tomb was watched with close attention; every day brought new insights into ancient Egyptian life and death.

10–11 Detail from the Golden Throne. The brilliance of the colored inlays heightens the impression of regal elegance.

12

The atmosphere, already heavily charged with the tension of discovery, was clouded by the inadequacy of the channels of information, controlled by the agreement made by the Earl of Carnarvon with The Times. And then, when the opening of the Burial Chamber, and the realization that an intact burial lay within, were followed by the tragic death of Lord Carnarvon, rumor and suspicion took over, and allowed those who find esoteric forces in all Egyptian things to indulge in a welter of fanciful imagination and fertile invention. And so it went on: the progress of the clearance was dogged by drama, tragedy, misunderstanding, and bad temper. Howard Carter was a hero, and he was fêted wherever he went; but he was also a sad, disillusioned man, whose success never quite brought him to the haven of content and happiness which he deserved.

In the last thirty years there has been a remarkable surge of interest in Tutankhamun. International exhibitions have brought selected treasures to the fascinated gaze of millions of people. The huge increase in tourism to Egypt has allowed waves of visitors to swamp the Valley of the Kings, to gaze in wonder at the coffin in the young king's tiny tomb; and in Cairo to view the overwhelming riches in the Egyptian Museum. Books have proliferated; Carter has been honored and vilified; the treasures have been lauded, and occasionally scorned. In this volume, a wider range of material than usual is offered for close examination in a series of outstanding photographs.

12–13 The head of Queen Ankhesenamun from the Golden Throne – Amarna art survives in the new reign.

14–15 Part of a pectoral with the prenomen of Tutankhamun incorporating a winged scarab.

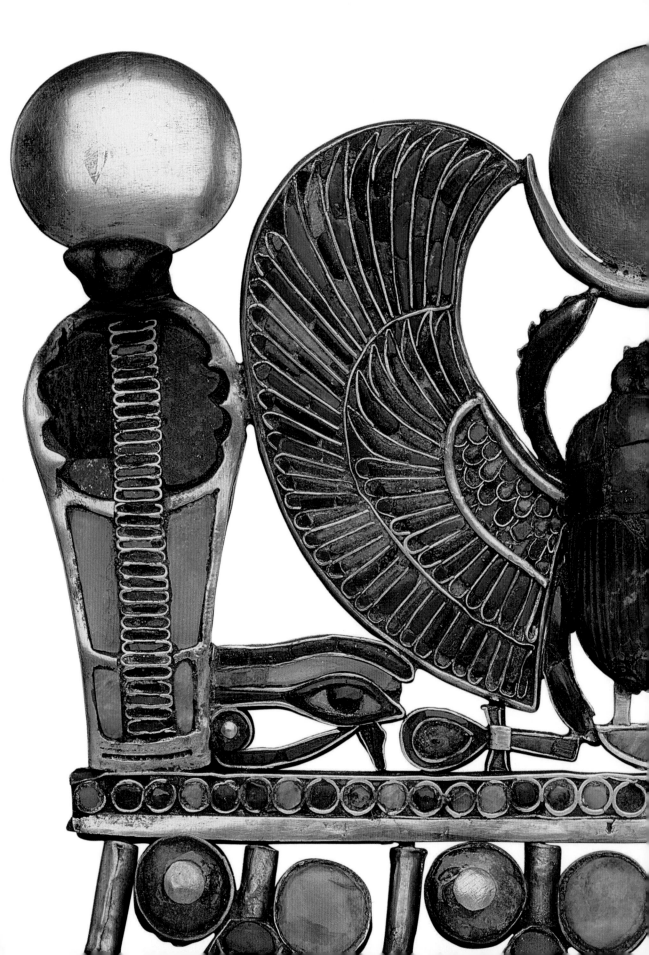

Tutankhamun and His Times

THE HISTORICAL BACKGROUND

When the Earl of Carnarvon and Howard Carter entered the Antechamber of Tutankhamun's tomb on November 27, 1922, they found themselves standing in what looked like a rather superior furniture store, abandoned for three thousand years. It was both thrilling and worrying: as Carter later wrote, 'everywhere the glint of gold'. But what problems faced them! In due course, reinforced with help from specialists loaned by the Metropolitan Museum and the Egyptian Government, Carter set about untangling the jumble of objects which were placed and stacked topsy-turvy in that confined space. Among the pieces which caught his eye on first inspection was the chair standing beneath the great couch with hippopotamus heads. Now often called the Golden Throne, it impressed the excavators with its dazzling splendor and sheer beauty. The panel forming the back of this chair was its most striking part. Carter claimed that it 'was the chief glory of the throne and I have no hesitation in claiming for it that it is the most beautiful thing that has yet been found in Egypt'. What concerns us here, however, is one element in the decoration of the panel which would certainly have been spotted by Carter at first sight. It is the sun disk at the top of the scene, sending down its life-giving rays on the seated king and his wife. Although Carter may not have taken much scholarly interest in the developing historical debate about the Amarna Period and the rise and fall of the deity, the Aten (or Aton), he can scarcely have failed to make a connection with what he had seen in his early days in Egypt.

When he was excavating with Flinders Petrie in the spring of 1892 he would have met this motive of the Aten during the excursions he made with Petrie, visiting the rock-cut inscriptions set up by the king, Akhenaten, to mark the sacred area of his new city. He would remember his drawing of that scene in the tomb of Akhenaten which was used by Petrie to illustrate his report in the *Daily Graphic*; it too contained the Aten motif. He would also recall the short time he spent with Percy Newberry in January 1893 when they began an abortive campaign to copy the scenes and inscriptions in the northern group of private tombs at El-Amarna. The life-giving rays of the Aten were ubiquitous, and Carter drew several scenes containing them before work in the tombs was brought to a halt. Carter retained an affection for the site, although he did not, it seems, revisit it until March 1918, after his first short season in the Valley of the Kings. At that time Carnarvon was actively looking for a second site at which to work. Carter pressed the case for El-Amarna very strongly: 'For you it is an ideal site, convenient in every way... with a dahabiyeh you would never be more than a mile from the scene of operations, beautiful desert, light and clean digging and one need hardly say with luck the chance of beautiful things'. In the years before the First World War, the Germans had worked there, and found much important sculpture, including the famous head of Nefertiti.

Howard Carter, therefore, was well aware of the significance of that sun disk when he saw it on the back-panel of the Golden Throne, but he may have been puzzled at finding such a potent symbol of recent heresy on such a striking object in the tomb of the king in whose reign normality in Egypt's religious affairs had been re-established. The taint of Atenism was undoubtedly difficult for the Egyptian monarchy to eliminate at this point and in due course it would lead to the removal of Akhenaten, Smenkhkare, Tutankhamun and his successor Ay from the official record of dynastic succession. Only with King Horemheb could the legitimate sequence recommence; he at least seemed to have a paternity unblemished by heresy, although he had served in high office under Tutankhamun. But all these problems and consequences arose from what had developed in the shining reign of Amenophis III.

To understand, in so far as is possible, it is necessary to go back to that glorious time when Egypt's power abroad was at its height, and the splendor of its culture at home was evident in most aspects of life, and especially in the arts of sculpture, relief, painting, in the small crafts of ceramics, metalwork, glass-making, and in the production of small, intimate items which enhanced the private lives of those who could afford them.

16–17 *The face of Tutankhamun's Golden Mask: a portrait by a master artist in beaten gold.*

18 *One of the two lion heads placed on either side of the seat of the Golden Throne; they represent the east and west horizons over which they stand guard.*

19 *A scene of intimacy between Tutankhamun and Ankhesenamun on the back of the Golden Throne. The queen anoints the king with perfumed ointment from a stemmed vessel.*

It was the first half of the fourteenth century BC. After the successful military campaigns of the earlier kings of the Eighteenth Dynasty, in Asia and Nubia, a state of equilibrium had been established in the eastern part of the Egyptian empire. It was not an empire of domination by military might, of the kind so often found subsequently in the ancient world. The Egyptian king maintained his influence by threat of intervention and by the lavish use of subsidies paid to the small rulers whose territories made up the empire. Powerful neighbors to the east were equally restrained from attacking by means of dynastic alliances and again by the dispensation of valuable gifts – in effect subsidies – from the Egyptian king. The parade of power and wealth by Egypt encouraged the expectations of subordinate powers, and also the more powerful neighbors. The King of Mitanni, writing to Amenophis III, expressed what was no doubt the common view in saying that 'gold was like dust in my brother's land'.

The possession of empire affected Egypt in many ways, and among those that are less easy to quantify were those involving religion. Egyptian religion, diverse in its variety of deities and local traditions, was not easy to export to other countries. In this respect the Egyptians were not a proselytizing people. There was, however, always the possibility for additional traditions from elsewhere to be imported and grafted directly or by partial assimilation into the body of Egyptian religious ideas. It seems likely that a need developed which required the acceptance of a conception of divinity of more universal application. The course of change led, almost imperceptibly, to the evolution of parts of the traditional Egyptian cult of the sun into a breakaway sub-cult in which the disk of the sun itself, the Aten (the Egyptian word for sun disk) became the principal, even the sole, object of worship.

The signs of this kind of sun worship can be traced back to at least the reign of Tuthmosis IV (c. 1400–1390 BC); but its growth became more marked in the reign of Amenophis III (c. 1390–1352 BC), when some important officials included Aten references in hymns which glorified the sun as the creator and sustainer of life. It is possible that this development may have been promoted by the king's chief wife, Queen Tiye, who exercised unusual influence in many areas of life. Amenophis III, who may have suffered long periods of ill-health, seemed content to allow this apparent transfer of power, while he restricted his activities to the domestic sphere. It has often been suggested that he succumbed to luxury and soft living – *la dolce vita* – but it is not easy to prove that this was the case.

20 *Portrait-head of King Amenophis III wearing the blue crown. It is made of painted plaster, and was found in the great deposit of sculpture in the Karnak temple.*

21 *Head of Queen Tiye, found in Sinai. In spite of the very small scale, the sculptor has succeeded in conveying the strong character of this determined lady.*

What is certain, however, is that his son and successor, also called Amenophis, readily embraced the growing cult of the Aten, and began its promotion, perhaps even before he became king. His mother, Queen Tiye, who continued to be a powerful political influence after his accession to the throne, may have been an encouraging agent in the move towards Atenism. An even greater supporter was the new king's wife, Nefertiti. Some historians believe that Amenophis III elevated his son to be a co-regent with himself some years before his death, but the evidence is mostly circumstantial. It must be admitted that historical evidence for the whole of the so-called Amarna Period is often inexplicit. Nevertheless, the more acceptable view is that the son became king after the death of his father in about 1352 BC. He retained the name Amenophis 'Amun is content' for the first few years of his reign, and then changed it to Akhenaten 'who is beneficial to the Aten'. In Thebes his father had built on a grand scale in honor of the great imperial god Amon-Re, and it was in Thebes that Amenophis IV, supported by his wife Nefertiti, began his campaign to establish the primacy of the Aten cult. Here he built an entirely new and original temple in honor of the Aten very close to the great temple of Amon-Re at Karnak. In design it was quite unlike the normal Egyptian temple, and in its decoration, in its reliefs and sculptures, it departed from what was conventional both in style and in content. It was a very provocative act, and it brought the royal family into direct opposition with the traditional priestly colleges, and also the established bureaucracy, which itself was closely integrated into the religious establishment.

It is not difficult to imagine the state of tension which built up in Thebes after this revolutionary turn of events. There could be no peaceful co-existence between the old and the new religious regimes. The formal suppression of the ancient cults followed, but no act of this kind could destroy old beliefs and allegiances; the situation in the capital must have become unbearable for both sides.

22 *The exaggerated facial features of this colossus shows Akhenaten in the style of his early reign, almost in caricature but strikingly dramatic. From Karnak.*

23 *Sculptor's trial or model showing Akhenaten, Nefertiti and two daughters making floral offerings to the Aten. From the royal tomb at El-Amarna.*

As far as the king was concerned, nothing but a complete break with the past, religiously, politically and territorially, would do. His own beliefs in the Aten, the divine and sole creator of the universe, had developed in these early years, and, as he claimed himself, the full practice of life under the Aten would have to be continued in a place unsullied by the old religions. And so, in his sixth year, having changed his name to Akhenaten, he moved his capital from Thebes to a place in Middle Egypt, about 350 kilometres to the north. Here the new life could be practiced, purged of all past associations. The chosen place was a virgin plain set in a great bay of rocky hills on the east bank of the Nile. Here the sun daily could be observed to rise in a dip in the hills. It was to be called Akhetaten, 'horizon of the Aten'.

The precinct of the Aten, the area delimited as the domain of the god, was marked by a series of boundary stelae – inscriptions setting out the limits of Akhetaten, and establishing the principles by which life would be lived there by the royal family, and consequently by those who chose to follow the king to the new city. The laying out of Akhetaten was one of the earliest pieces of conscious town-planning in the ancient world. The great Aten temple was the focal point; it was quite unlike the traditional Egyptian temple, an open structure with many altars for offerings to the god.

There were palaces, processional ways, huge administrative buildings, areas given over for fine villas for the high officials. There were districts for servicing the city with food and with industrial products such as pottery and glass. Outlying satellite villages housed workmen who, living apart from the main city and undoubtedly unfamiliar with the nature and rituals of the new religion, practiced their own personal cults in much the way that Egyptians in lowly levels of society had always done.

In Akhetaten the devotees of Atenism could follow the new life without being constantly aware of the disapprobation of those whose traditions were being destroyed. Akhetaten became a kind of cocoon in which the king and his family could promote and serve the Aten, loyally supported by those who ran the new bureaucracy and serviced the city. Every aspect of life was dominated by the Aten, whose worship became, seemingly, the supreme, even the sole, purpose of existence. The great hymns which contain the essence of the new

You establish every man in his place, making their sustenance... tongues made different in speech... their complexions distinct, for you have differentiated country from country... You make the seasons to allow all that you have created to prosper...'

At the end, Akhenaten's own position in the scheme of things is established: 'There is no one else who knows you except your son, Neferkheperure-Waenre [Akhenaten's prenomen]. You have made him skilled in your ways and in your power.'

In the early years of the twentieth century the publication of significant texts, like that of the great hymn, led scholars to study the nature of the Aten revolution. Historians like James Henry Breasted were so impressed by the Atenist hymns and their similarities to some of the Biblical psalms that they not only proclaimed the monotheistic nature of Atenism, but even saw in it the germs of Christianity. Modern Egyptologists are inclined to make more modest claims. It is

theology, and usually considered to be the compositions of Akhenaten himself, provide the evidence by which Atenism may be judged. The greatest of these hymns is found in the unused Amarna tomb of Ay, 'master of all the king's horses', who later succeeded Tutankhamun for a few years. Here is the flavor of Atenism:

'You arise beautiful in the horizon of heaven, O living Aten initiator of life when you shine forth in the eastern horizon, filling every land with your beauty... The earth grows bright when you have arisen in the horizon... The whole land performs its work. All cattle are content in their meadows. Trees and pastures flourish... All animals gambol on their feet... The one who makes men's fluid grow in women.... bringing to life the son in the body of his mother.... How various are your works!... Sole god, like whom there is none other...

now generally accepted that Atenism was monotheistic, perhaps the first religion with a single nature to its deity; but to consider it in any way as a precursor of Christianity presses the evidence beyond possibility. Verbal similarities are very seductive, but establish very little. If the content of the Amarna hymns is examined it can be shown that the phraseology of the praise to the Aten, and the claims made on its behalf, can be found in earlier hymns addressed to other Egyptian gods, especially the sun-god Re. What is special at Amarna is the exclusive focus of worship, and the emphasis placed on Akhenaten as the conduit for the delivery of the divine power of the Aten to the Egyptian people. Atenism was in effect wholly identified with Akhenaten and his family; the impression gained is that the new creed was tailor-made for them.

The rest of the dwellers at Akhetaten and elsewhere in Egypt could participate only through Akhenaten. Atenism placed almost all its emphasis on worship, and not on morality in the Judaeo-Christian sense. You were to order your life in accordance with the Egyptian principle of *ma'et*. In Amarna terms this meant living by order, by strict balance, by conformity with the proper regularity of life.

It was a kind of reinterpretation of the idea of truth embodied in the goddess named Ma'et, who played an important part in the ordering of conventional Egyptian life, and in the idea of judgement in the after-life.

A new and unusual feature of Atenism and life at Akhetaten was the emphasis placed on the inner circle of the royal family, on Akhenaten, his wife Nefertiti, and the six daughters of their marriage. In almost every scene in which the king is shown,

he is accompanied by Nefertiti, and often by a selection of children. Many surviving scenes represent the king and queen in intimate, affectionate relations, usually with daughters sitting on laps, climbing over them, being held up for embrace, standing beside them. The impression is given that the family was unusually close-knit, and more loving than was common for the period; it undoubtedly formed part of Amarna propaganda that this aspect of royal family life at Akhetaten should be emphasized.

In all probability it was in the wider circle of the extended royal family that Tutankhamun was brought up. He was at first named Tutankhaten, 'living image of the Aten', this name, with such a positive reference to the Aten, indicates that he must have been fairly closely connected with the principal royal family of Akhenaten and Nefertiti. But his parentage has never been convincingly established.

26 *Family life at El-Amarna. Akhenaten and Nefertiti lounge casually on cushioned stools entertaining three of their daughters, all irradiated by the Aten.*

27 *Unfinished statuette from El-Amarna showing Akhenaten kissing someone on his lap – a daughter or Nefertiti or his secondary wife Kiya, possibly Tutankhamun's mother.*

There is only one reference to him from the time of the reign of Akhenaten: on a block from one of the destroyed buildings of Akhetaten he is described as 'king's son of his body'. Such a statement establishes royal parentage, but it does not make his mother Nefertiti. It is very likely that Tutankhamun was fathered by Akhenaten, but by a secondary wife. The probable candidate is Kiya, the very existence of whom became known only in fairly recent years. She is referred to as 'the greatly beloved wife of the King of Upper and Lower Egypt... beauteous child of the living Aten who will live for ever and ever'. It is possible that some of Kiya's funerary equipment was included among the confused collection of Amarna material found in tomb 55 in the Valley of the Kings, which had been discovered by Theodore Davis in 1907; it lay not very far from the tomb of Tutankhamun. It is unlikely that the young king's parentage will ever be determined with certainty unless good new textual evidence is found. Even scientific evidence at present can do little more than confirm a family relationship.

Tutankhaten therefore will have spent his early years in the royal harem at Akhetaten, brought up, presumably, in a culture dominated by the cult of the Aten. He would have had little reasonable expectancy of becoming king; but he may have been seen by some ambitious officials, and even his mother, as having good prospects. In these early years he could have absorbed much of the grace and color of the palace environment in which he lived. In its prime, which lasted for such a short time, Akhetaten was undoubtedly a place of vibrant beauty. The pitiful remnants of the city, which had been utterly devastated after the collapse of Atenism, have been painstakenly retrieved by excavation over the last century, and they show how strikingly the palaces and villas were enlivened with wall decorations in which a new, naturalistic style of painting conveyed much greater freedom and vivacity than in preceding

panel which carries a scene wholly in the tradition of Akhenaten's reign. The intimacy suggested in the queen's approach to the king is apparent; the whole is dominated by the Aten, its descending rays ending in little hands, some of which hold the *ankh*, the hieroglyph for 'life'.

It might be thought that life in Akhetaten was idyllic; that, no doubt, was what Akhenaten hoped to achieve. Unfortunately, much as he might have wished it, it was impossible for him, King of Upper and Lower Egypt, to shut himself away from the business of state, or from the problems arising in the Egyptian vassal states in Asia Minor. There is little evidence from the time of how the greater part of Egypt fared during the Amarna years, but it is probable that a fairly tight control was exercised. Some indication of the efficiency of this control is provided by the way in which, at a late stage in the reign, royal agents scoured the

times. The standards of craftsmanship and perfection of design which characterized the art of the reign of Amenophis III were still in evidence, but now distinguished by a degree of free expression quite alien to conventional Egyptian art. Innovations were introduced in the early years of Akhenaten's reign, but much of what was then produced had a gauche, unfinished, quality to it. But as the reign advanced, and after the move to Akhetaten, artists came to terms with the changes in style and convention and, still employing the skills they had acquired in their years of apprenticeship under the old regime, began to produce works of surpassing beauty, especially in the field of sculpture. The best of what was new in the Amarna style was not jettisoned when Akhetaten was abandoned, and many of the objects found in the tomb of Tutankhamun incorporate the freedom of design and the intimacy in the representation of royalty which distinguished Amarna art. Again we may return to that Golden Throne and its back

country seeking out and destroying in visible inscriptions the names of the old gods, and particularly of Amun. Wherever that last hated name occurred it was cut out, even at the tops of obelisks, and the highest point of temples. Such a successful campaign needed remarkable organization, even though a flavor of desperation may be detected in it.

No such attention to detail was applied to foreign affairs. A surprising survival from the subsequent destruction of Akhetaten was part of the state archive consisting of clay tablets containing letters and dispatches from vassal rulers, written mostly in Accadian, the diplomatic *lingua franca* of the period. The subject rulers complain of their neglect by the Egyptian king, and they set out the problems they faced from powerful rulers like the Hittites in the north. The failure of Egypt to maintain its presence in Asia Minor also encouraged the warlike intentions of some of these vassals to renew old antagonisms with their small neighbors.

When Akhenaten died in about 1336 BC he did not leave a united country or a settled empire. A strong hand was needed to keep the ship of state steady, and to re-establish Egypt's authority in the East. An attempt to secure continuity for the Atenist revolution had been made by Akhenaten, who had a co-regent appointed in advance of his death. Paucity of evidence again prevents a certain identification of this co-regent. The name was Neferneferuaten; for long it has been thought that this person was a half-brother of Akhenaten called Smenkhkare; it has more recently been suggested that it was none other than Nefertiti herself, whose prenomen in cartouche was also Neferneferuaten. Nefertiti's disappearance from the Amarna scene towards the end of Akhenaten's reign has otherwise been ascribed either to her death, or to her disgrace for reasons unknown. The matter cannot satisfactorily be solved without further, more explicit evidence. What remains clear, however, is that during the short

independent reign of Neferneferuaten the first moves were made to re-establish relations with the old bureaucracy and the suppressed (but certainly not destroyed) priestly cadres at Thebes and elsewhere. It might be thought surprising if such moves towards reconciliation took place under a ruler who might have been Nefertiti; she had seemingly been so closely associated with Akhenaten in the development of Atenism. However, the interpretation of slim evidence from antiquity is always subject to uncertainty, and can lead to mistakes.

30 *Carving on the back of the trial of a head of Nefertiti. Here a person, even the queen, kneels with arms raised in adoration. From El-Amarna.*

31 *Quartzite face of Akhenaten from El-Amarna, made to fit into a relief of the king with inlays of different materials. The eyes and brows were separately inlaid.*

32–33 *Wonderfully stylish head of Nefertiti carved as a trial for a larger-scale relief for the temple at Karnak. She wears her characteristic crown with pendent uraei and flowing ribbons.*

34 *Greywacke statue of the god Khonsu shown as a mummiform figure wearing the side lock. Here the face has the unmistakeable youthful features of Tutankhamun. From the temple of Khonsu at Karnak.*

After a very short reign Neferneferuaten died in about 1336 BC, to be succeeded by Tutankhaten. He was very young, probably no more than eight years old; but he had royal parentage, and therefore the necessary legitimacy to succeed. His position was strengthened by an early marriage to Ankhesenpaaten, the third daughter of Akhenaten and Nefertiti. She had been born before the move from Thebes to Akhetaten in the sixth year of her father's reign, so it is unlikely that she was much less than fourteen or fifteen when she became the wife of the much younger Tutankhaten. She was, nevertheless, approaching an age when she could have given useful support to her juvenile husband. She would, much later, after his death, display an

independence of mind which was wholly in the character of the royal women of the Amarna Period. At the start of the reign, however, there had to be more mature support than that of a wife in her early teens. The position of regent was occupied by Ay, who had been closely associated with the royal family at least since its move to Akhetaten. Under Akhenaten he had been 'master of all the king's horses'; in the new reign he took the title 'god's father' and he is also credited with the secular title 'vizir' on one of the gold fragments found in the deposit which Theodore Davis thought was the tomb of Tutankhamun.

The usual shortage of evidence makes it difficult to chart with any detail the course of events which

followed the accession of Tutankhaten. Early in his reign, however, he and his wife, presumably on the advice of their advisers, changed their names to Tutankhamun and Ankhesenamun. With the Aten element replaced by Amun it would be easier to proceed politically to the reconciliation with the representatives of the old regime. There seems to have been a particular problem as far as Thebes was concerned. At Thebes, the old political center, the Atenist revolution had begun; at Thebes were the greatest temples in the land; Thebes was the city of Amun. At Thebes, no doubt, resentment against the heretic regime was strongest; the move to El-Amarna had certainly affected Thebes not only religiously, but also, and perhaps even more so, economically. Thebes, therefore, was not a promising place in which to establish the royal Residence and Court for the new reign. Consequently, in Tutankhamun's second year the move was made to Memphis in the north. This city had always been a place of major importance in Egypt; it had been so since it was founded as the first capital of the united land of Upper and Lower Egypt by King Menes at the beginning of the First Dynasty (c. 3100 BC). Memphis had remained an important commercial city, and during the Eighteenth Dynasty it had become the base of the Lower Egyptian vizir, and the center of a developing administrative and military bureaucracy. From Memphis it was easier to mount expeditions and control military operations in Asia Minor than from Thebes. Memphis was also the cult-center of the great god Ptah, one of the oldest and most influential of Egypt's deities; he seems to have avoided many of

the worst indignities suffered by other deities during the Amarna Period. Memphis was a very cosmopolitan city where new influences could be absorbed without causing resentment. It seems to have taken Atenism in its stride. A temple to the Aten was established there, and also at nearby Heliopolis, the great cult-center of the sun-god Re. The trauma of Thebes was absent from Memphis, and the latter was in most ways the obvious choice for the new royal Residence. Meanwhile, the brilliant city of Akhetaten was abandoned, and over the years its stones were pillaged for buildings elsewhere; its palaces, offices and villas were allowed to crumble; the temples of the hated Aten were laid waste. Blown sand covered the site and kept it hidden for three thousand years. Akhenaten was anathematized as the 'criminal of Akhetaten'.

In spite of the later blotting-out of the memory of the Amarna Pharaohs, something of what was accomplished in Tutankhamun's reign can be discovered. Any initiatives were of course not taken by the young king, but by his advisers. Above all, in seniority at least, was the regent Ay. Probably more important were powerful officials like the Treasurer, Maya, and, particularly, the General, Horemheb. Such men controlled policy and its execution, in the name of the king. Apart from the moves towards reconciliation there were more practical matters like the reconstruction of damaged sanctuaries. The most important evidence of what happened comes from one surviving inscription from Karnak. Its date is not known, and it has survived due to the fact that Horemheb, when he became king after the death of Ay, appropriated the text, inserting his own name wherever that of Tutankhamun occurred. Happily there are enough surviving traces of the young king's name to confirm that the inscription belongs to his reign.

The theme of this inscription is reconciliation. In the semi-circular lunette at the top of the stela Tutankhamun is shown before Amon-Re of Karnak and his divine consort Mut. The god bestows divine power on the king. The representations are carved in the fluid artistic style of the late Amarna Period. In the preamble to the main text the king's full titulary is given, followed by a long series of epithets in which, among other things, he is said to be beloved of Amon-Re, Lord of the Thrones of the Two Lands, of Atum of Heliopolis, of Re-Herakhty, of Ptah and of Thoth; here there is no religious discrimination. The text then goes on to state, 'When his Majesty arose as king, the temples of the gods and goddesses, from Elephantine [in the south] to the marshes of the Delta [in the north] had fallen into decay; their shrines fallen into desolation, overgrown with weeds; their sanctuaries as if they had never existed; their halls had become foot-paths'. In consequence, the king took counsel to see what could be done to please Amun and the other gods. Cult-statues of gold and precious stones were made, temples repaired and rebuilt, endowments of land and people were renewed, so that 'the gods and goddesses who are in this land are joyous in heart; the owners of shrines are glad; lands are in a state of jubilation and festivity; joyfulness exists throughout the country; a happy state has come about'.

35 Red quartzite colossal statue made for Tutankhamun's unfinished and abandoned funerary temple. It was later usurped by Ay and Horemheb and set up in their funerary temple at Medinet Habu.

36–37 *By a magical fiction Tutankhamun drives his chariot with prancing horses into the confused mass of his Nubian enemies. With bow and arrow and the help of his dogs and soldiers he smites 'this land of vile Cush'.*

36 bottom *On both ends of the painted box from which these details are taken Tutankhamun is shown as a destructive sphinx, wreaking havoc on behalf of Egypt. Here he tramples the Asiatic and the Nubian.*

was reasonably thought that these reliefs, like the colonnade itself, had been executed in the reign of Horemheb. His name could be read everywhere, and then, before the discovery of Tutankhamun's tomb, it could hardly have been conceived that such fine work could have been produced in the reign of a royal nonentity. Subsequently it has become increasingly clear, as a result of scholarly scrutiny of texts, that Horemheb freely appropriated from Tutankhamun, substituting his name for that of his young predecessor. This was not uncommon in ancient Egypt, but in the case of Horemheb and Tutankhamun its extent points very clearly to a conscious attempt by the former to eradicate the latter from the record.

Horemheb himself probably first achieved high office in the reign of Akhenaten, but he did not exercise great authority until Tutankhamun came to the throne. From the many titles, civil and military, which he held, and which are enumerated in the tomb he had constructed as a commoner at Saqqara, it is clear that he had a controlling hand in most spheres of government. He may have throughout his career been based at Memphis, enabling him to keep the regime at Akhetaten at arm's length; but under Tutankhamun he was Chief General, Deputy of the king, High Steward, Overseer of all the works of the king, Overseer of all divine offices. The tomb of Horemheb at Saqqara, high on the desert escarpment close to Memphis, is decorated with reliefs of the finest quality, very much in the style of the Luxor reliefs copied by Howard Carter, but

even outdoing them in the representation of individuals and in the grouping of figures. Craftsmen in the Memphite area had always excelled in the carving of fine relief in good quality limestone. Traditional Memphite style had, it seems, remained largely uninfluenced by the grossest mannerisms of early Amarna art, but it had assimilated the fluid grace of the later period, as is evident in the reliefs in the tombs of Horemheb and his contemporaries at Saqqara.

There is some evidence to suggest that small military operations were conducted in Asia Minor and Nubia during the young king's reign. Here can be detected the initiative of Horemheb, although he may not have supervised the campaigns personally. Much needed to be done to repair the condition of the Egyptian empire, but it

37 Tutankhamun was not alone in his campaigns. Here an Egyptian foot soldier stabs a Nubian. Note the difference between the Egyptian and Nubian shields, and the rare full-face depiction of one fallen enemy.

Positive evidence of work carried out at Thebes, the heartland of Amon-Re, can be seen in the temple of Luxor, one of the most beautiful of Egyptian temples, founded by Amenophis III. In the great hall containing a massive colonnade, Tutankhamun's agents arranged for a wonderful series of reliefs, possibly started under Amenophis III, to be completed; it was in celebration of the Feast of Opet in which the sacred marriage between Amon-Re and his consort Mut was solemnized annually. These wonderful sunk reliefs depict the processions by land and river of the divine image of Amon-Re from Karnak to Luxor. These were the reliefs which Howard Carter was commissioned to draw for the publication planned by Alan Gardiner, but sadly never completed. At the time – it was during the First World War – it

is unlikely that any large-scale expeditions could be mounted while the country of Egypt was recovering from the neglect and physical destruction of the reign of Akhenaten. While there is very little direct evidence to demonstrate the steps taken under Tutankhamun to return the country to a pre-Amarna state of affairs, confirmation that much was successfully achieved is provided by the apparently settled position of the country during the reigns of Horemheb and of his successors, the first kings of the Nineteenth Dynasty.

When Tutankhamun's tomb was discovered in 1922 there were at first some expectations that it might contain papyrus documents which would provide unique historical information about his reign, and perhaps even preceding reigns. The Earl of Carnarvon even wrote to Alan Gardiner immediately after the discovery to say that papyri had been seen. Disappointingly, the papyri turned out to be rolls of linen. The hope of finding historical papyri was probably quite misplaced. Such documentation would not normally form part of the funerary equipment. Texts for the deceased's future in the after-life were what was needed, whether on papyri, or on tomb walls, or, as in Tutankhamun's case, on shrines. So no further historical light was cast on the reign of this young king by the contents of the tomb. It is, however, interesting to contemplate the tomb itself, and to consider how the return to royal burials in the Valley of the Kings came about.

Amenophis III was buried in the West Valley of the Kings in about 1352 BC. Akhenaten had a large tomb prepared for himself and his family in a remote *wadi* to the east of his chosen city of Akhetaten. It should be assumed that he, and possibly his wife Nefertiti (whether or not she succeeded him as Neferneferuaten), were buried there, he in about 1336 BC. Shortly afterwards, Tutankhaten became king, and soon, as Tutankhamun, nominally organized the reconciliation with the ancient gods of Egypt, Amon-Re in particular. Akhetaten was abandoned and the court moved to Memphis. What then should be done in preparation for

38 bottom left The long south wall carries scenes preparing the king for his afterlife. Here he is shown as Osiris, with whom he is identified in death. His successor Ay, with ritual implement, restores his faculties.

38–39 The Burial Chamber of Tutankhamun with scenes painted in tempera. In the center stands the quartzite sarcophagus which still holds the outermost of the royal coffins, containing the king's mummified body.

39 top On the west wall of the Burial Chamber: above, the solar bark with Khepri, the sun at dawn, with kneeling Osirises; beneath, baboons of two of the twelve hours of the night through which the king must pass.

39 bottom The east wall of the Burial Chamber shows part of the funeral cortege of the king. His mummy, lying in a kiosk is dragged by 'the great officials of the palace', including the two vizirs of Egypt (with bald heads). They say: 'Nebkheperure, Come in peace! O God, protector of the land!'

40-41 Ay, successor to Tutankhamen on the throne of Egypt, officiates the rite of mouth opening towards the Pharaoh shown as a mummy.

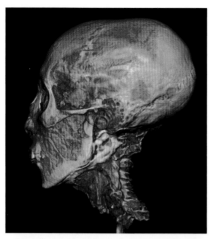

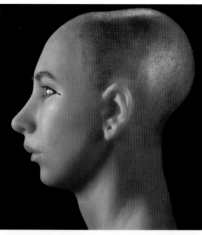

42 top left This 3-D image of Tutankhamun's skull was obtained by subjecting his mummy to an ultrasound scan: analysis of the data made it possible to rule out the theory that the young king had suffered a blow to the head.

42 top right Data from the ultrasound scan made it possible to produce a hypothetical reconstruction of the young pharaoh's facial features. The sculptress Elisabeth Daynès made the skull mold, using clay to reproduce tissue.

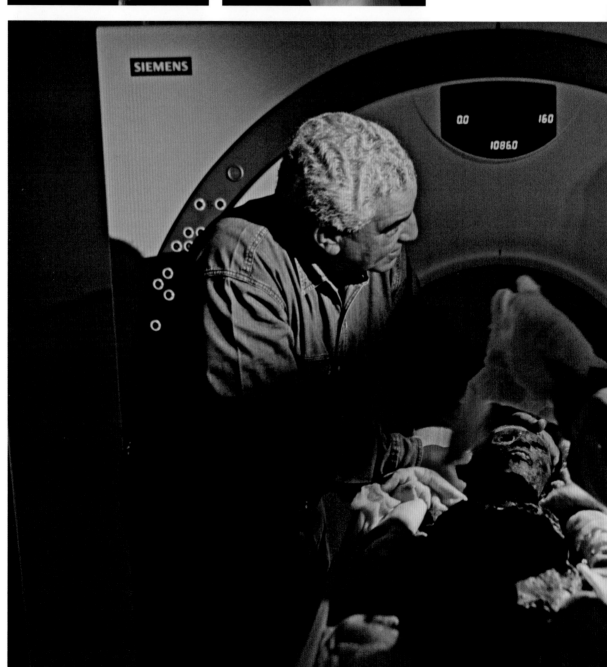

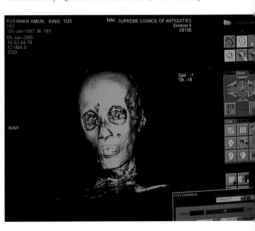

42-43 and 43 *Zabi Hawass, secretary general of the Supreme Council of Antiquities, accompanied Tutankhamun's mummy to the CAT scan equipment, where his body was subjected to its first-ever ultrasound examination, using computerized axial tomography. The screen shows the 3-D images of the king's skull, obtained from processing the data collected using the CAT scan. These images made it possible for experts to determine that some of the cranial traumas, once thought to prove Tutankhamun's murder, were actually caused by mummification operations.*

44-45 *Valley of the Kings, looking south.*

the future burial of the king? It must be assumed that the event was not thought to be imminent. He had been brought up as an Atenist, but had renounced his old religious attachments when reconciliation commenced. It is foolish to think that any of these moves were carried through in consultation with, or even with the acceptance of, a child of under ten years of age. But they happened. After the process of reconciliation it was probably considered logical to return to Thebes and the Valley of the Kings as the proper place for the burial. The return to the Valley may first have been tested by the placing of some of the funerary equipment of Amarna royalty in the cache known as KV 55; there was at least one body in a coffin; there was material from the burial of Queen Tiye, consort of Amenophis III and mother of Akhenaten; there may have been parts of the burial of Kiya,

Tutankhamun's putative mother. Sealings suggest that this deposit was made in Tutankhamun's reign. The return to the traditional Eighteenth Dynasty royal burial ground had begun.

Then Tutankhamun died. It was probably unexpected. Certainly the tomb in which he was buried had not been cut specially for him. It has been suggested that it was originally planned for Ay, his regent, but this is not certain. Ay, however, supervised Tutankhamun's burial. Many of the objects included formed part of earlier royal equipment; some objects from earlier reigns, often described as heirlooms, were included. This practise may always have been followed. In any case, the burial cannot be described as inadequate. The splendor and lavishness of its contents speak for themselves.

Investigations performed in 2005 on the Tutankamen's mummy, whose remains were subjected to an ultrasound scan, cast new light on his age, his state of health and the cause of his death. Results confirmed that the Pharaoh was about 19 when he died and that he was in good health overall at the time of his death. In addition, the various theories about a violent death attributable to murder have now been set aside.

Who should succeed? A pre-emptive move was made by Queen Ankhesenamun, who was by

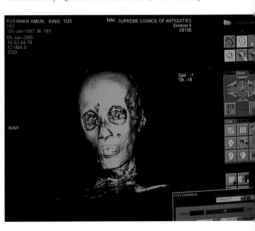

now about twenty-five years old. She was the last surviving member of Akhenaten's family, and, uncertain of her future, she turned to the king of the Hittites, Shuppiluliuma, in a letter asking him, 'Had he a son who could marry her and be the next king of Egypt?' A son was sent, but never reached Egypt, presumably assassinated on the way. The way was then clear for Ay to succeed. His reign (c. 1327–1323 BC) made little mark, and in due course he too would be expunged from the record. He was buried in a tomb – possibly one that had originally been planned to receive Tutankhamun – in the West Valley of the Kings. It was then the turn of Horemheb to take up the threads of royalty, to rule with real authority, overcoming his non-royal origins by pragmatic engagement with the problems facing Egypt at home and abroad.

The Amarna Period was over. The idyll of Akhetaten had finished. The great warrior kings of the Nineteenth Dynasty were in the wings, ready to follow Horemheb in restoring Egypt's security and empire.

The Discovery of the Tomb of
Tutankhamun

46–47 The moment of truth: At last the doors of the four shrines in the Burial Chamber have been unsealed and opened. Howard Carter, kneeling in front, points towards the sealed quartzite sarcophagus, not knowing what to expect next. Behind him stand his assistant Arthur Callender and an Egyptian workman.

In his work diary for his new season of excavation in November 1922, Howard Carter lists as the first discovered object 'Item 433', continuing the numbering series of finds which he had begun in February 1915. This last was the date when he took up the concession for excavation in the Valley of the Kings on behalf of his employer, the 5th Earl of Carnarvon; the first object, 'Item 1' was a fragment of a *shabti* figure of Queen Tiye found near the entrance to the tomb of king Amenophis (Amenhotep) III. From February 1915 until November 1922, with a long period of inactivity during the First World War, the harvest of objects, therefore, was a very modest 432. The laconic entry for Item 433 was 'Entrance of tomb of', and on the opposite page Carter wrote: 'in bed rock floor of water course (below entrance of R VI). Discovered 4th Nov. 1922.' After the clearance of the steps leading down to the blocked entrance of the tomb, Carter telegraphed Lord Carnarvon: 'At last have made wonderful discovery in the Valley. A magnificent tomb with seals intact. Re-covered same for your arrival. Congratulations. Carter.'

There is no mention of Tutankhamun, and the identity of the owner of the newly discovered tomb was not revealed until his name was read in some of the seal impressions on the lower part of the blocked entrance, when the excavation was resumed after Carnarvon's arrival in Luxor later in November. Carter was at first not able to make an identification, but he may have suspected, even

hoped, that Tutankhamun was the king in question. He quite probably had earlier suggested to Carnarvon that Tutankhamun's tomb was a likely candidate for discovery. How else can one explain the question put to Alan Gardiner, the great British grammarian of the ancient Egyptian language, by Carnarvon on the day after the telegram had arrived: 'Carnarvon asked me whether it could possibly be the tomb of Tutankhamun. I replied that I was not well up in the history of the Valley and that we should have to wait and see.'

Carter's belief in the identification of the tomb owner will be examined a little later. But now let us consider how the Amarna Period, the time of heresy, of which Tutankhamun's reign marked the turning point back to what for most ancient Egyptians was normality, in strange ways impinged on the career of Howard Carter from its very beginnings.

Samuel John Carter, a very good naturalistic artist in the Victorian tradition, taught all his many children to draw and paint. Howard, his youngest son, was brought up to think of no other career than that of an artist, not perhaps a successful painter of portraits (like his older brother William), or genre paintings (like his father), but someone who could do a good professional piece of work – a jobbing artist, in fact. While still young he showed a good mastery of line and a promising ability to paint in water-colors. When he was still only seventeen he

48 Carnarvon arrives in Luxor. The first steps to the tomb were found on November 4, 1922, and Carter immediately telegraphed the good news to his patron in England. With all haste Carnarvon left for Egypt accompanied by his daughter Lady Evelyn Herbert. In those leisurely times it took many days for them to arrive in Egypt, and a few more before they reached Luxor. Here they are met outside Luxor station by Carter and the Governor of Qena province. Carnarvon, not in good health, is warmly dressed for Egypt in November.

49 top Lord Carnarvon photographed at ease on the porch of Carter's house in Western Thebes. In Egypt he preferred to live in luxury in a good hotel, in Luxor at the Winter Palace. Carter's house served as a comfortable haven away from the newspaper reporters and importunate tourists, where he could retire from time to time for peace and quiet.

49 center Detail from the 1924 painting of Howard Carter by his brother William, a most accomplished portrait painter. The bow tie was one of Carter's characteristic articles of dress. Here he may seem to be at ease, but his eyes suggest a certain deep-set anxiety. It was a difficult time for him.

49 bottom The entry in Howard Carter's work diary for November 24, 1922. The Carnarvon party had reached Luxor and Carter's workmen, supervised by Arthur Callender, had begun to clear completely the stairway down to the first blocked entrance to the tomb. At last the whole plastered wall was visible and the prenomen cartouche of Tutankhamun could clearly be read.

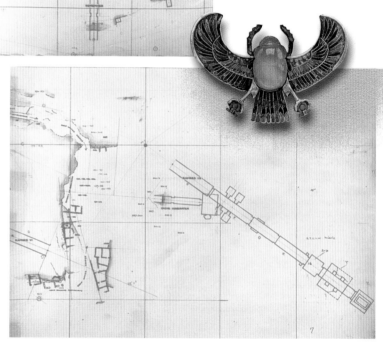

50 Parts of the detailed map of the Valley of the Kings made by Howard Carter. The two sections shown here are adjacent to each other. In the upper section the main features are the tombs or Horemheb and Ramesses VI, the line of the former running beneath the latter. It demonstrates how carefully the ancient tomb-cutters had to work. In following the line of the best limestone they were constrained by the existence of earlier tombs. In this case the tomb of Ramesses VI was cut at a higher level. In the lower section the remains of the workmen's huts built over Tutankhamun's tomb can be seen at the lower left. On the right in the middle is Tomb 55, the so-called Amarna cache, near the entrance to the tomb of Ramesses IX.

obtained a modest position which was to lead to great things. The Egypt Exploration Fund, a recently established British private organization for archaeological works in Egypt, needed an artist to help record the scenes and inscriptions in tombs at Beni Hasan and El-Bersha in Middle Egypt. Carter already had some knowledge of Egyptian antiquities from being allowed to draw in the collection of William Amhurst Tyssen-Amherst (later Lord Amherst), a rich landowner in Norfolk. He had, however, never been to Egypt, had indeed scarcely travelled beyond London and Norfolk, when he was sent to Egypt in the Autumn of 1891. Within a few weeks he was sent to assist in the excavations at El-Amarna conducted by Flinders Petrie, who was to become the most famous field-worker in Egypt in the early twentieth century.

El-Amarna had already been identified as the site of the ancient town of Akhetaten, founded by King Akhenaten (c. 1352–1336 BC), whose history was outlined in the previous chapter. In 1892 very little was known of the period and its religion, but interesting objects of unusual style had been found in the area, and Petrie was the first serious archaeologist to excavate there. Carter spent over four months with Petrie and they were momentous months in the early career of one whom Petrie first described as 'a good-natured lad, whose interest is entirely in painting and natural history.... it is of no use to me to work him up as an excavator'. This was perhaps rather a premature judgement by an experienced thirty-eight-year-old on an immature, inexperienced seventeen-year-old. At El-Amarna Carter first learned about Akhenaten and the Amarna Period, and was bitten by the bug of excavation. In his methods of work, and of life generally, Petrie was uncompromising, severe and methodical. He was also dogmatic and eccentric, and the young Carter did not appreciate many of his peculiar economies. Nevertheless, he watched the older man, listened to what he said, and understood the reasons for some of his oddities. It was indeed an acknowledgement that his 'pupil' of thirty years earlier was doing well (in the Petrie sense) that he could comment in 1923: 'We may only say how lucky it is all in the hands of Carter and Lucas'. And that was but two months after the discovery of Tutankhamun's tomb.

It was in this season with Petrie that Carter was introduced to his first royal tomb, that of Akhenaten himself, possibly the father of Tutankhamun. So the circle of interest started, although it would be foolish to claim that this early experience established the path that was to lead to the great discovery of 1922. Rumors of the finding of the Akhenaten tomb had been circulating for several months in 1891, and it was in December that the Egyptian Antiquities Service announced the event. In February 1892 Petrie took Carter to see it. They walked for many miles, mostly up a rocky *wadi* or valley, and what was to be seen did not excite the young man. He wrote to his mentor Percy Newberry: 'The tomb... is a great sell [anti-climax], is very rough and unfinished... I have made some drawings for Mr. Petrie of the Valley and the Tomb.' Indeed the tomb at first sight is not very impressive, and not nearly as spectacular as the private tombs Carter had been working on at Beni Hasan. It was dark, and the few reliefs not easy to make out. The drawings Carter made were published with an article Petrie wrote for a London newspaper, the *Daily Graphic*, on the March 23 – the very first published drawings of the budding archaeologist. One of them shows Akhenaten and his wife Nefertiti mourning their dead daughter Meketaten. Above the king the divine sun-disk,

51 View of the entrance to Tutankhamun's tomb taken some time after its discovery. The large tomb entrance in the middle of the picture marks the tomb of Ramesses VI, in front of which ran the regular tourist path into the Valley which inhibited excavation in the area. A newly built low wall surrounds the small area leading down to the tomb of Tutankhamun. The boxes and timber lying to the right are part of the excavator's equipment. The path on the left runs up to the tomb of Amenophis II which was robbed while Carter was Chief Inspector in Thebes. At the point where another path turns off to the left is the deep entrance to the tomb of Horemheb which runs into the cliff beneath the line of Ramesses VI's tomb. Holes just above the tent mark other Carter investigations. His searchings were very thorough, but accompanied by little success until the end.

the Aten, pours down its life-giving rays, an idea Carter would meet again, most notably on the back of the Golden Throne found in the Antechamber of Tutankhamun's tomb. In spite of the lack of light in the tomb, Carter's drawing is remarkably accurate for a quick sketch by someone who had scarcely served his apprenticeship as an archaeological artist. Carter completed his work with Petrie at the end of May 1892. His taste for excavation was established; he had worked with the best of instructors and survived. By the end Petrie would discuss objects with him, and even sometimes seemed to respect his opinion. Carter would never forget those months at El-Amarna, and he would, if only subconsciously, carry in his mind the experience of working in the area of the Great Temple of the Aten in Akhenaten's city, where Tutankhamun passed his childhood. And there he first met Amarna art, finding many examples of Amarna sculpture, all sadly damaged, but still showing the craftsmanship and exquisite lines of the finest art of the period.

The next step on the road which would lead him in the direction of his ultimate triumph came in late 1899, when Carter was appointed Chief Inspector of Antiquities for Upper Egypt with his base in Thebes. It was an unexpected promotion for him, and not welcomed by many of his British colleagues. This was not surprising. Carter had not readily been accepted into the British archaeological community for several reasons. He was poorly educated, and had few apparent talents apart from an outstanding ability to draw. Unlike most of his contemporaries he had not attended a good school and been to one of the older universities; he had not, as it seemed, made noticeable efforts to learn systematically about ancient Egypt. He was also less well mannered than those with whom he came into contact professionally and socially in Egypt. By temperament he did not make friends easily among his Egyptological colleagues, and sought rather the company of artists and foreign visitors to Egypt who might not expose his Egyptological uncertainties. But he had proved his worth as a practical worker in the field, especially during the six years he spent at Deir el-Bahri as principal artist, and as virtual deputy to Edouard Naville,

director of the excavation and reconstruction of the great temple of Queen Hatshepsut. In all practical matters he worked successfully for Naville, and it was probably Naville who recommended Carter to Gaston Maspero, Director-General of the Antiquities Service of Egypt.

Although Howard Carter was not book trained, he was an observant and pragmatic person who clearly learned lessons quickly from the knowledge and practices of others. He may never have learned the intricacies of the ancient Egyptian language, but he was a brilliant copier of hieroglyphic texts. Naville once wrote about the work done by Carter and his assistant Percy Brown on one series of reliefs at Deir el-Bahri: 'Most of the inscriptions copied had been erased (in antiquity), and were difficult to read, but owing to the familiarity which the artists had acquired with hieroglyphs at Deir el-Bahari, and to their skill in recognizing a sign from a few broken lines or a small colored fragment, it has been possible not only to correct the former publications of Mariette and Duemichen, but here and there to add materially to what had been deciphered previously by those scholars'.

So far in his career in Egypt Carter had mostly been an employee of the Egypt Exploration Fund, carrying out tasks assigned to him, and only occasionally having the freedom to act independently. But his independence had always been circumscribed. Now at last, from December 1899, he was virtually his own master, operating far from Cairo, and capable of setting his own priorities, except in matters involving the substantial expenditure of money. Shortage of funds was a constant problem. Excavation was the activity that attracted Carter most. At Thebes, after many decades of inactivity, work had been resumed in the Valley of the Kings in 1898 by Victor Loret, Maspero's predecessor as Director-General. His most important find was the tomb of King Amenophis II (c. 1427–1400 BC), which turned out to be a cache containing a group of very important royal burials.

In January 1900, as one of his first official tasks, Carter supervised the removal of the royal mummies to Cairo, leaving in the tomb only that of Amenophis II in his sarcophagus.

52 The ancient steps descending to Tutankhamun's tomb seen from top and bottom. To find the first step was the moment when anticipation began. Most royal tombs in the Valley were cut into the side of the rocky wall roughly at ground level. Pit tombs, of which Carter had investigated several, tended to be for non-royal persons, and were usually disappointing. Here was something different, and it was surely with great reluctance that he filled in the stairs to await Carnarvon's arrival.

52–53 Excavation in Egypt was a very labour-intensive activity in Carter's day. There were skilled workmen who could be entrusted with tasks needing experience and care; there were general workmen who did most of the labouring; and there were basket-boys who carried away the excavated spoil to be dumped elsewhere. The work was supervised by a reis, or foreman, who can be seen here on the level platform on the left of the picture; he controlled, encouraged and bullied the team, and was in charge of the dig when the excavators might be elsewhere.

54–55 The doors of the second shrine in the Burial Chamber were fastened by rope passing through bronze staples, and secured with a mud sealing. When Carter saw these doors, closely shut and protected magically by the sealing, he realized that whatever lay within had surely remained undisturbed since the time of Tutankhamun's funeral. The seal impression shows the recumbent Anubis jackal above the figures of nine kneeling captives – the standard design for the necropolis seal. Behind the jackal's head is a cartouche containing Tutankhamun's prenomen.

56–57 Howard Carter assigned names to the four chambers in the royal tomb, which through usage have become established, although they do not all properly reflect the functions of the rooms.

The first room, the Antechamber, was not just the room of approach to what Carnarvon called the 'Holy of Holies', but a storeroom of miscellaneous material. Facing the entrance were the three great ritual couches with dramatic animal heads. Above and beneath them were items of furniture, the Golden Throne, fine chairs and stools, smaller beds, boxes filled with linen and items of clothes, calcite jars of unguents, white-painted, egg-shaped containers for food to sustain the dead king. To the right, by the blocked entrance to the Burial Chamber, stood the guardian statues and on the floor, the painted box, one of the greatest treasures in the tomb. The other end of the room was mostly filled with parts of chariots, dismantled at the time of the funeral. The entrance to the Annexe lay behind the hippopotamus-headed couch. Its floor was much lower than that of the Antechamber, and it contained an even more confused mass of material, deposited in a haphazard manner which cannot wholly be attributed to tomb-robbers. Here there were remarkable pieces like the so-called Ecclesiastical Throne, other fine furniture, weaponry, boats, chests of shabti-figures, and many more containers of food and the king's 'cellar' of wine for the afterlife.

The extraordinary assembly of shrines and coffins in the Burial Chamber is described on the next page. This room was alone in having wall paintings of ritual purpose. It also contained items of special funerary significance, and, in each wall, a magical brick.

Out of the Burial Chamber opened the Treasury, so called because of its precious contents, chief of which was the Canopic Shrine protecting the king's embalmed entrails. There were also many chests containing divine and royal figures, boxes of shabti-figures, a fleet of boats sailing to the West, more chests of linen and jewelry. And over all brooded the impressive Anubis jackal on a shrine-shaped pedestal.

In the confined area of the Burial Chamber there was little space for movement; everything had to fit, and Carter found evidence that in some cases adjustments had to be made to get everthing into place. First, the quartzite sarcophagus was centrally set, ready to receive the three coffins which were lowered into it one by one, resting on a wooden bier. Then around this sacred container were assembled four shrines of gilded wood decorated with funerary texts and representations. The sides were certainly placed against the walls of the chamber in advance, because they could scarcely have been manhandled into position from outside. Around the second shrine was then placed a gilded wooden frame on which was hung a fine linen pall decorated with gilt-bronze marguerites. The final assembling was of the first, outermost, shrine, which, when in position, scarcely allowed a person to walk around.

56

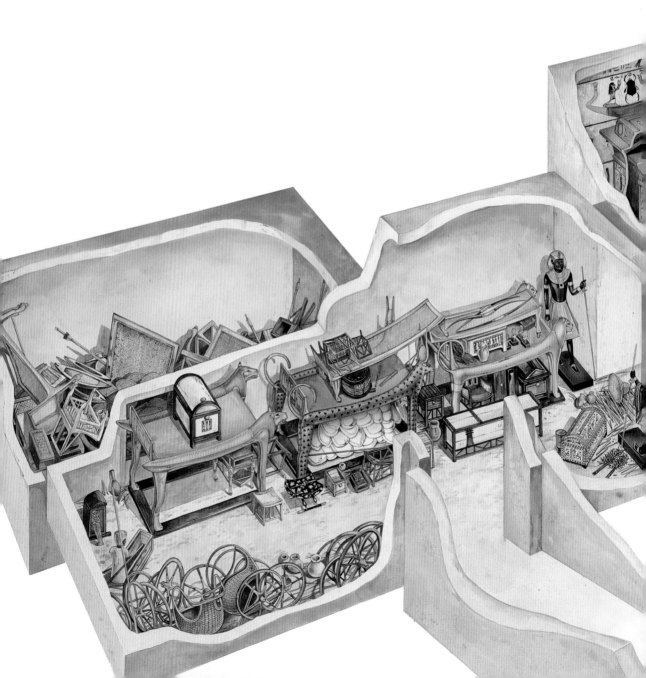

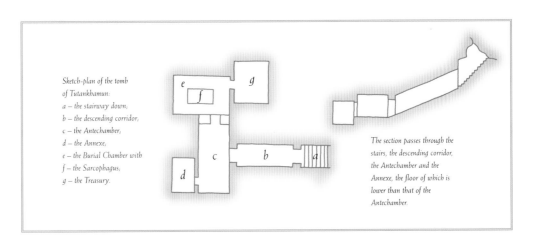

Sketch-plan of the tomb
of Tutankhamun:
a – the stairway down;
b – the descending corridor;
c – the Antechamber;
d – the Annexe;
e – the Burial Chamber with
f – the Sarcophagus;
g – the Treasury.

The section passes through the
stairs, the descending corridor,
the Antechamber and the
Annexe, the floor of which is
lower than that of the
Antechamber.

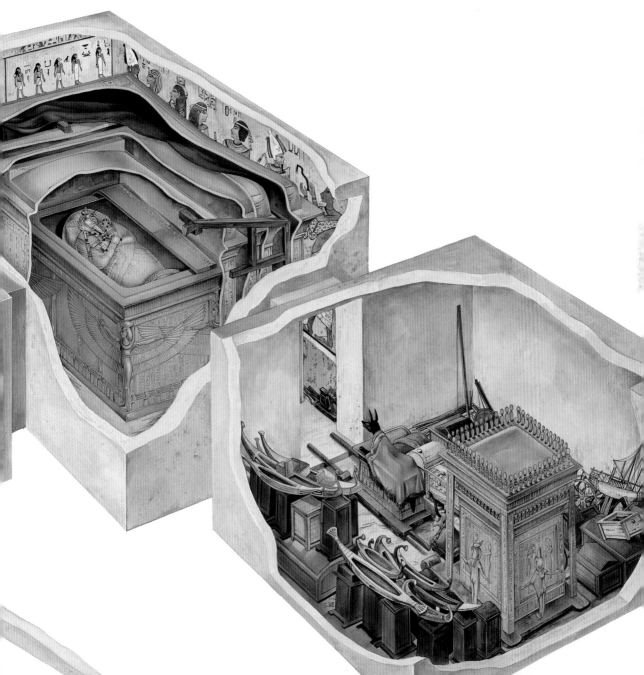

This was Carter's first involvement in the Valley of the Kings, and for the rest of his career the Valley was to occupy a central position in his thoughts, if not in his day-to-day activity. Its pull took time to develop, but by chance and design the Valley fixed itself in his mind, and cast its spell on this young, scarcely formed archaeologist. There was, it seems, a strong romantic element in this fascination, which was over the years to develop into an obsession. For no good reason, and with unrealistic expectation, Carter came to believe that there was – there must be – one undiscovered tomb, unplundered, he hoped, which dogged determination would in the end yield to his passion. To begin with it is unlikely that a special burial occupied his thoughts. In fact any burial would do. Could he ever have the chance to make that discovery? Would someone else get there first?

In his few years as Chief Inspector in Upper Egypt, some opportunities came his way. His first independent excavation was not in the Valley of the Kings, but in the plain before Deir el-Bahri where Maspero allowed him to investigate a hole in which his horse had tripped a year or two earlier. This 'Tomb of the Horse', as it came to be known, turned out to be in some way connected with the temple of Nebhepetre Mentuhotpe II (c. 2055–2004 BC), also in Deir el-Bahri just to the south of Hatshepsut's more famous temple. It did not turn out to be the unviolated tomb Carter hoped it might be, and its one significant object, a remarkable life-size seated statue of the king dressed for the *sed* or jubilee festival, was no consolation for the general disappointment of a practically empty sepulchre. But it was his first royal tomb, or perhaps cenotaph.

His next involvement with a royal tomb brought him back to the Valley of the Kings, and in even less happy circumstances. On the evening of November 24, 1901, while Carter was away from Thebes on a tour of inspection, robbers broke into the tomb of Amenophis II, only recently discovered. Local rumor had it that the tomb still contained precious objects, and the mummy of the king, still lying in its sarcophagus, was carefully cut open in a search for gold jewelry. Although there was good forensic evidence pointing to the guilt of members of a well-known local Qurnawi family, with a fully justified reputation for tomb-robbing, no successful prosecution followed. Carter was in no way to blame, but the episode left a stain on his reputation which could subsequently be used by those who resented his presence in Luxor.

Victor Loret's work in the Valley of the Kings had shown that there were royal tombs still to be found. Although Carter had no further funds for excavation himself, he carried out much needed work in the Valley, clearing tombs, fitting steel doors, and installing electric light. He had the best of opportunities to get to know the place in detail, and to observe likely places where more tombs might be found. It was a chance to survey and to reconnoitre – the best of preparations for serious work; this might be considered the period when the seeds of his final harvest with the Earl of Carnarvon were sown. There was a way, however, by which even then he could involve himself in excavation. With Maspero's encouragement he sought out a wealthy sponsor who could finance excavations in the Valley, to be conducted on his behalf by Howard Carter. It was not at all difficult to persuade the rich American businessman Theodore Davis to be that sponsor, and in 1902 there began the Davis excavations in the Valley which were to continue until 1915. Carter remained in charge of the work until he left Thebes for Cairo at the end of 1904. In that time he demonstrated that there were more tombs to be discovered and, perhaps more importantly for his own archaeological development, that he was an excavator ideally suited in skills and temperament for this kind of work.

Carter's best success with Davis came in January 1903 when he found his first royal tomb in the

58 bottom left One of the two life-size guardian or
ka-statues placed on either side of the blocked
entrance to the Burial Chamber. When discovered
they were partly covered with linen sheets, as were
many other objects in the tomb. The black-painted
wooden figures with gilded headdresses, kilts and
staves made a dramatic effect.

58–59 and 59 top 'As my eyes grew
accustomed to the light, details of the room
within emerged slowly from the mist, strange
animals, statues, and gold – everywhere the
glint of gold'. So wrote Carter of his first
impressions. 'A roomful – a whole museumful it
seemed – of objects.' To the left was a tangled
mass of chariot parts, to the front were three
huge ritual beds with monstrous heads and
beneath them chests of personal possessions,
egg-shaped boxes for food offerings, and pieces
of furniture, some quite simple in design, others
grand beyond imagination.

59 bottom To the right the excavators could
see the unmistakeable signs of a blocked
entrance, flanked by the two guardian figures.
On the floor was the magnificent painted box,
then even more brilliant in its colors which
after essential conservation became darkened.
And, against the wall a round basket
concealing a hole into the Burial Chamber,
through which Carter, Carnarvon and Evelyn
Herbert would later squeeze to view the 'Holy
of Holies'.

Valley. It had been prepared for King Tuthmosis
IV of the Eighteenth Dynasty (c. 1400–1390 BC),
and had, one may say inevitably, been ransacked
in antiquity. Nevertheless, considerable remains of
impressive painted wall reliefs still remained, and
there were large quantities of fine, but mostly
damaged, antiquities. Carter carefully stage-
managed the official opening, having himself
made in advance preparations to ensure a
relatively comfortable experience for the
distinguished visitors, and as little damage as
possible to the tomb and its contents. Electric
light, an almost unheard of luxury in a newly
excavated tomb, had been installed. Mrs. Emma
Andrews, close companion and relative of Davis
and the social chronicler of their annual trips on
the Nile, described what happened on the
February 3. The whole event must have been
difficult, dangerous, thrilling and at times
hilarious. She went in with Gaston Maspero,
Director-General. There were two long inclines:
'Maspero being so stout had actually to lie down,
with his feet sometimes on Carter's shoulders'.
They crossed the deep well – a characteristic
feature of Eighteenth Dynasty tombs – by a
precarious suspension bridge. The great burial hall
'was strewn with a mass of beautiful debris...
Carter placed boards along which we walked and
were requested not to step off them'. Getting out

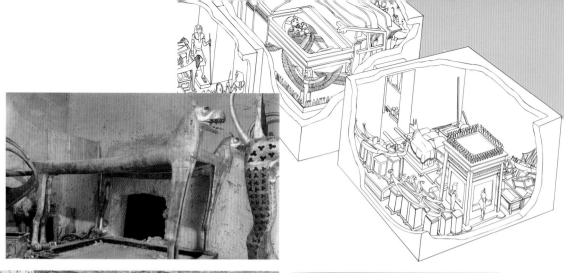

was even more difficult. After a late lunch they returned to Davis's house-boat: 'We were glad enough to have tea'.

Changes in the appointments of Chief Inspectors were, however, to bring Carter's work with Davis to an end. It had been Maspero's intention to switch the Lower and Upper Egyptian Inspectors after four or five years, and he decided to make the change in 1904. It could not have pleased Carter, although no adverse comment by him has survived. He was now a government official and had to do what he was told. But for ten years Thebes had been the center of his life in Egypt, and for recent years the focus of his professional interest had been the Valley of the Kings. Royal tombs were what he enjoyed discovering, and there would be none in the North where pyramid investigation was quite another thing, and not on offer in any case. If he had at that time a particular tomb in mind it was that of King Amenophis I (c. 1525–1504 BC), which, according to indications in ancient Egyptian papyrus records, lay outside the Valley of the Kings. He could therefore conduct a search for it as Chief Inspector without compromising Theodore Davis's concession in the Valley. For funds Carter approached his old patron Lord Amherst: 'I can do it this summer before I leave for Lower Egypt'. In the event he could do little more

60 top left *After the clearance of smaller items from the Antechamber, in the wall behind the great hippopotamus couch, it could be seen there was a low square entrance to another room. This small storeroom, the Annexe, lay at a level lower than the Antechamber and it was so full of objects that it could not be entered at that point.*

60 bottom left *The first object to be seen in the Treasury was the great Anubis shrine, the recumbent jackal figure of the god on duty for eternity, protecting the most precious Canopic Shrine and embalmed internal organs of the king. The finely modeled head of the god, with gilded eyes and ears, made a profound impression on the first modern visitors to the tomb.*

than scratch around on the heights of Dra Abu'l Naga, a hill overlooking the plain running east from Deir el-Bahri, and the known site of small royal tombs of the Seventeenth Dynasty. To find the tomb of Amenophis I became something of an *idée fixe* with Carter; it was something he could later interest the Earl of Carnarvon in, while they waited for the Valley concession.

The move north in late 1904, accepted if not welcomed by Carter, soon brought calamity. He was still only thirty years old, mature in experience but not easy in his ways. Maspero described him as 'entêté', obstinate. Called to intervene in a dispute between Antiquities Service guards and a group of visitors to Saqqara, Carter failed to resolve the matter before a brawl occurred and blood was drawn. The outcome, greatly exacerbated by his unwillingness to compromise, led to his being moved to Tanta in the Delta. He was not happy, and in the autumn of 1905 he resigned from the Antiquities Service.

For three years he became an outcast from the archaeological community. He scraped a living by selling his water-colors to European and American visitors, many of whom were wealthy, and pleased to employ him as a guide to the ancient sites, with very special professional knowledge. He returned to Thebes, living, it has been suggested, sometimes on the charity of his former Egyptian employees. He was helped a little by some of his old associates like Theodore Davis, who had made his best discovery in the Valley in February 1905, only a few months after Carter had left Thebes. The tomb of Yuia and Tjuiu, parents of Queen Tiye, favourite wife of Amenophis III, contained the largest quantity of well preserved

funerary furniture, including their intact coffins, ever found in the Valley. Davis in due course asked Carter to make water-colors of some of the most spectacular objects in the tomb, and they were used to illustrate the subsequent publication. Undoubtedly it was all very galling for Carter, and Davis's commission was small compensation for what might have been his own success. Had he stayed in Thebes for another three months he might have made that discovery. But the success fell to his colleague James Quibell, with whom he had exchanged Inspectorships.

For the time being, therefore, all Carter could do was to stay in Thebes picking up small pieces of work, and observing the not infrequent triumphs over the hill in the Valley of the Kings. Each royal discovery by the Davis team meant one less discovery to be made in the future. And would Carter ever have the chance to work there again? Triumph followed triumph for Davis. In late 1905, no doubt on the advice of his newly engaged full-time excavator, Edward Ayrton, Davis had decided to systematize his operations in the Valley, 'exhausting every mountain and foot-hill' – a pattern of work which would be carried through more thoroughly by Carter himself after 1917. Ayrton was eight years younger than Carter and less experienced; but he joined Davis before Carter had resigned. It is piquant to think that Carter might have received the Davis appointment if he had known about it at the time when he was feeling so dissatisfied with his life in Tanta. In late 1905 the tomb of King Siptah (c. 1194–1188 BC) was discovered, but not fully cleared until some years later. In January 1907 a tomb used or reused as a cache for funerary furniture and equipment was opened. This controversial deposit, famously known by its Valley of the Kings number, KV 55, contained material belonging to royal individuals closely connected to Akhenaten and the Amarna court. In February 1908 Ayrton discovered the spectacularly decorated tomb of Horemheb, last king of the Eighteenth Dynasty (c. 1323–1295 BC). One by one the tombs of the kings of the New Kingdom were being found; but the lure of the Valley did not diminish for Howard Carter. It is unlikely that he lay in bed at night counting on his fingers the missing sepulchres. It would be some years before he made researches into the history of

the Valley, investigating the possibilities of further
discoveries. But it would not have escaped him
that there could be other non-royal tombs like
that of Yuia and Tjuiu, unexpectedly located in the
Valley and still unplundered.

In January 1909 Howard Carter wrote to Mrs.
Kingsmill Marrs of Boston, one of his wealthy
American clients: 'At the Tombs of the Kings Mr.
Davis found a small tomb pit but nothing of great
interest in it beyond some gold foil'. In the light of
later events, Carter should perhaps have taken
greater interest in what had been found. It is of
course likely that he had not seen the discovery
when he wrote the letter. Some of the gold
fragments bore the name of Tutankhamun, and
others the name of Ay, his short-reigned successor

(c. 1327–1323 BC), and Davis and his new excavator Harold Jones, identified this very modest tomb pit as the actual burial place of Tutankhamun. It was later published as such, but the evidence did not support the identification, and it was not generally accepted. At the very least, however, it brought forward the name of Tutankhamun. For Carter's immediate future, however, what he later said to Mrs. Marrs in the same letter was of particular significance: 'I have just been offered an enormous fee by Lord Carnarvon to undertake a month's excavation (February) at Drah abou'l Neggeh a site no doubt you will remember between Deir el-Bahari and the mouth of the valley of the Tombs of the Kings – to try to find the Tombs of Amenhotep I and Aahmes

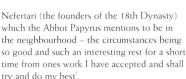

Nefertari (the founders of the 18th Dynasty) which the Abbot Papyrus mentions to be in the neighbourhood – the circumstances being so good and such an interesting rest for a short time from ones work I have accepted and shall try and do my best'.

So, with apparent reluctance Carter showed himself ready to return to excavation, and to take up the project which he had proposed to Lord Amherst five years earlier. He must have been thrilled at the prospect of excavating again in the Theban Necropolis, although he might have had some misgivings arising from his unhappy experiences in the past as a government official. Furthermore he seems to have enjoyed his time as an artist and high-class dragoman; he was very much his own master, and he had gained much social confidence through mixing with rather grand clients. No longer was he the gauche, awkwardly mannered, young man; he could more than pass as a gentleman. As such he would fit reasonably well into the kind of life enjoyed by the Earl of Carnarvon, who did not expect to live in discomfort or enjoy pointless economies like Petrie. Further, there was the attraction of 'an enormous fee'. In a letter to Percy Newberry in 1911, Carnarvon mentioned that he paid Carter £200 'per mensem'; it is unlikely that he was paying much less in 1909.

62–63 On February 17, 1923, Howard Carter and Arthur Mace, in the presence of distinguished guests and officials, breached the sealed blocking between the Antechamber and the Burial Chamber. When this picture was taken, most of the blocking had been removed and the visitors were faced with the wall of the great outermost shrine with an open-work pattern of djed and tyet amuletic hieroglyphs, signifying endurance and life. The background is made of blue faience of a wonderful purity of color.

63 top and right These two pictures illustrate the care with which the objects in the tomb were prepared for the short journey to the tomb of Sethos II where conservation took place. But this journey involved the negotiating of the exit from the tomb, and Carter took no chance in ensuring that adequate packing material and carrying trays were available. Here the guardian statues are prepared by Carter and Callender.

Carter came to work with Carnarvon with the blessing of Gaston Maspero. He had been very disappointed when Carter resigned in 1905, and had done his best to persuade him to stay. So, when Carnarvon came to him in 1908 and asked him to find a 'learned man' to help him with his excavations, it gave Maspero a wonderful chance to effect Carter's rehabilitation as an archaeologist. Carnarvon had been conducting modest excavations in the Theban Necropolis since 1907. He supervised his workmen himself, but overall control was exercised by Arthur Weigall, the current Chief Inspector for Upper Egypt. Weigall was a clever man and a good Egyptologist who did not suffer fools or incompetents gladly. He was not sympathetic to Carnarvon and did little to help him work in places where he might find something. He confessed to Francis Llewellyn Griffith, the leading British Egyptologist of the day: 'I placed him on the rubbish mounds of Shekh abd'el Gurneh, where of course he worked for the season without finding anything, though I had hoped that he might find a good painted tomb which would have been a useful find, without much to damage in it'. In his second season in early 1908 Carnarvon had greater success. He had negotiated, without the unhelpful advice of Weigall, a much more promising area for excavation; he found a number of interesting antiquities and several tombs, including one dating to the early Eighteenth Dynasty, made for a mayor of Thebes, Tetiky. His success annoyed Weigall, who had been to some extent side-lined. He complained to Griffith: 'Lord Carnarvon does his best, and sits over his work conscientiously; but that is not enough… He is a good sort, but perfectly irresponsible.' Weigall had a good point to make. Rich men do not necessarily make good excavators. Carnarvon himself had his doubts. He could see that he was wholly unequipped technically to conduct successful excavations, and without proper support from the representative of the Antiquities Service he had to find his own man. Carter it would be.

In this way began an association which would last for fourteen years, culminating in the greatest discovery in the history of Egyptian archaeology. Carter turned out to be just the right man. He and Carnarvon came from very different strata of society, but Carter had the abilities and personal qualities which Carnarvon appreciated. And, in addition to being an accomplished excavator, Carter was an unusually skilled handler of antiquities and a fine artist; he was totally at home in the Theban Necropolis. He knew the Qurnawis well, and understood their strengths, comprehended their weaknesses, and was trusted by them sufficiently for them to bring him advanced knowledge of good illicit finds. So he was often able to acquire for Carnarvon's growing collection objects of exceptional quality before they were passed into the general antiquities market. But Carter was not, as he had hoped, to work on finding the tombs of Amenophis I (Amenhotep) and his mother Queen Ahmes Nefertari.

Carnarvon's concession in the Theban Necropolis had begun to yield very interesting material, and there was every reason to continue work in the same area. For the next six years Carter worked steadily to the east of the Deir el-Bahri temples. Work was on a large scale, but tight control was exercised; excellent procedures in the technical operation of the excavation were developed. At last Carter was gaining the experience of serious excavation which he had not been able to acquire in his early years of clearance in the Valley. In 1912 a fine volume describing the results for the years 1907–1911 was published. It

was issued under the joint authorship of Carnarvon and Carter, but it is certain that it was master-minded by the latter. By 1912 a certain repetitive quality to the finds began to persuade Carnarvon that a change was necessary. He considered sites in other parts of Egypt. Carter kept his eye on the Valley of the Kings, where Theodore Davis still retained the concession. Davis was now well into his seventies and not in the best of health. He could scarcely continue his annual visits to Egypt much longer. Discoveries in the Valley had been trivial in recent years; yet he hung on to his concession as if he too believed that one great discovery was there to be made.

In 1912, as a diversion, Carter dug a short season at Sakha in the central Delta, site of the ancient city of Xois. In 1913 he investigated Tell el-Balamun, a vast mound in the northern Delta. Neither place proved very profitable, and neither was further investigated by Carter. A certain aimlessness seemed to overcome the Carnarvon-Carter enterprise. Other sites, very desirable, could not be obtained. Carter was the professional, and for the sake of his own future he had to pay attention to his employer's wishes. Then chance intervened, reviving the possibility of

the discovery of the tomb of King Amenophis I. In an essay Carter wrote in the 1930s he told the story of how he was put on to the exact location of the tomb – long sought for by himself – by a member of one of the most successful tomb-robbing families of the Theban Necropolis. In his best florid style he described how he was sitting on a bench outside the new house he had built near the entrance to the Valley of the Kings. It was evening in the late spring of 1912: 'The setting sun had shed its rich yellow beams over the landscape... The Arabian desert opposite, beyond the fertile valley, had assumed opalescent tints... The evening was fast closing... when far away across the broken tract of desert between my house and the fertile plain, the figure of a man was slowly approaching.' Gad Hassan was bringing Carter a basketful of alabaster fragments, some inscribed with the names of King Amenophis I and Queen Ahmes Nefertari. As is evident from his account, Carter knew exactly how to deal with an approach of this kind. He negotiated the purchase of the fragments, and then persuaded Gad Hassan to show him where they had been found. It turned out to be a tomb, difficult of access, in a position high on Dra Abu'l

66 top and 66 left The clearance of the tomb continues. Howard Carter and Arthur Callender work together in moving objects to the conservation tomb. The two made a good team. Carter, undisputed director, experienced in all aspects of field activities, Callender, by training and profession an engineer, a good practical assistant, wholly reliable. Carter did not mind getting his hands dirty, and when it was necessary to move an object with particular care he would be there to do it himself. Here he and Callender gently lower one side of the great Hathor (cow) couch into a prepared tray, and again the two themselves carry a chest to Sethos II's tomb.

Naga, in a position which could just be reconciled
with the ancient description given in the Abbott
Papyrus in the British Museum.

The tomb was in a wretched condition: 'Every
remnant of the old grandeur and divinity had
gone... The walls were sullen and black from the
fires lit by its dynastic desecrators. The charred
remains of its equipment were but evidence of base
minds that had wrought revenge upon the
illustrious dead.' It was, however, still worth careful
examination, and in due course, at what seemed to
be the right moment, Carter proposed its
clearance to Carnarvon. In the event, it was the
last piece of work to be undertaken by Carnarvon
and Carter before the outbreak of the First World
War. A short season began in late February 1914;
it was not promising and the results were
disappointing – mostly more fragments of stone
vessels and *shabti* figures; identification was not
certain, but Carter himself was convinced that it
had been the burial place of Amenophis I and his
mother.

After the completion of that piece of work,
Carnarvon gave up his concession in the Theban
Necropolis, and planned to move operations to
Hawara, at the entrance to the Faiyum depression
much further north. But at the same time, almost
precisely, Theodore Davis surrendered his licence
for the Valley of the Kings. He was seventy-seven;
recent results had been negligible. In 1912 he had

written 'I fear that the Valley of the Tombs is now
exhausted'. He was echoing what Giovanni Battista
Belzoni had written nearly a century earlier: 'It is
my firm opinion that in the valley of Beban el
Mulook there are no more tombs than are now
known in consequence of my late discoveries'.
Maspero also considered the Valley completely
worked out. How could Howard Carter expect any
further success? Well, he could have argued,
Belzoni was wrong, why not Davis and Maspero
also? Carnarvon was persuaded to apply for the
licence, and it was granted to him in June 1914.

It may be imagined – for there is no
contemporary evidence to show to the contrary –
that Carter was both delighted and disconcerted
by this development. What should his strategy be
in tackling this difficult area? Where should he
begin? Had he a precise objective? As it happened,
no immediate decisions had to be made, for war
broke out in the summer, and it became clear that
nothing systematic could be started while
hostilities continued. The Earl of Carnarvon would
not be returning to Egypt for the time being.
Carter, still retained, at least nominally, by
Carnarvon, and comfortably equipped with his
own house, decided to remain in the country,
offering himself for whatever war-work might
become available, and making only rare visits to
Britain. It seemed proper, however, in order to
clinch the concession, to carry out one small task

68 left After the removal of the sealed wall, the remainder of the wall on either side had to be taken down to make room for the shrines to be dismantled and removed without damage. In this picture it is clear that the shrines were protected with planks while the wall was taken down. Carter here works with his Egyptians and Callender.

68 right The removal of the sealed blocking in the Antechamber was a tricky operation, requiring great care to avoid damage to the shrines, and also to ensure that the archaeological evidence of the blocking should be properly recorded. In this view Carnarvon himself can be seen participating, helping Carter to remove parts of the sealed area.

tomb, but not all of it as he subsequently claimed; but he did find foundation deposits in front of the entrance to the tomb, and also, most interestingly, part of a fourth buckle.

The month's work, although disappointing in general, provided a good example of Carter's shrewd interpretation of what may have happened when Davis's excavators had been at work; there can be little doubt, as Carter surmised, that the buckles came from this tomb, stolen by Davis's workmen.

For nearly three years Carter was unable to resume work for Lord Carnarvon. He was not, however, entirely idle from the archaeological point of view. Whenever he came south to Thebes from Cairo, where he was engaged in work for Military Intelligence, he had time on his hands. 'Glad to say well occupied with drawing and painting.' Some of his drawing resulted from a commission he received to copy the very interesting, and artistically very fine, reliefs in the colonnade of the Temple of Luxor. Alan Gardiner planned a *de luxe* volume, the core of which would be Carter's drawings. Carter entered whole-heartedly into the work. The scenes, although always referred to by Gardiner as Horemheb's, had in fact been started in the reign of Amenophis III, and were completed under Tutankhamun. So, by

in the tomb of Amenophis III, which lay not in the main Valley of the Kings, but in the side *wadi* known as the West Valley. In 1912 Davis's men had done some work near the entrance to this tomb, which had been known since the time of the Napoleonic Expedition to Egypt in 1799. Nothing much had been found by Davis, but Carter subsequently purchased in Luxor for Lord Carnarvon three fine openwork plaques or buckles: 'They are two of carnelian and one agate cameos of Amenhotep III. I should say without a doubt from his tomb in the second Valley of the Kings (which as you know has never been properly cleared neither inside or out)...' So he reported to Carnarvon, and in February 1915 he followed up his hunch with a month's season in this tomb. The work carried out was perhaps a little perfunctory. He cleared some parts of the

coincidence, if not by planning, Carter found himself involved in material produced during the young king's reign. The project, sadly, was never completed because of the resumption of his work for Lord Carnarvon in late 1917. The drawings were among the finest he had ever made.

While he was staying in his house in Thebes, he was able to keep an eye on the activities of the local antiquities-hunters. Lax control during the war years offered rare opportunities for substantial initiatives in clandestine archaeology. Carter exploited his local knowledge and his acquaintance with the Qurnawi, and was able to salvage much useful archaeological information from the confusion caused by illicit tomb-robbing.

He also, more unusually, began a piece of serious research, probably the first in his lifetime, compiling a comprehensive dossier on the history

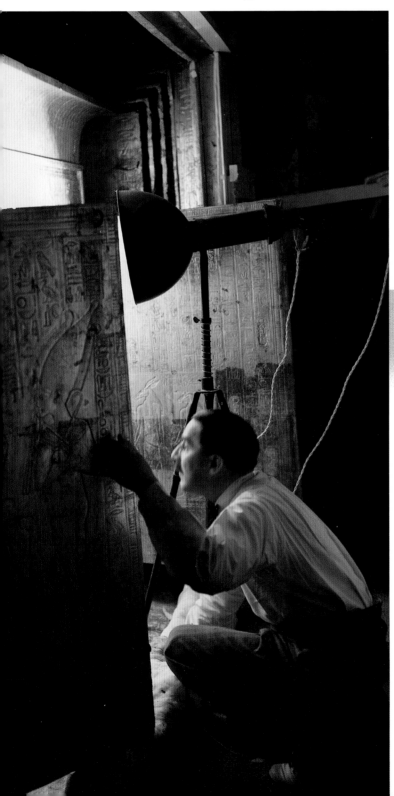

of the Valley of the Kings and its exploration. In Cairo he had access to good libraries, and he engaged the help of specialists to deal with evidence beyond his capabilities. Thus, he sought permission from the Metropolitan Museum Egyptian Expedition to ask their classical archaeologist, Hugh Evelyn-White, 'to help me later on the Classical stuff re Valley of the Kings. Among other reports of our work there which I trust will be exhaustive to the end – or as far as we can go – I aim... to publish in parts a kind of *Record of the Royal Theban Necropolis.*'

It is quite impressive to observe how Carter was preparing himself scientifically for the resumption of work in the Valley. It is now probably the right moment to consider whether Carter had at this time – the war years – seriously considered Tutankhamun's tomb to be a possible candidate for discovery. In his general book on the first season when he discovered that tomb, he states: 'at the risk of being accused of *post factum* prescience, I will state that we had definite hopes of finding the tomb of one particular king, and that king Tut.ankh.Amen'. He then goes on to justify this claim by setting out the archaeological evidence available at the time. All the relevant discoveries had been made by Theodore Davis. In the season of 1905–6 Ayrton found a small blue faience cup bearing the name of Tutankhamun; it lay 'at a depth of twelve feet from the surface' at a point

about half way between the tomb of Ramesses VI and that of Amenophis II. It was an isolated find at the time. On December 21, 1907 Ayrton opened a small pit in the hill above the tomb of Sethos I. It contained what seemed to be a collection of ancient refuse – pottery jars, bags of natron, floral collars, mud trays with the remains of food, seal impressions, fragments of linen. Davis showed no interest in these rather dreary objects (although some of the jars were of fine shape), and he subsequently allowed Herbert Winlock, a senior member of the Metropolitan Museum Egyptian Expedition, to carry the whole collection off to New York. In due course Winlock published a study of this material, concluding that it was indeed a mass of ancient refuse, but refuse deriving from the burial processes of the Tutankhamun inhumation. His name occurred on many objects, and much of the material, especially the natron, was undoubtedly waste from the embalming of the king. The traces of food were remnants of the final royal funerary feast. Winlock believed that the deposit was made some distance from the actual tomb so as not to contaminate the latter. The third piece of evidence pointing towards a tomb for Tutankhamun in the Valley was the cache of objects, including gold foil, about which Carter wrote to Mrs. Kingsmill Marrs in 1909, and which Davis had mistakenly published as the tomb of Tutankhamun.

Tutankhamun's name, and they, therefore, were as good evidence for the existence of his tomb as the blue faience cup and the inscribed gold fragments. His own studies of the history of the Valley of the Kings could also have revealed Tutankhamun as being a prime candidate for an undiscovered tomb. But he was a rather insignificant king. James Henry Breasted, the great American historian of ancient Egypt, had found scarcely anything to say about him in his *History of Egypt* (1905, new edition 1909). If his tomb were to be found, could it possibly be in the same class as those of his predecessors of the Eighteenth Dynasty? And could it possibly be intact? There is plenty of room for speculation about Howard Carter's thinking way back in 1914, or even 1917 when he was seriously to start his search. But it scarcely amounts

70 left Three views of the shrines in the process of dismantling. The top picture looks over the cornice of the outermost shrine on to the linen pall with gilt-bronze marguerites. The removal of this pall involved rolling it onto a specially made wooden roller. When it was removed to the tomb of Sethos II, it was laid out for conservation in front of the tomb, and there it suffered damage at the time when Carter was locked out of the tomb in 1924. In the center, a view of the top of the quartzite sarcophagus lying within the innermost shrine, the walls of which are carefully protected with padding.

All these pieces of evidence indicated that there was a tomb for Tutankhamun in the Valley. But can it be believed that Carter had made the right connections as early as his first survey of the Valley with the Earl of Carnarvon after the licence to dig there had passed to them? As far as the burial refuse is concerned Winlock, in his study of 1941, states that he did not fully appreciate what the objects truly signified until the early 1920s. 'Eventually I gave Howard Carter further information about the find and he used it in *The Tomb of Tut.ankh.Amen...*' It is quite possible that Carter was being less than accurate in claiming that he knew about Winlock's findings earlier than seems likely, but it is not unreasonable to believe that he knew that some of the objects carried

to much when the final triumph of his discovery is considered.

He opened his first campaign on the first of December 1917: 'Beginning in the small lateral valley situated between the tomb of Ramses II and Ramses VI, and running approximately N.W.–S.E.' It was not far from the entrance to that part of the main Valley which was occupied by the royal tombs. Opposite the opening to this 'small lateral valley' was KV 55, which had contained the extraordinary and enigmatic cache of Amarna Period funerary material found by Davis in 1907. The site was cut on its south side by the regular tourist path into the Valley on account of which excavation there had been strictly limited to avoid inconvenience to visitors. Here Carter first began

70 right Working in the confined space of the tomb to remove objects which were not in first-class condition required great delicacy and patience – virtues which Carter had in abundance. The removal of the top of the first shrine was particularly difficult. It was 5 metres long and over 3 metres wide, but was made up of three sections; there was little head-room for manuever. Here Carter and Callender supervise the operation. The original task of assembly after the funeral must have been equally difficult, although the timbers were not then warped.

to put into action his plan to clear down to bed-rock, the only certain way, he reckoned, by which he could be sure that no tomb entrance was missed. And here in a small triangular area below the entrance to the tomb of Ramesses VI he uncovered the remains of a group of stone structures, workmen's huts connected undoubtedly with the cutting of the adjacent royal tomb. At this point he did not clear down to bed-rock, being anxious to complete his season's work without further inconveniencing visitors to the Valley. He would not return to those huts until November 1922. Generally, the season had not been encouraging; few objects had been found, and Carter's worries were compounded by disturbing news of Lord Carnarvon. Later, in a letter to Albert Lythgoe of the Metropolitan Museum, Carter

wrote, 'Poor Lord Carnarvon, as no doubt you have heard, has had a very poor time. He nearly died this spring – saved only by an immediate operation for septic appendix.'

It is as well to bear in mind this crisis in the health of Lord Carnarvon, and to recall it when his mortal illness overtook him in 1923. He had first come to Egypt to recuperate from illness in 1903, and he always needed to watch his health. He was frequently accompanied by his personal physician when he came to Egypt. Yet illness did not prevent him from taking a strong interest in Carter's work. The War was not yet over, but the signs of final victory were beginning to appear as 1918 advanced. Carnarvon still wanted to excavate somewhere other than Thebes, and while the War continued he applied for and received a

71 top Carter sits at the entrance to the Burial Chamber making notes and considering his next move. The scaffolding and timber used to dismantle the shrines shows how little room there was to work comfortably. He greatly relied on Callender's practical experience as an engineer. Most of the second season was spent dismantling the shrines, and some of the shrine parts can be seen carefully packed against damage. They were not removed from the tomb, but left there to be dealt with finally in 1932, when, consolidated, they were transported to Cairo.

71 bottom Here the lid of the first coffin has been removed, revealing the second coffin. It is seen in this picture after the removal of garlands and the shroud that covered it. Preparations have been made to lift this coffin out of the shell of the first. Silver pins securing the lid of the coffin were partially pulled out and copper wires from the scaffolding were attached; these can be seen in the picture. So suspended, the coffin was left hanging clear while the shell of the first coffin was lowered. This was a typical example of Carter's ingenuity.

concession to work at Meir in Middle Egypt. Here there were rock-cut tombs of the Old and Middle Kingdoms, and it was worth giving the place a try. Carter proposed to carry out a limited, economical excavation for a few weeks – a trial dig. In late November 1918 he began work at Meir with a small body of workmen, and he continued until mid-January. The results were not encouraging, and Carter was happy to return to Thebes. He opened work again in Carnarvon's principal concession on February 19, but continued for one week only, clearing an area deep in the Valley, below the tomb of Tuthmosis III. The shortness of the season appears to have been not the paucity of finds, but the eruption of civil disturbances throughout Egypt. Carter was recruited to act as a political officer for the Nag Hamadi district to the north of Luxor.

The troubles calmed down after a few weeks, and Carter was able to return to England on leave, his first visit home for three years. Returning to Thebes in the autumn he renewed the work in the Valley on the January 5, 1920. Apart from a brief investigation in the 'canyon' (as Carter called it) above the tomb of Tuthmosis III, at the far end of the Valley, in which he detected traces of what he considered to be debris from the cutting of a tomb, and needing further exploration, the work during this ten-week season was concentrated near the entrance to the Valley. Here, between the tombs of Ramesses II and Ramesses IV there were huge deposits of debris, dumped there from earlier excavations. A very large team of workmen was needed, assisted by a length of Decauville rail with trucks to move the spoil well away from the parts to be investigated. Carter had first encountered such a light railway when he assisted Naville in the clearance of the Deir el-Bahri temple of Queen Hatshepsut. The experience he then gained in shifting vast quantities of deposit with the help of large numbers of men proved to be of considerable value in his work in the Valley. He had to vary the pace of the work between large-scale clearance and the careful examination of promising places when the bed-rock had been reached. But by his strategy he found intact foundation deposits

72 top and 73 Successive stages in the revealing of the third gold coffin. A reddish colored shroud covered it. The gold face was uncovered, arranged around the nemes-headdress was what Carter described as a linen napkin. An elaborate collar of beads and real flowers covered the neck and chest. When these had been removed, the lid of the gold coffin could be seen, disfigured by solidified unguents, but promising wonderful decoration when cleaned.

of Ramesses IV, and, as in most areas, numbers of inscribed and sketched *ostraca* – fragments of limestone used for casual sketches, memoranda, etc.

In mid-February Carnarvon, in much better health, joined Carter, staying, surprisingly, in Carter's house, while Lady Carnarvon and their daughter Evelyn Herbert stayed in the Winter Palace Hotel. Carter then shifted the focus of work to the area in front of the tomb of King Merenptah of the Nineteenth Dynasty, where again there were ancient, untouched, deposits. Here, in the presence of the Carnarvon family, he made what he described as 'the nearest approach to a real find that we had yet made in the Valley'. It was a collection of thirteen large alabaster vessels inscribed in ink with texts naming Merenptah and his father Ramesses II. They had held sacred oils used in the funerary ceremonies of Merenptah. 'We were naturally excited, and Lady Carnarvon, I remember, insisted on digging out these jars – beautiful specimens they were – with her own hands.' It is not surprising that Carter did not greatly welcome their presence on the dig; eager but untrained hands could easily cause damage.

Part of his plan for this season was to commence the clearance of the workmen's huts below the entrance to the tomb of Ramesses VI. But time ran out, and he decided to leave the huts until the next season, which he proposed to start in the autumn of 1920. Work began at the beginning of December. Once again he continued bed-rock clearance in the lateral valley between the tombs of Ramesses II and Ramesses VI, and he began work on the triangular site containing the huts. Fate was not on his side.

In his excavation diary entry for January 2, 1921 he notes: 'As one is unable to cut away the path in front of T9 (RVI) [i.e. the tomb of Ramesses VI] during the tourist season and the coming visit of the Sultan [] have removed men for the time being to another portion of the valley'. He had, in spite of good intentions, started his season too late, and VIP visits would at that time always take precedence over ordinary archaeology, as he was to find to his cost after he had made his great discovery, and was overwhelmed by grand visitors. Most of the rest of the season, which ended on March 3, 1921, was spent working a number of sites at the far end of the Valley, near the tomb of Tuthmosis III. This area exercised a notable attraction on Carter, who returned to it again and again, but always with negligible results.

His intention once again to start early in the autumn of 1921, to anticipate the arrival of tourists, was sadly frustrated by his own poor health. In October he wrote to Frederic Whiting, Director of the Cleveland Museum of Art, for whom he was acting as an antiquities adviser:

73

of condition. The yield of fine objects from these recent years had been considerably less than the harvest from the years of work in the lower slopes of Dra Abu'l Naga before the War. It was time to call a halt. Carter was summoned to Highclere Castle. The only evidence of this crucial meeting in the summer of 1922 is contained in Charles Breasted's biography of his father, James Henry Breasted, *Pioneer of the Past*, written in 1948. Breasted senior had given Carter much help over the inscriptions found in Tutankhamun's tomb, and while he was in Egypt at that time his son acted as his secretary, and had ample opportunity to talk to Carter. What he wrote about the meeting at Highclere he claimed to have heard from Carter himself. Carter knew in advance what the issue was, and understood the possible outcome. Understandably he did not want to stop the work until he was satisfied that nothing lay beneath those huts which had escaped investigation on so many occasions. He discussed his plans with

74 left Because the mummy was held solidly in the coffin by the unguents poured over it during the burial ceremonies there was no possibility of removing it for unwrapping. Carter therefore was obliged to conduct his examination of the mummy within the confined space of the coffin. It was a slow, nerve-racking and painstaking process, and it tested Carter's skills and patience to the utmost. Colleagues marvelled at his dexterity and at the cleverness of the many drawings he made of the successive stages in the unwrapping. Layer by layer he stripped the body of its bandages. Between each layer he found wonderful objects, unexpected treasures, many designed to protect the body from adverse forces in the king's afterlife. In all there were over 150 objects. By his successive drawings Carter compiled a stratified record of his examination. In this illustration the pommel of the golden dagger can be seen.

'unfortunately I have been indisposed for this last few weeks and I am now obliged to undergo a serious abdominal operation'. It would be the removal of his gall bladder, carried out by the same surgeon who had dealt with Lord Carnarvon's appendix in 1918. Carnarvon had become very much Carter's role-model in most things non-archaeological! He spent six weeks in hospital and six weeks convalescing before he could return to Egypt on January 25, 1922. Work started on February 8, the day after Lord Carnarvon had joined him. It was much too late for those tiresome but tantalizing workmen's huts, so Carter directed his men further into the Valley to the 'east side of the foot hill containing the tomb of Siptah'. Here Theodore Davis had worked in 1905, and Carter noted: 'The greater part of this spot was covered with large mounds of rubbish thrown out during the excavation of Siptah's tomb'. Carter also noted: 'Its removal took 10 days with 40 men and 120 boys'. The season ended in early March – Carter was still recovering from his gall bladder operation – and the results were minimal and again disappointing. Carnarvon, who had stayed on in Luxor for two weeks, while Carter visited Cairo, had time to reflect, and brood, on the way his excavation was going. It was not at all encouraging.

Later in the year, back in England, Carnarvon had further time for reflexion. Carter had been working in the Valley since late 1917 – over five years. It had not been such an intensive campaign as has sometimes been suggested, in total just about eight months on the ground. Nevertheless, work had at times been very concentrated, large numbers of men were employed, and the expense had been considerable. Carnarvon himself was not old, just fifty-six in June 1922; but his health was not good, and his finances, after the difficult years of the First World War, were not in the best

Carnarvon and, according to Breasted, offered to pay the costs of the final season himself. Carnarvon could not accept this generous offer, and agreed to finance the work. It was probably not going to be as expensive as has often been suggested. At Meir in 1918 Carter was spending only about five Egyptian pounds a day for a small workforce. For his final season at Thebes the labour costs could scarcely be much higher; living expenses would be minimal; equipment was already there in the Valley.

On October 11, Carter arrived in Egypt, and spent two weeks trawling the antiquities shops of Cairo on Carnarvon's and his own behalf. So much for urgency! On October 27 he reached Luxor, and on the November 1 opened his season in front of the tomb of Ramesses VI – the fateful untouched triangle of land. First came the planning and then the removal of those workmen's huts, completed by the evening of November 3. Carter could trust his experienced local workmen

to carry out the next stage without initial supervision. Under their foreman, Ahmed Gerigar, they began on the next day to remove the debris beneath the huts, working down to the bed-rock. By the time Carter joined the dig a frisson of expectation indicated that something had happened. The first step down to the tomb had been uncovered. With his knowledge of the arrangements of the entrances to tombs in the Valley, he had to be excited. In the course of the day enough steps had been uncovered to reveal the top of the plastered blocking, which without question indicated the entrance to a tomb. At that point Carter could not make out any royal names in the great seal impressions stamped on the mud plaster, but he could recognize the jackal and nine bound prisoners of the Royal Necropolis seal. Here at last was something to reward him for his persistence and faith, and Carnarvon for his support. Now he must contain his curiosity; and so, filling in the stairs, he crossed the river to Luxor, and sent off the fateful telegram quoted at the beginning of this chapter.

The Earl of Carnarvon and his daughter, Evelyn Herbert, reached Luxor on November 23. Carter and his new assistant, Arthur Callender, had everything ready to resume the clearance. By the afternoon of the 24th the whole blocked entrance was visible, and seal impressions towards the bottom clearly gave Tutankhamun's name. The removal of the blocking revealed a corridor leading down quite steeply and filled with rubble. There was disturbing evidence that this filling had been burrowed through on at least two occasions, and as the excavators removed the rubble, fragments of antiquities were found. Some of these carried royal names, which suggested that whatever lay beyond had been robbed, and that the contents might have been material from more than one royal burial – possibly another cache. After about eight metres a further mud-plastered blocking with seal impressions was reached. It was November 27. Carter wrote:

The decisive moment had arrived. With trembling hands I made a tiny breach in the upper left hand corner. Darkness and blank space, as far as an iron testing rod could reach, showed that whatever lay beyond was empty... Candle tests were applied as a precaution against foul gases and then, widening the hole a little, I inserted the candle and peered in... At first I could see nothing... but presently, as my eyes grew accustomed to the light, details of the room within emerged slowly from the mist, strange animals, statues and gold – everywhere the glint of gold. For the moment... I was struck dumb with amazement, and when Lord Carnarvon, unable to stand the suspense any longer, inquired anxiously. 'Can you see anything?' it was all I could do to get out the words, 'Yes, wonderful things'.

Now the great work of investigation and clearance could begin.

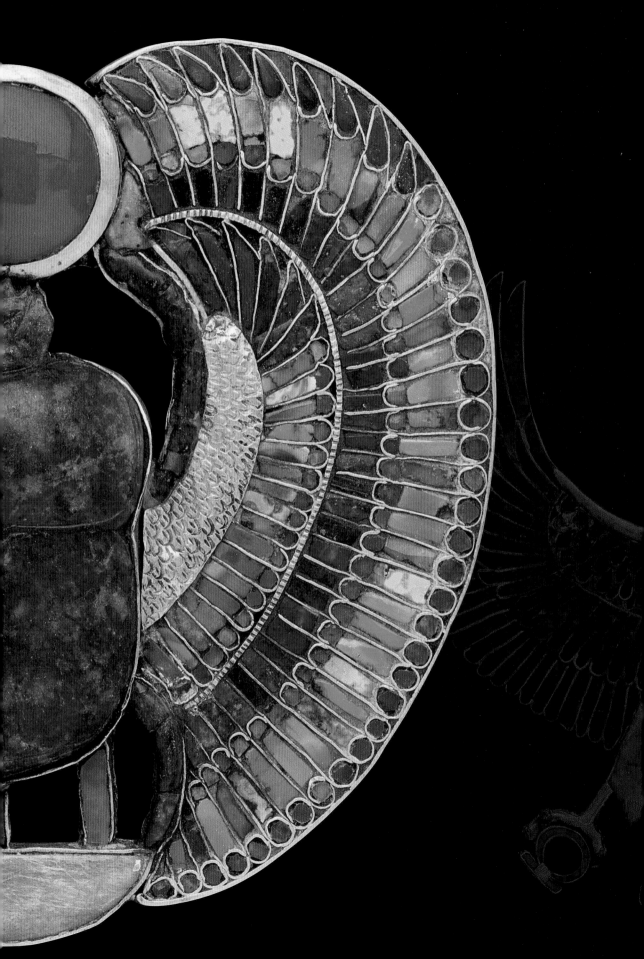

A Treasure above
All Treasures

76–77 *A pectoral from a jewel box in the Treasury. Its main form of a winged scarab incorporates the prenomen of Tutankhamun. The cloisonné inlays are of semiprecious stones and coloured glass, the scarab itself being a fine single piece of lapis-lazuli.*

78 *A calcite stopper from the Canopic chest. It is a royal head which is surely not that of Tutankhamun; it was possibly prepared originally for the burial of his predecessor Neferneferuaten.*

79 *A carnelian bird, a swallow or a swift, with a sun-disk on its back. It is mounted on a gold bangle placed within the king's mummy wrappings. The bird may represent a transformation of the sun-god.*

When Howard Carter was asked by Lord Carnarvon what he could see through the hole he had made in the blocked entrance to the tomb, he claims to have said 'wonderful things'. These may not have been his precise words at the time, but they have come to represent what he could have said, words which were in any case very appropriate for the discovery. The tomb was not in the state it would have been at the time of the king's funeral, and for Carter and Carnarvon that implied that it was not intact. According to the terms of his licence to excavate, Carnarvon could expect a substantial share of the tomb's contents, and there can be little doubt that he ever thought otherwise. Carter from the first had felt that the whole tomb equipment should go to the Cairo Museum, but he was Carnarvon's man, and he could advise but not decide.

His examination of the many boxes in the Antechamber which had been broken into, rifled, and repacked carelessly by the Necropolis guards convinced him that a very large number of fine and precious objects had been stolen. His view

was reinforced when he came to examine the Treasury. Here again there was scarcely a box that had not had its seal broken and been ransaked. In the tomb only the innermost shrines, the sarcophagus and coffins, the royal mummy itself and the Canopic shrine were in the positions and condition in which they had been left on the day of burial.

So, Carter concluded, the majority of fine objects, including most of the best jewellery, had gone, and he was left to deal with the residue. What a residue! Carter never complained about the 'meagre' material with which he and his co-workers had to deal. A residue indeed, but still what riches! It took ten years to clear, clean, conserve and document the objects, with many lost months when official difficulties prevented work at Thebes. It is doubtful whether any other archaeologist of the time would have had the pertinacity and patience to keep the process going for so long: certainly not Sir Flinders Petrie, brilliant but impatient; not even George Reisner of Harvard and Boston, meticulous but restless.

80–81 One side of the palm of the ostrich-hunt fan found in the Burial Chamber. Here Tutankhamun is depicted in heroic form. He stands alone in his chariot, driving his team of horses at full speed in the chase after ostriches in the Eastern Desert. Two birds have been shot with the king's arrows, and his hound bounds forward to retrieve them. A fine symbolic touch in the design is the ostrich fan carried behind the chariot by a personified ankh-sign.

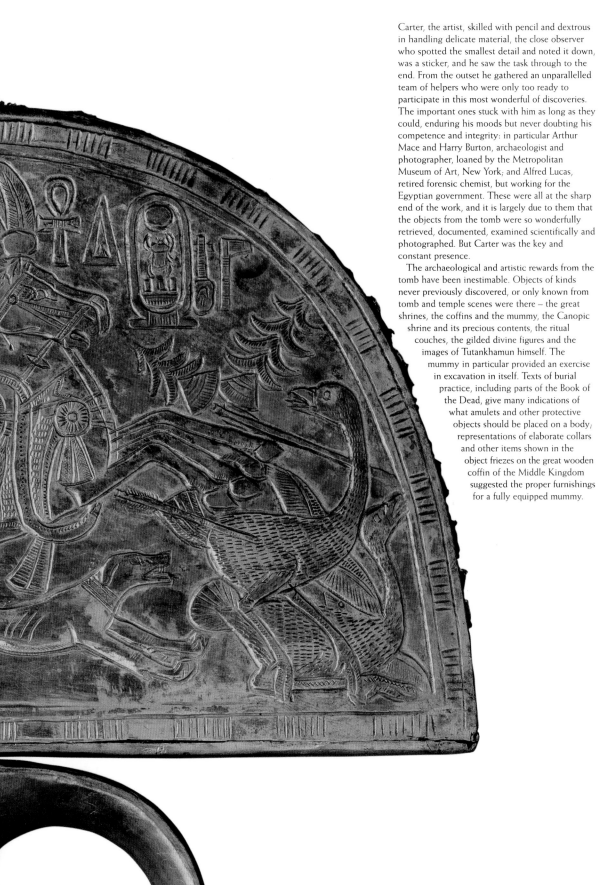

Carter, the artist, skilled with pencil and dextrous in handling delicate material, the close observer who spotted the smallest detail and noted it down, was a sticker, and he saw the task through to the end. From the outset he gathered an unparalleled team of helpers who were only too ready to participate in this most wonderful of discoveries. The important ones stuck with him as long as they could, enduring his moods but never doubting his competence and integrity: in particular Arthur Mace and Harry Burton, archaeologist and photographer, loaned by the Metropolitan Museum of Art, New York; and Alfred Lucas, retired forensic chemist, but working for the Egyptian government. These were all at the sharp end of the work, and it is largely due to them that the objects from the tomb were so wonderfully retrieved, documented, examined scientifically and photographed. But Carter was the key and constant presence.

The archaeological and artistic rewards from the tomb have been inestimable. Objects of kinds never previously discovered, or only known from tomb and temple scenes were there – the great shrines, the coffins and the mummy, the Canopic shrine and its precious contents, the ritual couches, the gilded divine figures and the images of Tutankhamun himself. The mummy in particular provided an exercise in excavation in itself. Texts of burial practice, including parts of the Book of the Dead, give many indications of what amulets and other protective objects should be placed on a body; representations of elaborate collars and other items shown in the object friezes on the great wooden coffin of the Middle Kingdom suggested the proper furnishings for a fully equipped mummy.

As Howard Carter removed the bandages from the royal corpse, he uncovered layer after layer of protective objects – representations charged with divine power, amuletic objects invested with magical forces by appropriate texts. Here for the first time was a practical demonstration of what the texts had indicated. Even now the full implications of the mummy accoutrements have not been adequately appreciated or studied.

In many respects the contents of the tomb gave the impression of being a haphazard collection of objects from the palace and the royal storerooms. Did a royal burial provide an opportunity to dispose of royal objects which were no longer of any use, but could not just be thrown away? Why, for example, was a wine jar included which dated back to the reign of Amenophis III? Was it full of wine when deposited in the tomb? Could the wine have been drinkable? Was it just an opportunity to dispose of a jar of royal wine well past its consumable date?

The questions are manifold, and there remains much scope for the analysis and examination of the tomb's contents. What cannot be denied, however, is that the range and excellent condition of so many objects, made by the best craftsmen, using the best materials, provide huge opportunities for the elucidation of technical processes, and the study of styles and even of taste. Let us consider the remarkable calcite vessels used to hold unguents and perfumed oils. For years these extraordinary containers were singled out as examples of bad taste. They were florid, over-decorated, intricate beyond the requirements of utility: in short, they demonstrated the decadence of artistic appreciation at the end of the Eighteenth Dynasty. They lacked the purity of form which seemed so characteristic of Egyptian design in the Middle Kingdom and in the earlier years of the Eighteenth Dynasty. Nowadays it is easier to consider such objects as being creations of their time, made for their particular function according to the principles of contemporary appreciation. Why should our good taste be the same as the good taste of the ancient Egyptians? Some people may not like them, but they are what they are, the remarkable products of remarkable craftsmen who understood the capabilities of their materials and exploited them to the best of their abilities.

The tomb's contents are infinite in their ability to teach, to surprise, to enthral. They make up a cornucopia of treasure, sacred and profane. They are indeed wonderful things.

82 The shape of the pomegranate was a favourite of Egyptian vessel makers of the New Kingdom, examples occurring in glass, calcite and ivory. This little vase, made of silver with a substantial proportion of gold, is one of two such vases in the tomb, the other being made of ivory. It bears bands of chased decoration incorporating cornflowers and vine leaves.

83 A gilded wooden standard of the divine falcon named Gemehsu. It was stored with the standard of Sopdu in one of the black-painted wooden chests in the Treasury. The Gemehsu falcon, shown in mummified form with a royal flail protruding from its back, may represent in form one of several Egyptian divinities so transformed. The details are made of glass inlay.

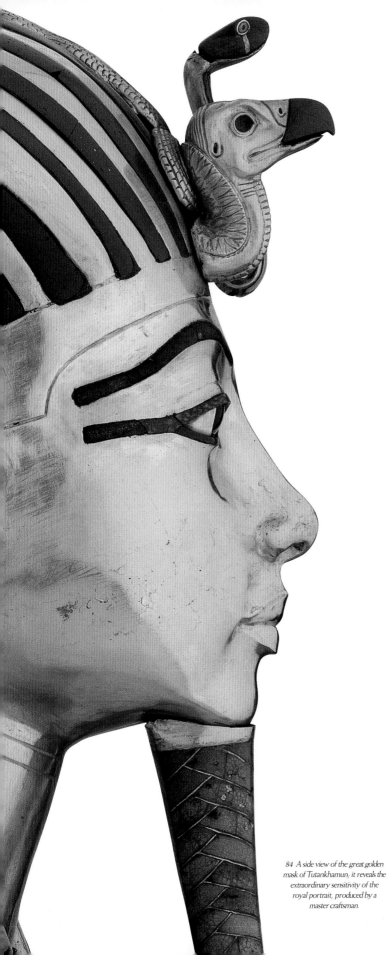

Personal Funerary Equipment

The most important object in a tomb was the mummy of the deceased. The most important purpose of the burial was to ensure the preservation of the mummy so that the dead person could pass to and be equipped for the after-life. The greatest care was therefore taken to protect the mummy.

In the tomb of Tutankhamun was found the most complete set of protective measures discovered in any burial. The mummy was contained within three coffins, all placed in a stone sarcophagus, which in turn was enclosed within four shrines. A hint of such an arrangement had been found by Carter and Alan Gardiner in a tomb plan on a papyrus in the Turin Museum which they had published in 1917. In this plan the sarcophagus is surrounded by six rectangles, which they had tentatively thought to be steps. In retrospect they could see an arrangement of sarcophagus and shrines like those provided for Tutankhamun.

Tutankhamun's ensemble fitted so neatly into his small burial chamber that it must be concluded that the shrines were almost certainly made after the king's death, when the layout was known.

A secondary part of the personal funerary equipment concerned the mummified internal organs of the deceased. These were usually placed in four vessels called Canopic jars. In Tutankhamun's case the organs were placed in four miniature coffins put in a calcite chest. A gilded wooden shrine covered the chest, and the shrine was protected by an open canopy with an elaborate cornice. The whole shrine was placed under the protection of four gilded figures of the protective goddesses Isis, Nephthys, Selkis and Neith – among the most enchanting and seductive figures to have been found in Egypt, or any other ancient culture.

The Canopic shrine, because of the lack of space in the Burial Chamber, was placed in the adjacent room, which Carter called the Treasury.

84 A side view of the great golden mask of Tutankhamun; it reveals the extraordinary sensitivity of the royal portrait, produced by a master craftsman.

1

THE FIRST
GILDED SHRINE

(CARTER 207, J.D'E. 60664; LENGTH 508 CM,
WIDTH 328 CM, HEIGHT 275 CM)

When Howard Carter began to take down the blocking between the Antechamber and the Burial Chamber, the observers gathered in the tomb were dazzled by the gradual revelation of this shrine, a spectacular gold wall with openwork decoration consisting of the amuletic signs *djed* and *tyet*, 'endurance and life', with a background of bright blue glazed faience. The great shrine subsequently revealed had a roof with two humps, somewhat resembling the sign for the horizon. As a whole the shrine also resembles the pavilion used during the *sed* or jubilee festival of the king, composed of two chapels placed back to back. Its walls are inscribed on the inside and on the doors with texts from the Book of the Dead and passages from a composition for royal burials known as the Book of the Divine Cow. Nine vultures with outstretched wings decorate the ceiling. Within this shrine, and embracing the second shrine was the frame supporting the linen pall with gilt-bronze marguerites.

THE SECOND GILDED SHRINE

(CARTER 237, J.D'E. 60660; LENGTH 374 CM, WIDTH 235 CM, HEIGHT 225 CM)

Between the first, outermost, shrine and this second shrine was the linen pall with gilded bronze daisies draped over a wooden frame. The form of the shrine itself, with sloping roof, is that of the *per-wer*, traditionally the Upper Egyptian shrine. The wooden structure is covered with gesso-plaster, carved with fine relief representations and inscriptions, and then gilded. The texts on the inside and the outside are taken from traditional royal compositions like the Pyramid Texts of the Old Kingdom, and also from the more recent compilations, like the Book of the Dead. There are also texts written in hieroglyphs used enigmatically, where incomprehensible switchings of signs are used, presumably to confuse the hostile forces which the king might meet in his journeys after death. Carter detected changes in cartouches which to him suggested re-use from the Amarna Period. The representations, however, are not in the Amarna style.

3

4

THE THIRD GILDED SHRINE

(CARTER 238, J.D'E. 60667; LENGTH 340 CM, WIDTH 192 CM, HEIGHT 215 CM)

Like the second shrine, this one is also in the form of the Upper Egyptian palace shrine, the *per-wer*. In the usual royal tomb of the Eighteenth Dynasty, the walls of the various rooms and corridors were decorated and inscribed with scenes and texts from the newly devised royal compositions to enable the dead king to pass through the Underworld by night, to achieve union with the sun god at dawn. The tomb of Tutankhamun, a makeshift refuge for a king prematurely dead, it seems, was cramped, and the only room to be decorated was the Burial Chamber. In consequence, some of the important texts of divine passage were inscribed on the great shrines. On the outer walls of this third shrine are shortened versions of two of the sections of the composition 'What is in the Underworld', a small part of which is painted on the west wall of the Burial Chamber. There is also an utterance from the Book of the Dead for providing sustenance to the *ka* of the deceased in the underworld.

THE FOURTH GILDED SHRINE

(CARTER 239, J.D'E. 60668; LENGTH 290 CM, WIDTH 148 CM, HEIGHT 190 CM)

This shrine has a vaulted roof, taking the form of the pre-dynastic Lower Egyptian palace shrine, the *per-nu*. When it was erected in the tomb it made a tight fit around the sarcophagus, which had not been positioned with precision; parts of it therefore had to be trimmed to permit its erection. The walls of the shrine have reliefs containing deities closely associated with the protection of the king after death, and the care of his separately mummified internal organs.

All the Canopic deities are shown: Isis, Nephthys, Selkis and Neith; and the genii of the entrails: Amsety, Duamutef, Hapy and Qebhsenuef; also those deities found on the sides of royal sarcophagi: Thoth in two forms, Geb, Anubis and Horus. The main text is Utterance 17 of the Book of the Dead, a long rambling composition concerning the sun god and his doctrinal significance, with many comments on the god and on the deceased.

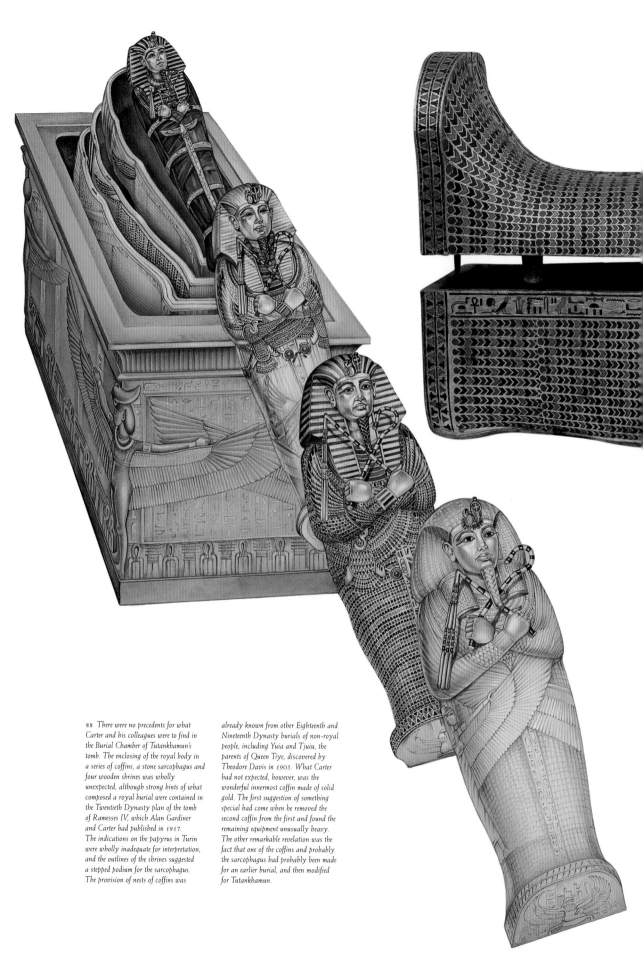

88 There were no precedents for what Carter and his colleagues were to find in the Burial Chamber of Tutankhamun's tomb. The enclosing of the royal body in a series of coffins, a stone sarcophagus and four wooden shrines was wholly unexpected, although strong hints of what composed a royal burial were contained in the Twentieth Dynasty plan of the tomb of Ramesses IV, which Alan Gardiner and Carter had published in 1917. The indications on the papyrus in Turin were wholly inadequate for interpretation, and the outlines of the shrines suggested a stepped podium for the sarcophagus. The provision of nests of coffins was already known from other Eighteenth and Nineteenth Dynasty burials of non-royal people, including Yuia and Tjuiu, the parents of Queen Tiye, discovered by Theodore Davis in 1905. What Carter had not expected, however, was the wonderful innermost coffin made of solid gold. The first suggestion of something special had come when he removed the second coffin from the first and found the remaining equipment unusually heavy. The other remarkable revelation was the fact that one of the coffins and probably the sarcophagus had probably been made for an earlier burial, and then modified for Tutankhamun.

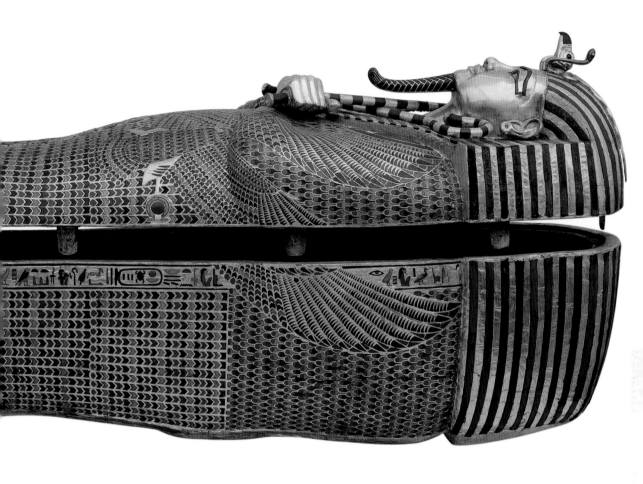

THE MIDDLE COFFIN

(CARTER 254, J.D'E. 60670; LENGTH 204 CM, MAX. HEIGHT 78.5 CM; MAX. WIDTH 68 CM)

The fine outer coffin of Tutankhamun, of gilded and inlaid wood, now lies in the sarcophagus in the king's tomb in the Valley; it contains the royal mummy.

When Carter returned to Thebes in the autumn of 1925, his first task was to open up the coffin to retrieve and examine the mummy. What he did not appreciate was that there would be three coffins nesting each within another. When the lid of the outermost coffin was raised, he found the middle coffin covered with a linen shroud and garlands of flowers – olives, lotus, cornflowers – attached to strips of papyrus. After removal and cleaning, the coffin presented a magnificent sight.

It is made of wood and covered with sheet gold. The decoration of the body is carried out in a cloisonné technique, which involved the inlaying of pieces of coloured glass and semiprecious stones in cells or cloisons made by soldering thin strips of gold to the main body of the coffin. The inlays are individually cut to fit the cloisons. Dark blue glass, light blue glass and red glass represent lapis-lazuli, turquoise and red jasper or carnelian. The principal decorative motif is a feather design, called *rishi*, which here looks like chevrons. On the upper part of the coffin inlaid figures of the cobra and vulture deities with outstretched wings protect the body within.

On the lid of the coffin, the king is shown with royal accoutrements, and the headdress known as *nemes*, in reality probably made of folded cloth. On his brow are the two royal protective deities, cobra and vulture heads. The plaited beard with turned up tip is closely associated with Osiris, god of the dead.

The features of the king here are markedly different from those on the outer and innermost coffins, which suggests that this coffin may not have been made originally for Tutankhamun.

THE INNERMOST COFFIN

(CARTER 255, J.D'E. 60671; LENGTH 187 CM,
HEIGHT 51 CM, WIDTH 51.3 CM, WEIGHT 110.4 KG)

90

The excavators were much puzzled by the great weight of the coffins when they were removed from the sarcophagus. The mystery was solved when the lid of the middle coffin was raised and they found a third coffin made of solid gold. After the removal of its contents and cleaning, it was found to weigh 110.4 kg. It is quite the most impressive coffin ever found, but apart from its bullion value it is an outstanding piece of craftsmanship; the head is particularly well done, the features being distinctly those of the young king. Again he is shown with the *uraeus* and vulture on his brow, and holding the crook and flail, symbols of royalty. Around the neck, separately added, are necklaces of disk beads of gold and coloured glass; on his chest is an elaborate collar made up to represent eleven rows of tubular beads of coloured glass.

When this coffin was placed in the middle coffin, large quantities of bituminous resin were poured over it,

which in time fixed it firmly in place. It took Carter and his assistants much time to soften and chip away this material, in order to separate the two coffins. The hot bitumen had damaged some of the inlays, and caused deterioration in some elements of decoration, including the calcite whites of the eyes.

The decoration of the main body of the coffin is again *rishi*-work, but here in the form of chasing rather than inlay. Splendid figures of the cobra Wadjyt and the vulture Nekhbet with outstretched protective wings are shown on the chest, and further down on the sides of the legs are delicate relief figures of Isis and Nephthys, traditional guardians and mourners of the dead, also with protecting wings. On the foot of the coffin is another figure of the goddess Isis with outstretched wings, beautifully designed to fit the available space. She is shown kneeling on the sign for 'gold', and is described as 'Great Isis, mother of the god'.

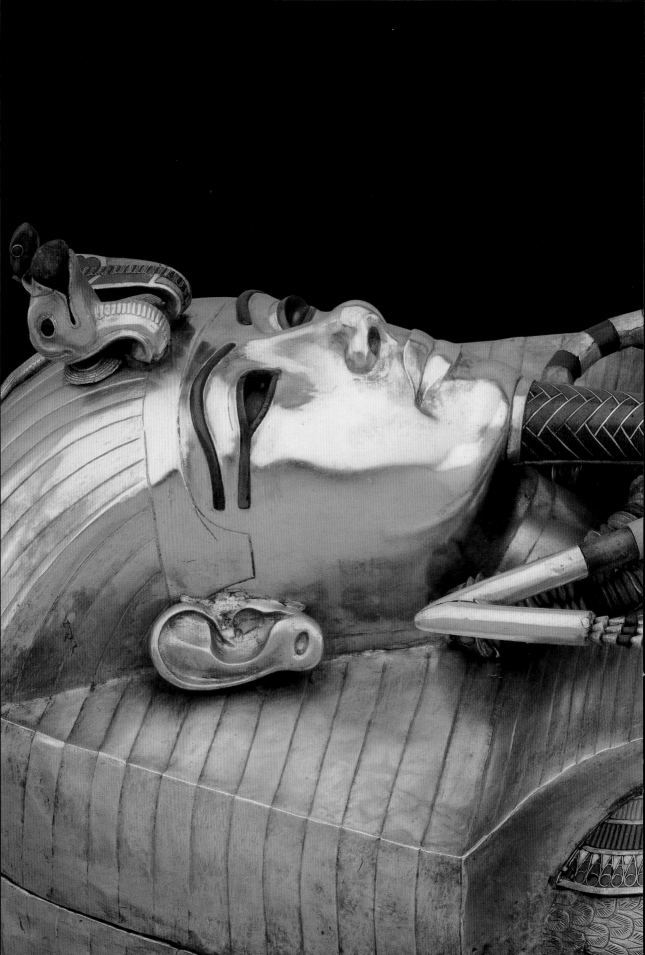

The gold mask

(CARTER 256A, J.D'E. 60672;
HEIGHT 54 CM; WEIGHT 11 KG)

No object from the tomb evokes the tragedy and magnificence of the young king more than this gold mask. It is without a doubt a masterpiece of portraiture and a supreme example of the skill of Egyptian goldsmiths. When the solid gold coffin was opened the excavators were faced with a mummy covered with quantities of unguents; but 'in contradistinction to the general dark and sombre effect, due to the unguents, was a brilliant, one might say magnificent, burnished gold mask or similitude of the king, covering his head and shoulders...'

It was some time before the mask could be removed from the king's body. Because everything was fixed firmly in the coffin by the unguents, Carter decided to examine the mummy before removing it; this involved the removal of the wrappings and the careful mapping end extrication of the many pieces of jewellery and other items contained within the wrappings. When the mask was available for examination it was found to consist mainly of two sheets of gold, raised into shape and then joined together by hammering. The surface was finished with chased detail and embellished by burnishing. The king is shown wearing the *nemes* headdress, its striations inlaid with blue glass; on the brow are the protective deities Nekhbet and Wadjyt, both in solid gold with inlays of glass, carnelian and lapis-lazuli.

The broad collar with falcon terminals on the chest has twelve rows of beads represented by inlays of semiprecious stones and glass. The realistic eyes are composed of white quartz and black obsidian; their rims and brows are inlaid with lapis-lazuli. The ear-lobes, pierced for ear-rings, were covered with gold foil when discovered.

The back flap of the mask is inscribed with a magical text designed to protect the various parts of the mask which are identified with specific deities: thus, 'your forehead is Anubis; your right eye is the night boat (of the sun-god Re); your left eye is the day-boat; your eyebrows are the company of nine gods'.

THE CANOPIC SHRINE

(CARTER 266, J.D'E. 60686;
HEIGHT 198 CM, LENGTH 153 CM, WIDTH 122 CM)

The purpose of this shrine was to protect the embalmed internal organs of the dead king. The shrine itself is placed under an open canopy on a sledge. All components are made of wood and gilded. The corner posts of the canopy are inscribed inside and out with Tutankhamun's full titulary. The posts support a heavy cornice with a dramatic frieze of *uraei* with sun-disks, inlaid with blue, red and green glass; the effect is spectacular.

Between the posts on each side is a figure of one of the goddesses charged with protecting the containers of the entrails: Isis is identified by a seat on her head, Nephthys by a basket on an enclosure, Selkis by a scorpion and Neith by two bows. The figures are among the most appealing of Egyptian sculptures. Each goddess is shown with a slender, slightly elongated body, designed in accordance with the proportions associated with the art of the Amarna Period. Each is shown wearing a tight-fitting pleated garment with short sleeves; her head is covered by a cloth; her hair, which hangs down the back, being drawn together just below her neck. Most exceptionally, each head is turned to the left in an attractive but quite un-Egyptian manner. Eyes and eyebrows are dramatically marked in black.

The shrine itself also has a cornice and frieze of *uraei*. Each side shows a scene of a god or goddess stretching out a hand towards one of the Canopic deities or genii, identified with the various organs: Isis to Amsety, Geb (the earth god) to Duamutef, Ptah-Sokar-Osiris to Qebhsenuef, and Nephthys to Hapy. The effect of Amarna-style conventions can again be observed in these divine figures; it is particularly noticeable that their heads are exaggerated in size.

100 The arrangement of coffins and shrines, provided for the protection of the mummy of the dead king, has been compared with the idea of 'Chinese boxes' or 'Russian dolls' – a diminishing series of containers, one within another. A similar, but less complicated, arrangement was prepared for the protection of those parts of the royal body which could not be included in the coffins. The diagrammatic illustration here shows clearly the sequence of the protective elements. An open canopy surrounds the shrine proper, which is supported by the four Canopic goddesses, charmingly and sensitively posed. Within the shrine was the Canopic chest with lid, made from two pieces of finely zoned calcite. On the removal of the lid four royal heads become visible. These form the stoppers of four cylindrical depressions cut into the calcite of the chest, each depression containing a solid gold miniature coffin decorated in the cloissonné technique, and containing the mummified internal organs of the king.

THE CANOPIC CHEST

(CARTER 266B, J.D'E. 60687; TOTAL HEIGHT 85.5 CM,
WIDTH OF EACH SIDE OF THE BASE 54 CM)

The very earliest known Canopic chest was made for Queen Hetepheres, mother of Cheops the builder of the Great Pyramid, who lived more than a thousand years before Tutankhamun. It was made of calcite and of very simple design. Tutankhamun's chest is also made of calcite, but more elaborate in design. It was found inside the Canopic shrine, covered with a linen cloth.

In the Eighteenth Dynasty most Canopic chests had compartments containing jars for the internal organs, each with a human head stopper. This royal chest has four cylindrical depressions cut into its mass to receive the Canopic coffins, and each is topped by a stopper in the form of a royal head, finely carved with a few details picked out in black paint, and the lips rouged. The heads seem to be portraits. But of whom? There is good reason to believe that they do not show Tutankhamun, but perhaps his predecessor. This question is discussed further in connection with the Canopic coffins.

The chest is carved from a finely veined block of calcite in the form of a shrine; it has a sloping lid which was fastened to the chest by cords passed through staples and sealed. The chest stands on a gilded wooden sledge, and its lower part is carved with a gilded dado made up of the amuletic *djed* and *tyet* signs connected with Osiris and Isis. At the corners of the chest figures of the four protective goddeses are carved in high relief: Isis, Nephthys, Neith and Selkis. Each figure is quite unusual in that it is folded around its corner with one arm stretched on the two adjacent sides of the chest. Each is shown apparently nude, with very slender elongated limbs, but without the usual protecting wings. The inscriptions carved on the sides of the chest are filled with blue pigment which contrasts sharply with the waxy-yellow colour of the calcite. The texts invoke the protection of the four deities.

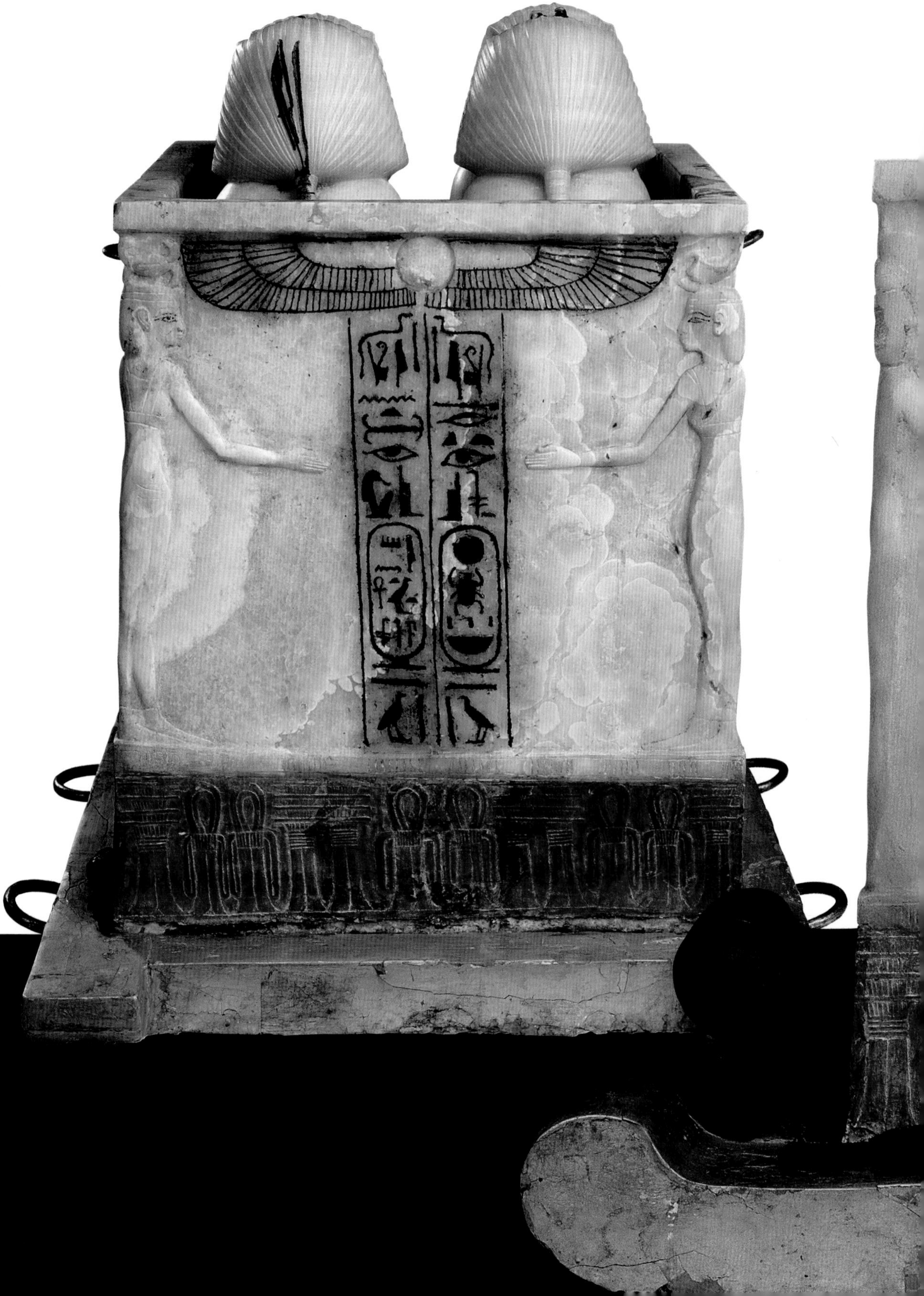

104 The two sides of the Canopic chest shown here carry statements by Canopic goddesses. The left-hand picture shows the back of the chest, and the statements are addressed by Neith (left) and Selkis (right) to Tutankhamun, whose names are in the cartouches. The figures of the appropriate goddesses are carved on the corners of the chest.

105 The principal picture shows one side of the chest with invocations by Neith (right) and Isis (left) to their Canopic genii, Qebhsenuef and Amsety respectively. Above is the sloping lid of the chest.

106–107 Two of the Canopic lids representing Tutankhamun, but probably portraits of his predecessor Neferneferuaten.

CANOPIC COFFINS

(CARTER 266, J.D'E. 60690, 60689;
HEIGHT 39 CM, WIDTH 11 CM, DEPTH 12 CM)

The term Canopic jar is strictly incorrect. Early scholars saw in these human-headed jars confirmation of the ancient story of Canopus, pilot of Menelaus, who was buried at Canopus and worshipped locally in the form of a jar with a human head. Jars were not, however, used for Tutankhamun's internal organs, but miniature coffins. Those illustrated here, protected by Nephthys and Neith, held the king's lungs, identified with the genius Hapy, and his stomach, identified with the genius Duamutef.

Each small coffin is a remarkable example of the Egyptian goldsmith's skills. Made of solid gold, most of the body is covered with the feathered *rishi*-pattern, carried out in the cloisonné technique, with tiny cloisons inlaid with individually cut pieces of coloured glass. The upper part of the body is shown to be enveloped by the wings of two vultures, one with the head of Nekhbet, the other with the *uraeus* head of Wadjyt. A line of text on the lid contains a statement by the appropriate deity: 'I embrace with my arms what is within me; I protect Hapy (or Duamutef) who is in me, Hapy (or Duamutef) of the Osiris King Nebkheperure [prenomen of Tutankhamun], justified before the great god'. The inside of the lid has a figure of the appropriate deity in protective attitude; the body of the coffin contains a long magical text on behalf of the king.

Careful examination shows that changes have been made to the cartouches inside the coffins. Traces indicate clearly that the name in the prenomen cartouche was first Ankh-kheperure, prenomen of Neferneferuaten, predecessor of Tutankhamun. The chest and miniature coffins were clearly made originally for this predecessor; they were either never used or recycled for the young king. The physiognomy of the human-headed stoppers and of the little coffins, so distinctly different from that of Tutankhamun, as shown by his innermost and outermost coffins and many other images in the tomb, provides strong confirmation of this re-use.

Servant Figures

The burial of every Egyptian of means would include a figure in mummiform which was magically to assist the deceased in carrying out certain manual duties in the afterworld. In the Eighteenth Dynasty many burials were provided with fine *shabtis* in various materials, and later in the dynasty they begin to be called *shawabtis*. They are usually shown carrying hoes, mattocks and baskets – the tools of their trade.

The few surviving *shabtis* of kings of the Eighteenth Dynasty had shown that fine examples were made; but these could in no way have prepared the excavators for the great numbers found in Tutankhamun's tomb: in total 413, mostly stored in black painted boxes, eleven in the Treasury (with 176 figures) and fourteen in the Annexe (236); one which had 'escaped' from the Annexe was found in the Antechamber. Where a figure is named, it is called *shabti*. A common analysis of the 413 establishes 365 as being for single-day duty, thirty-six for duties overseeing groups of more than ten, and twelve as monthly overseers. It is not easy, however, to apply this distribution to the figures themselves. There is a huge diversity in material, size, iconography and inscription. Some are plain wood with a few details emphasized in black paint; gold leaf used sparingly enhances others; some are of wood, wholly gilded. There are many faience examples with different coloured glazes; some are carved of stone – calcite, limestone, granite etc. There are many headdresses, all the principal royal crowns being represented. Some hold royal insignia, but not usually working tools. But large numbers of model hoes, mattocks, yokes and baskets in metal, faience and wood were also found in the Treasury and the Annexe.

The finest figures are of carved wood, large, and presented for the king's burial by the general and royal scribe Nakhtmin, or Minnakhte (five), and the treasurer Maya (one): tokens of devotion in life and beyond the grave.

110 left Plain wooden shabti *with a broad collar and armlets of gold foil, wearing a Nubian wig with bronze* uraeus *and vulture heads.*

110 right Gilded wooden shabti *wearing the white crown of Upper Egypt and holding a bronze crook. Bodily features suggest that this figure was made for a woman.*

111 Turquoise glazed shabti *with details picked out in black. This is an overseer or* reis *figure, and it holds the characteristic flail and folded cloth.*

SHABTI WITH BLUE CROWN

(CARTER 318A, J.D'E. 60830;
HEIGHT 48 CM)

There is nothing ordinary about this *shabti*-figure. It is a fine small sculpture in its own right, made from a close-grained wood, mostly left plain, but highlighted with a discreet use of gold leaf on the broad collar, head band, *uraeus* and flail. The figure is mummiform, and the king is shown wearing the blue crown, the *khepresh*. The eyes and eye-brows are marked in black and the pupils of the eyes marked with white paint. He holds the crook and the flail, symbols of royal power, in his hands. Two lines of text running down the body contain just part of the common *shabti*-text, in which the figure is charged by the deceased to answer for him if he is conscripted for field-work in the after-life. Of particular interest is the short text underneath the feet: 'Made by the servant, loved of his lord, the general Minnakhte, justified'. It is one of five *shabtis* similarly inscribed, indicating that they were made for Tutankhamun's burial as tokens of respect by Minnakhte, and this accounts for the fine quality of the carving.

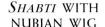

SHABTI WITH NUBIAN WIG

(CARTER 326A-F, J.D'E. 60835;
HEIGHT 54 CM)

SHABTI WITH TWO FLAILS

(CARTER 325A, J.D'E. 60838;
HEIGHT 52 CM)

This plain wooden *shabti* with some gilding differs from some of its comparable fellows in a number of respects. To begin with, it shows both hands holding gilded bronze flails. It is impossible to determine whether it was placed in the tomb so equipped, for at the very least it might have been expected that one of the flails should have been replaced by a bronze crook. The figure would then have been truly furnished with the insignia of royalty. And yet the Nubian wig, which fits the head, lacks any royal mark – the *uraeus* or the vulture head and *uraeus* which occur together on many of the larger Tutankhamun *shabtis*. Apart from the gilded flails, gold is used for the multiple bead collar on the chest and the bracelets on the wrists. A thin gold band separates the wig from the brow. Like some other of the large wooden *shabtis*, this figure carries four vertical columns of text containing a fairly full Eighteenth Dynasty *shabti* text, invoking the figure to work on behalf of the dead king if his name is called in the corvée.

In some respects the *shabtis* from the tomb made just of wood, or of wood with some gilding, are much more attractive artistically than those heavily gilded. This example is particularly fine, conveying an extraordinary feeling of dignity. It is a simple wooden mummiform figure, beautifully carved, with just enough gilding to enhance the overall effect. There is a thin gold head band, a collar of quite substantial gold foil, and one gold bracelet. The headdress is interesting. It is a kind of wig sometimes called 'Nubian', with some royal connotations, worn both by men and women. Tutankhamun, for example, wears it in scenes on the golden shrine, in activities some of which could be described as informal, such as the king with his queen shooting birds in the papyrus swamp. In tomb 55 in the Valley, often called the Amarna cache, a set of Canopic jars has stoppers with this wig; they may belong to a woman. The coffin in that cache also wears it. It is something of a puzzle. On the brow of this *shabti* there is not just the *uraeus*, but the double insignia of vulture and *uraeus*. A fairly full *shabti*-text occupies four lines which run the full length of the figure.

SHABTI PRESENTED BY MINNAKHTE

(CARTER 230J, J.D'E. 60828; HEIGHT 52 CM)

This *shabti* is another of the group of five which the general Minnakhte presented for the king's funeral. Such presentation pieces could be regarded as indications of true loyalty and affectionate piety, directed at a young king who had not lived long enough to gather enemies against him. Like the other presentation *shabtis* it is made simply of wood with just a trifling use of gold: here a thin head band and a gilded bronze *uraeus*. Of the two royal emblems he carries, the crook is of bronze only, while the flail is of gilded bronze. The carver of this piece was a true sculptor, and the royal features are so well and sensitively delineated that there is good reason to think that the ancient craftsman was aiming to show not just a royal head but a portrait of Tutankhamun. He is shown wearing the *nemes* headdress with blue stripes. Over his chest is a multiple broad collar, lightly incised, and below, obscured partially by his folded arms, is a *ba*-bird with outstretched wings – the form of spirit which could move in and out of the tomb after burial. A full *shabti*-text occupies six vertical lines on the body.

SHABTI FROM THE ANTECHAMBER

(CARTER 110, J.D'E. 60825, HEIGHT 51.6 CM)

The large number of *shabti*-figures found in the tomb of Tutankhamun were deposited in two rooms, the Treasury and the Annexe, mostly placed in groups stored in black-painted shrine-shaped boxes. One, however, was found loose in the Antechamber where it had migrated probably from the boxes in the Annexe, not taken by the ancient tomb robbers presumably because it carried little of value on it. Nevertheless, it is a fine wooden example with some effective gilding. The *nemes* headdress which was the most common type of semi-crown worn by kings throughout the Pharaonic Period, is here gilded, but the vulture and *uraeus* heads on the brow are of ungilded bronze. Normally the Egyptian king wore only the *uraeus* on his brow, the embodiment of Wadjyt, the protective deity of Lower Egypt. It was not uncommon, however, for Tutankhamun to be shown with the vulture head also, Nekhbet the protective goddess of Upper Egypt. A carefully detailed gilded flail is held in the right fist; if there was originally a crook, it has not survived. Four lines of incised, yellow-painted text running the length of the body, contain the *shabti*-text in a fairly full form.

GILDED *SHABTI* WITH NUBIAN WIG

(CARTER 330H, J.D'E. 60833; HEIGHT 54 CM)

One of fifteen *shabtis* of different styles found in a white-painted chest in the Treasury, this example represents a group which carries a full version of the *shabti*-text, Utterance 6 of the Book of the Dead. The figure itself is made of wood in mummiform, and it is completely gilded except for those parts of the body which in this form are shown to be not covered by bandages, namely the face, neck and hands. The face is sensitively carved with eye details marked in black, and the whites are painted white; the lips are lightly rouged. It wears a tight short Nubian wig of ebony, with the tight curls clearly marked; a gold band encircles the top. The band on the brow is also gold. A broad collar is marked on the chest and shoulders, and a slightly incongruous, rather ordinary, bronze crook is placed in the left hand. There is no flail, but in the tomb were placed many loose crooks and flails, some of which belonged to *shabtis* like this one. There are four lines of text with the *shabti*-formula.

SHABTI WITH RED CROWN

(CARTER 330C, J.D'E. 60823; HEIGHT 63 CM)

Also found in the chest in the Treasury which housed the last *shabti*, this figure is one of the representative regal examples from the tomb. Here Tutankhamun is king even in death; he is shown wearing the so-called red crown, one of Egypt's oldest royal crowns. It is generally thought to have been made of thin copper, which, having a ruddy colour, could be termed 'red'. It is generally shown with a thin extension and curled end, rising forward from the bottom of the rear vertical projection; but it is often omitted from three-dimensional representations in stone because of the difficulty of carving it. In wooden examples it could be added in metal; but not here. Its absence does not seem to have been a problem. There is here an *uraeus* on the brow. The royal features are picked out in black and the lips are rouged. He carries a gilded bronze flail in his right hand, and a bronze crook in the left. The whole figure is gilded, apart from the face and hands. Two lines of text running down the body contain an abbreviated version of the *shabti*-text.

SHABTI WITH WHITE CROWN

(CARTER 330E, J.D'E. 60824A; HEIGHT 61.5 CM)

This is a fine *shabti*-figure of a very youthful Tutankhamun wearing a white crown, almost a companion piece to the last, from the same chest in the Treasury. There is, however, a significant difference between the two: whereas the last carries just an *uraeus* on the brow, here there are *uraeus* and vulture head in bronze. It has not been possible to discover if there is a significant distinction to be made between royal figures with the single and those with the double form of protective deities. It seems unlikely that a matter of this kind would be left to the whim of the craftsman making the piece, but no other explanation has been put forward.

As in other *shabtis* from the same chest, the whole of the body is gilded apart from the face and hands, which are left in the natural wood. An unusual feature is the raised eyebrow on the figure's right side, giving the face a somewhat quizzical look. Of the royal insignia only the crook has survived. There are four lines containing the *shabti*-text.

SHABTI OF TRADITIONAL FORM

(CARTER 608B, J.D'E. 60795, HEIGHT 26 CM)

Twenty-two gilded wooden *shabtis* were found in one of the black-painted chests in the Annexe. This example is very much of the common shape of Eighteenth Dynasty *shabtis* in which the body is mummiform, and the head equipped with what in Egyptian archaeology is termed the tripartite wig: this form has two parts with heavy tresses hanging on either side of the face down to the upper chest, while the third part hangs down the back. It is much used in funerary contexts, and is regularly shown as the headdress on coffins. The whole figure including face and hands is gilded and some details on the face are added in black. So also is the beard which is unusually long. The hands are shown holding hoes and baskets, to be used in the agricultural works for which it might be conscripted; this would be a working *shabti*. There is no *shabti*-text inscribed, but just a single line in which the king is 'bodily son of Re' and 'beloved of Anubis who is in the place of embalming'.

REIS SHABTI WITH NUBIAN WIG

(CARTER 496B, J.D'E. 60765, HEIGHT 32 CM)

Here is one of the more important *shabtis* in the hierarchy of funerary figures. He is a *reis* or foreman *shabti*, whose task it was to oversee the labouring activities of the ordinary *shabtis*. In later times, when it was regular to have large numbers of *shabtis* even in private burials, the *reis* figure was shown carrying a whip. In the present case, and with other *reises* from the tomb, the implement of control is the flagellum or flail, here carefully marked with its various strands. In the other hand he carries a folded cloth, the purpose of which is not certain – possibly so that the *reis* could wipe his hands if by chance he happened to get them dirty! The figure wears the Nubian wig in its more normal form, and there is an *uraeus* on the brow. A broad bead collar is marked out on the chest. Down the body runs a single line of text giving a simple royal titulary: 'the good god, lord of the two lands, Nebkheperure, son of Re, lord of diadems, Tutankhamun, ruler in southern Heliopolis, given life like Re'.

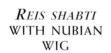

118

SHABTI WITH ROYAL BEARD

(CARTER 512C, J.D'E. 60800; HEIGHT 25 CM)

In its usual form the *shabti* is a mummy; it is the deceased as Osiris, and as such it is generally shown either with no beard, or with the long plaited beard with turned-up tip, the characteristic Osirian beard. This *shabti*, which is not otherwise particularly distinctive, is given a straight beard with cross-markings of the kind usually worn by the king. Such beards are not uncommon with *shabtis* of Tutankhamun, and one must concede that some confusion over beards is allowable. This is a working *shabti* made of wood and gilded all over, with some markings in black paint: the striations on the tripartite wig, the eyes and eye-brows, and the cross-markings on the beard. The indications of detail on the body are very lightly marked, but it can be seen that there is a broad collar and that both hands hold hoes; there are no baskets. A single line of text runs down the body contained within an incised frame with a sign for 'heaven' at the top: 'the good god, lord of the two lands, Nebkheperure, son of Re, Tutankhamun, ruler in southern Heliopolis, given life'.

GILDED REIS SHABTI

(CARTER 496B, J.D'E. 60758, HEIGHT 32 CM)

Another *reis* or overseer *shabti*, made of wood and fairly heavily gilded. Here he is shown as king, wearing the *uraeus* on his brow, attached to another headdress, the *khat*, which seems to be exclusively royal. In form it is not a crown in the strictest sense, but some kind of head cloth fitted closely perhaps over a special wig. It is not known whether it was made of cloth. It is neat and brings distinction of appearance, but it is not an obvious symbol of authority. The detail of the face is to some extent suppressed by the gilding, but even so it conveys an impression of great calm. There is no beard. Around the neck is a broad collar of beads, and in the hands are held the folded cloth and flail or flagellum, the characteristic symbols of authority held by the overseer *shabtis* of Tutankhamun. He is named in a single line of text as 'the good god, lord of the two lands' and 'the son of Re'; he is 'given life like Re'.

SHABTI WITH BLUE WIG

(CARTER 323N, J.D'E. 60851;
HEIGHT 23 CM)

Among the grand, well carved *shabtis* found in the Treasury, there were many much simpler examples, making up the body of workers who would, when called on, carry out the tasks required of the deceased. Even the king, it seems, was unable to avoid these posthumous chores. This *shabti* comes from a group of twenty-three stored in a chest in the Treasury. It is made of wood and very modestly decorated: the tripartite wig is painted blue with the ends of the front lappets painted white; the long spade-shaped beard of the kind worn by the living king is black, as are the eye markings. A broad collar is superficially indicated in white paint with no detailing. The areas of white paint on wig and collar clearly would have been gilded on superior examples. The single line of text describes the king as 'good god, lord of diadems' and 'beloved of Sokar-Osiris'. Sokar is a necropolis deity of the Memphite region.

SHABTI WITH GREEN WIG

(CARTER 319J, J.D'E. 60941; HEIGHT 22 CM)

This *shabti*, found in a troop of fifteen in one of the black-painted chests in the Treasury, is a simple worker figure. It is made of wood of a fairly ordinary kind, and painted. It was first given a wash of white paint on which details and text were then added in other colours. The head is covered by a tripartite wig painted a light green, with striations in dark green. Facial features are in black paint, as is the exceptionally long royal beard.

Details of the *shabti*'s adornments and implements are added in red paint: on the chest a multiple collar with drop-beads forming the outside row; a bangle or bracelet is marked on the wrist; the hands hold hoes and baskets, ready for menial tasks. Down the front of the body is a single line of text written within a frame topped by the heaven-sign: 'the good god, Nebkheperure, beloved of Anubis who is in the embalming chamber'.

SHABTI WITH NO IMPLEMENTS

(CARTER 323P, J.D'E. 60897; HEIGHT 22 CM)

This wooden *shabti*-figure is of ordinary form with a minimal amount of painting. The tripartite wig is not itself painted as in other simple examples: just the striations are delineated in blue on the bare wood. The eyes and brows, and the beard with its side straps, are painted in black. The vertical text is also painted straight on the wood in blue, a fairly standard statement set between framing lines topped by the heaven-sign. It reads: 'the good god, lord of the two lands, Nebkheperure, given life like Re for ever'. No implements are painted in the hands, but this *shabti*, and many others in the tomb without implements, would not go unequipped to clear ditches and move sand in the after-life. In the *shabti*-boxes in the Treasury and the Annexe, and also lying loose in the tomb, the excavators found 1866 miniature implements for them – hoes, mattocks or picks, baskets with yokes to carry them, made of bronze, faience and wood. There were 793 in the Treasury and 1073 in the Annexe.

SHABTI WITH GILDED WIG

(CARTER 323E, J.D'E. 60802; HEIGHT 26.2 CM)

Some of the simple workman *shabtis* are distinguished by certain details and features in their carving. This example, which is from the Treasury, demonstrates the interest that can be derived from a relatively ordinary object. It is of wood, with paint used to highlight some features. The face, to begin with, is remarkably strong; it is only remotely a likeness of Tutankhamun, with eye details marked in black; the beard is long and of the royal kind, with its end painted white. The wig is tripartite and gilded, with the lines of the striations painted in black. There is no broad collar. Both hands hold hoes and baskets which are painted black; they are quite specially delineated, the baskets in particular showing their structure, their handles strung over the wrists. The white painted text in a single column with no framing lines reads 'son of Re, Tutankhamun, ruler in southern Heliopolis, given life like Re for ever'.

SHABTI WITH MINIMAL DECORATION

(CARTER 418F, J.D'E. 60868; HEIGHT 23.4 CM)

The simplicity of plain wood often provides greater aesthetic satisfaction than gilded extravagance. This superficially plain piece is in fact a fine example of wood carving in which just enough basic detail has been added to give it life. It was found in a chest in the Annexe with nineteen other wooden *shabtis*. The tripartite wig on the head is without paint or detail; the face has eyes and brows marked in black, and the beard side straps which hold in place the long black spade beard of living royalty. A fine red painted line is used for the bracelet on one wrist, and for the hoes and baskets held in the hands. The single line of text, in blue paint running down the front of the body, has framing lines and the heaven-sign at the top. Both of Tutankhamun's cartouches are written, and he is 'the good god, lord of the two lands, possessor of joy'; he is 'son of Re' and is 'given life'. The chest containing this *shabti* also held a hundred miniature implements to equip those figures without any tools.

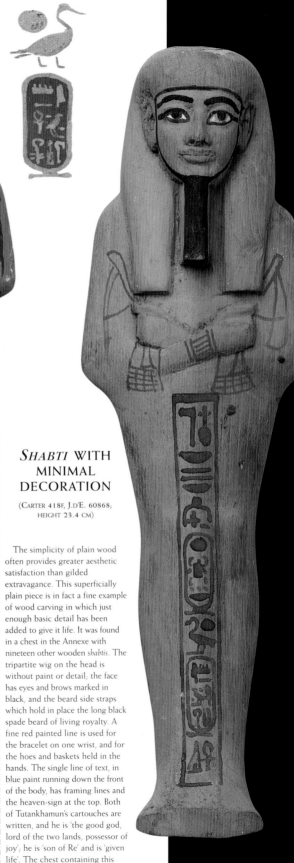

GRANITE *SHABTI* WITH GILDED HEAD

(CARTER 605F, J.D'E. 61040; HEIGHT 15.5 CM)

The majority of the *shabtis* found in Tutankhamun's tomb were made of wood, some entirely gilded, some in part. Stone figures are not common, and among these this black granite example is unusual. It is more solidly proportioned than the wooden *shabtis*, and its bodily details are more suggested than clearly carved, due no doubt to the hardness of the stone. The head is shown with the *khat* cloth headdress, which is gilded, with a bronze *uraeus* attached to the brow, inlaid with blue and red. Eyes and brows are outlined in blue paint with internal details in white and black. The simple royal designation is lightly carved on the front of the piece. It is interesting to consider the materials used for royal *shabtis* at this time: many of those made for Amenophis III were of serpentine; for Akhenaten, from whose tomb many broken examples were recovered, many different stones were used. Tutankhamun's sudden death probably required unexpectedly rapid manufacture, and *shabtis* of wood could be made more quickly.

LIMESTONE *SHABTI* WITH WHITE CROWN

(CARTER 605A, J.D'E. 61043, HEIGHT 20.7 CM)

A hard, close-grained yellowish limestone was used for this *shabti*, one of two found in a box in the Annexe along with twelve other *shabtis* and twenty-seven copper or bronze miniature tools. All the figures were made of stone, of five different kinds, from soft limestone to hard granite. Yellow limestone is found in both the Eastern and the Western Deserts of Egypt, but not in such deposits as could be used for building. This rather austere figure shows the mummiform king with his hands just appearing from his wrappings, with no royal regalia. On his head is the white crown of Upper Egypt, appropriately painted white; the *uraeus* on the brow shows the most adventurous markings: the details of the cobra's hood have small depressions filled with blue and red paint. Eyes and brows are marked in black, and there are traces of red colouring on the lips. The very simple text, in black, reads: 'the good god, lord of the two lands, Tutankhamun, ruler in southern Heliopolis, given life'.

LIMESTONE *SHABTI* WITH BLUE CROWN

(CARTER 605B, J.D'E. 61044; HEIGHT 22.5 CM)

Yellow limestone is used for this *shabti*; like the previous example it was found in a chest in the Annexe. Here the king wears the *khepresh*, or blue crown, a fairly recent addition to the repertoire of royal headgear in the New Kingdom. In its developed form, as seen worn by Tutankhamun in scenes on the painted box and the golden shrine, it is ornamented with little circles, possibly of metal, attached to the body of the crown, made possibly of leather. It is commonly shown as blue, hence its general designation.

It is also called the war crown because the king wears it in battle. On this *shabti* it is painted black, as are the facial details. The *uraeus* on the blue crown is usually shown with the coils of the body arranged in circles behind the hood of the cobra, with the tail running up the front of the crown. Here the hood is inlaid with blue and red colour. The simple text gives the king's prenomen, and his titles 'The Good God, Lord of the Two Lands'.

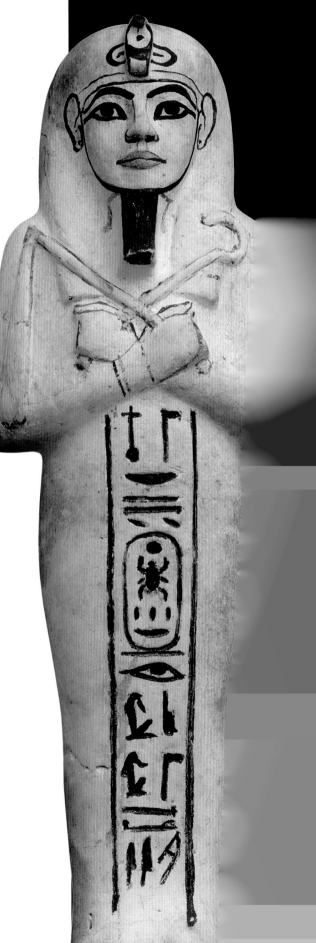

LIMESTONE *SHABTI*

(CARTER 330M, J.D'E. 61050; HEIGHT 28 CM)

The chest that contained this piece had a short hieratic text written on the lid: 'What is in it: smooth gold and *mry*-wood *shawabtis*'. In the box were found fifteen *shabtis*, eight of gilded wood, three of plain wood, four of stone, and seventy-five model tools. It is interesting that in this cursive text the figures are called *shawabtis*, a form which supercedes the older form *shabti*, the word used commonly on Tutankhamun's figures themselves. The hieratic scribe here was being rather up-to-date. This fine figure is shown wearing the tripartite wig, with an *uraeus* on the brow. He holds the crook and the flail in his hands, carved in high relief. Details are sparingly supplied in black paint: the coils and hood markings on the *uraeus*, the eyes, brows and ears, the lines of the head band. The mouth is lightly rouged, and the beard and beard straps are black.

In the simple inscription the king's prenomen and usual preliminary titles are given; he is described as 'beloved of Osiris, the great god'.

LIGHT BLUE FAIENCE *SHABTI*

(CARTER 519F, J.D'E. 61168; HEIGHT 17 CM)

Faience, a material which should more correctly be called glazed quartz frit, was used by the ancient Egyptians from the earliest historical times. Small moulded objects were ideally suited for this kind of manufacture, and *shabti*-figures were among the objects produced from the Eighteenth Dynasty onwards. In the later periods most *shabtis* were made of faience, often with a glaze very like that used for this example and a number of others in the tomb of Tutankhamun. During the reigns of Amenophis III and Akhenaten the production of fine quality glass and glazed objects reached a peak of quality, with a wide range of colours being developed. The colour of this *shabti* is not very special, but it is still a good example of the discreet use of glazing. The figure is shown wearing a tripartite wig with details marked out in black. The beard is long and royal; no implements are shown in his hands. The text gives the simple royal designation and prenomen, 'given life for ever'.

TURQUOISE GLAZED *REIS SHABTI*

(CARTER 519C, J.D'E. 87852; HEIGHT 30 CM)

One of the chests in the Annexe contained sixteen faience *shabtis*, of which six were *reises*, or foremen, rather more supervisors than their humble worker neighbours required. It is clear that no special care was taken to distribute *reis* figures evenly among the workers. When the time came, they would all by magical means know the order of things in the underworld, and appear on parade as required. This is a particularly fine *reis*, displaying striking dignity; one may even detect authority in his look, and consider how well he might wield the flail of control which he holds in one hand. In the other he holds the folded cloth. He wears the *khat* headdress with *uraeus*, and has around his neck a broad collar with droplet beads in the outermost row. Details are marked in black, as is the simple inscription containing both of Tutankhamun's cartouches: he is 'the good god, lord of the two lands' and 'son of Re, lord of diadems'. The material of the piece is high quality dense faience, with a light turquoise blue glaze.

A NON-ROYAL *SHABTI*

(CARTER 496D, J.D'E. 61108; HEIGHT 17.5 CM)

In the regular text inscribed on these *shabti*-figures, an identification is made between the figure and the named deceased person. Whoever is named is the one for whom the *shabti* will shout out 'Here I am' when the roll of the corvée is called. What then can one make of an anonymous *shabti*? Six such figures were found in Tutankhamun's tomb, three in the Treasury and three in the Annexe. All are similar to this example, light blue glazed, wearing the tripartite wig, with no tools, and a full *shabti*-text written in black in eight or nine horizontal lines. No identifying deceased person is named. The features of these figures are well modelled, but they do not appear to be in the style of the late Amarna Period, or of the reign of Tutankhamun. It seems possible that they were made either early in the Amarna Period or even in the reign of Amenophis III, as stock figures to be used in an emergency. But why were they used for Tutankhamun when several hundreds could be made for his burial? Who can tell?

REIS SHABTI WITH NUBIAN WIG

(CARTER 519A, J.D'E. 61054; HEIGHT 30 CM)

Two shades of blue glaze are used on this *reis* figure, with black employed for detail. It is one of the foremen *shabtis* found in the same box in the Annexe as the turquoise glazed piece. It is no duplicate, although they have much in common. This figure wears the Nubian wig, which here is carefully marked with its rows of tight curls. There is an *uraeus* on the brow. A collar, with five rows of beads, is marked on the chest, and in his hands are indicated the signs of office, the flail and folded cloth. These two instruments are marked rather superficially, although the hands emerging from the mummy wrappings and the arms are carefully modelled. The single line of text in lighter blue glaze contains an inscription similar to that on its fellow *reis*. Like so many *shabtis* from this tomb, the text is very simple, and includes no invocation that the *shabti* perform the necessary tasks in the underworld.

SHABTI WITH A TEXTUAL ERROR

(CARTER 602F, J.D'E. 87853;
HEIGHT 15.5 CM)

One of the boxes in the Annexe contained eight wooden *reis* figures, some with gilding, and thirty-one faience *shabtis* of worker status, with violet glaze, along with thirty-two miniature copper tools. This example is characteristic of the group, but has some features which are unusual. The striations on the tripartite wig are made in light blue glaze, and the same colour is used for the text, which is of the shortest kind found on the Tutankhamun *shabtis*. It contains his prenomen, the title 'good god, lord of the two lands', qualified with 'given life'. There is an error in the writing of the prenomen in the cartouche. The signs should be, from top to bottom, a sun-disk, a scarab beetle with three strokes indicating plurality, and a basket at the bottom. Here the three strokes of plurality have been omitted, subtly changing the meaning of the name from 'master of forms (or possessor of forms) is Re' to 'master of form is Re', a subtle theological distinction which could give rise to argument in the after-life.

SHABTI WITH *ANKH* SIGNS

(CARTER 327MM, J.D'E. 61120,
HEIGHT 16.4 CM)

Royal *shabtis* do not necessarily follow the simple rules of the *shabti* tradition either in iconography or in inscription. Those made for Akhenaten had very short texts, and there is no example known which carries anything like the conventional *shabti*-text from the Book of the Dead. It is not surprising that Akhenaten avoided the Osirian aspects of the *shabti* idea; it is surprising that he even contemplated the use of *shabtis*, unless their function was to be diverted towards a solar purpose. With Tutankhamun the *shabti* reverted to its subterrestrial function; Osiris was no longer abhorred. This modest violet glazed *shabti* with a simple text might be thought to be in the Akhenaten tradition, an idea strengthened by the presence of *ankh*-signs in the clenched hands. This feature is found on many Akhenaten *shabtis*. Could this have been noted by the priests of Amon-Re in Thebes?

Personal Ritual
Objects

The extraordinary mixture of objects placed
in the tomb of Tutankhamun defies simple
analysis. Many pieces seem to possess little
relevance to the main purpose of the burial of a
royal and divine person; some seem to have been
included almost as if to enlarge the size of what
might otherwise have seemed to be a meager
funerary equipment. Why so much furniture, so
many beds of ordinary kinds, so many boxes filled
with linen, clothes, jewels? It is as if the moving
men had been told to clear all unwanted things
from the palace storerooms. Was it the practice
to include all things bearing the deceased's name?
Unfortunately, just not enough is known about

Egyptian funerary procedure in this respect.

Other items in the burial, however, must have had great personal significance for the dead king; some may even have had ritual meanings which can not now be comprehended. Such is the nest of coffins; among other things it contained a tiny coffin bearing the name of Queen Tiye, mother of Akhenaten, which held a lock of hair. Was this just a keepsake or an heirloom, or did it have greater significance? Questions of similar kind apply to the other objects illustrated below.

Other objects not illustrated here invoke the word 'Why?' Is ritual involved, or personal piety? What, for example, is to be made of two further sets of miniature coffins, placed in a plain wooden box in the Treasury? They contained two mummified foetuses, both female and prematurely born. These pitiful little bodies had not been fully mummified, but had been carefully and piously prepared for burial. It is generally thought that they were the children of Tutankhamun and Ankhesenamun, but the parentage is not yet satisfactorily established. The connection must have been intimate, and would have justified the inclusion of the bodies in the most sacred and ritually important part of the tomb. How many more pieces in this remarkable tomb possess hidden significance!

128–129 Tutankhamun lies on his funeral bier, a mummy protected by the wings of a falcon and of his ba-bird – his spirit of movement after death. The wood-carver who made this piece exploited most cleverly the natural grain of the wood.

SQUATTING GOLD FIGURE OF THE KING

(CARTER 320C, J.D'E. 60702;
HEIGHT 5.4 CM, LENGTH OF CHAIN 54 CM)

This charming small royal figure was found in the miniature coffin illustrated later. It represents a squatting figure of a king cast in solid gold. He wears the *khepresh* or blue crown, and holds the royal insignia, flail and crook, in one hand. There is no lock of youth and it is difficult, therefore, not to see this piece as a person in some maturity. There is unfortunately no inscription to identify which king is represented. Because it was found with a lock of Queen Tiye's hair, Carter took the view that it was Amenophis III, and that both figure and lock of hair were in the tomb as 'heirlooms'. There is little evidence to support this view as far as this statuette is concerned, and it has been pointed out that the ears are pierced for earrings, a feature not found in royal ears before the reign of Akhenaten. It was designed to be worn as a pendant, and a ring on the back takes the gold chain used for suspension; the ends of the chain do not have a clasp, but are provided with tasselled linen cords for tying. Around the neck of the figure was a tiny necklace of glass beads. There seems no reason to believe that anyone other than Tutankhamun is represented; but the significance of the piece, apart from being decorative, is not easily determined.

BLUE GLASS FIGURE OF THE KING

(CARTER 54FF, J.D'E. 60718;
HEIGHT 5.8 CM)

A box of objects found in the Antechamber contained, among other things, parts of Tutankhamun's corselet, and this small figure. Like so many other pieces in the tomb it seems to have no obvious place among the tomb equipment. It shows a royal figure, squatting like the gold statuette shown to the left, wearing the *khepresh* or blue crown. He holds his right finger to his mouth in an attitude commonly associated in ancient Egypt with the young, and specifically with the young Horus, the god with whom the Egyptian king was identified in life. This then could be a figure of the child Horus (called Harpocrates in later times), or of the king as a child; presumably Tutankhamun, although Carter thought it might be Akhenaten. It is a rare case of glass sculpture from the Eighteenth Dynasty, a figure in the round, almost certainly molded, and then finished by working with abrasive materials. The glass itself is translucent, but not transparent, which suggests a different composition from the glass of the many inlays, beads, amulets etc. from this tomb, which are almost exclusively of opaque glass. The color of Egyptian blue glass was mostly obtained by the use of a copper compound, but some examples show traces of cobalt as the coloring agent.

THE KING ON A BIER

(CARTER 331A, J.D'E. 60720; LENGTH 42.2 CM, WIDTH 12 CM, HEIGHT OF BIER 4.3 CM)

Carved in the style of, and with the same artistry as, the best of the wooden *shabtis* of Tutankhamun, this figure was found packed into a small wooden chest in the Treasury, padded around with linen. It shows the king as a mummy lying on his funeral bed, the shape of which incorporates two elongated lions whose heads rise beside that of the king. He is mummiform, wearing the *nemes* headdress, the striations of which are marked in black, and with a gilded *uraeus*. This is the sole piece of gilding on the figure, and it therefore makes a striking effect. The body is lightly marked with a broad bead collar, and it is seen to be wrapped around protectively by the wings of a falcon and of a human-headed *ba*-bird, spirit of movement; bands of text, following the lines of mummy straps, carry a long traditional address by the sky-goddess Nut, and short statements in which the king is said to be 'revered by' the four Canopic genii, with Anubis, Osiris and Horus. Texts on the sides of the bier state that this figure was made for the king by Maia, the royal treasurer, whose own tomb was at Saqqara. He also presented a fine wooden *shabti*-figure to the burial equipment.

THE HEAD
ON THE LOTUS

(CARTER 8, J.D'E. 60723; HEIGHT 30 CM)

One of the most appealing images from Tutankhamun's tomb, this head is a masterpiece of wood sculpture, simple in its conception, complicated perhaps in its religious significance, but wholly engaging as a work of art. What function it served in the tomb is not known; where it was placed is not known. It was found by the excavators in the passage into the tomb, beneath the rubble, but discarded presumably by the ancient robbers, who could see no value in it. It is not thought that there was an illicit trade in works of art in ancient Egypt. The piece consists of a child's head emerging from an open lotus flower, and it is generally thought to represent the birth of the young sun-god at the beginning of time; then the lotus sprang up from the high mound rising from the watery chaos called Nun. It harks back therefore to distant times when earth came into being and the sun-god was born. In this subtle representation the sun-god is given the features of Tutankhamun, modeled very much in the Amarna tradition, with the elongated skull characteristic of the children of Akhenaten and Nefertiti. The carved wood is covered with a thin layer of gesso-plaster painted brown; the eye-brows and the surrounds of the eyes are blue.

MINIATURE COFFIN AND MINIATURE COFFIN LID

(CARTER 320, J.D'E. 60698; LENGTH 78 CM, WIDTH 26.5 CM)
(CARTER 320A, J.D'E. 60698; LENGTH 74 CM)

A nest of miniature coffins was found in the Treasury, providing one of the great mysteries concerning the funerary equipment of Tutankhamun. The outer coffin was black painted with inscribed gold bands and other gilded parts. It is described below, along with the puzzles raised by its contents. The second coffin was firmly fixed in the outer coffin by solidified unguents, and is inextricably stuck. The lid, however, can be removed, and is illustrated here. It is very reminiscent of the solid gold coffin which contained Tutankhamun's mummy, but lacks the detail and splendor which its full-size counterpart displays. The king is shown mummiform, wearing the *nemes* headdress, but with no *uraeus* on the brow. The piece is of wood, gilded on gesso-plaster, the color of the gold relieved only by the black outlines of the eyes and eyebrows. The body is shown to be wrapped around with the protective wings of two vultures, here probably representing the two mourning goddesses, Isis and Nephthys. As on a full-size coffin, the text down the body is an address by the king: 'O my mother Nut! Spread yourself over me, place me among the imperishable stars which are in you, that I may not die again.'

The miniature coffin, partly described above, takes the form of a standard Eighteenth Dynasty coffin, not necessarily of a royal person. It has an elaborate broad collar around the neck, and a vulture with outstretched wings beneath the arms. Part of the conventional address to Nut runs down the front of the body. The greatest interest in this nest of coffins rests on what was found within. Firstly there was a linen bundle containing the solid gold figure of a king, probably Tutankhamun, described above. Secondly there was a third small plain wooden coffin which contained yet a fourth tiny wooden coffin, wrapped in linen and doused with unguents. This last coffin contained a lock of hair – of auburn hair as Carter romantically described it. This tiny coffin, about 12.5 cm long, carried texts naming 'the great royal wife Tiye', her name in cartouche, and requesting all benefits of food, drink etc from the multiple funerary deity Ptah-Sokar-Osiris. It is more than reasonable to conclude that the hair belonged to Tiye, and had been included in Tutankhamun's burial for reasons of piety, but is not necessarily an indication that Tiye was his mother. The question is too intriguing!

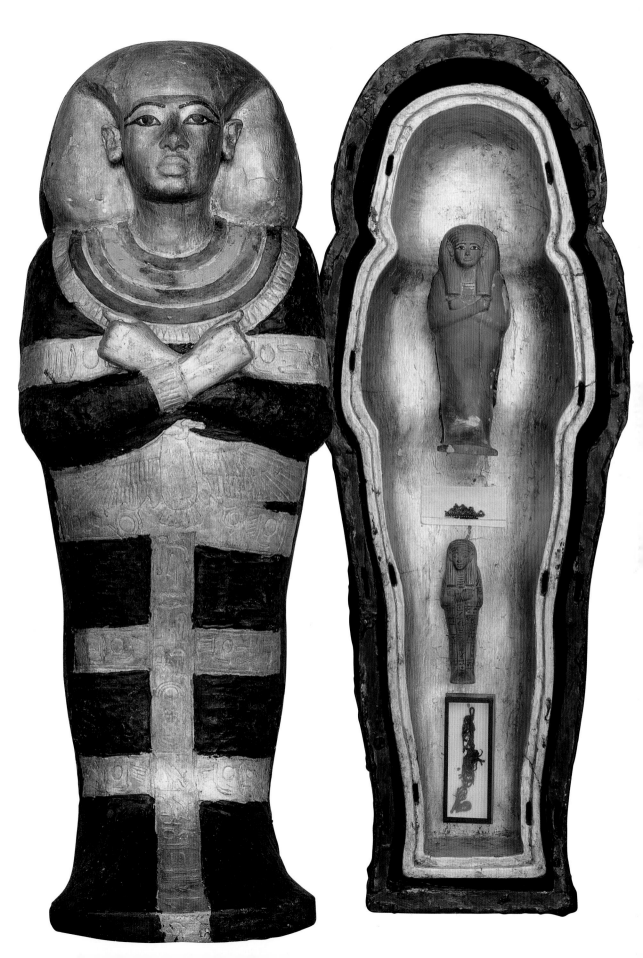

Ritual Furniture
and Objects

136 One of the lion heads from the ritual
couch of Meht-weret. The wooden base is
covered with gilded gesso, and the blue
details of nose and tears are made of blue
glass. The eyes are wonderfully rendered in
translucent quartz.

137 One of the two hippopotamus heads
from the ritual couch of Ammut, the 'gobbler
of the dead'. The teeth are made of ivory, and
the tongue of pink-stained ivory. The eyes
are of translucent quartz and black glass.

The impression of confusion which faced Carter on entering the tomb was caused chiefly by the untidiness left by the ancient intruders. Not all the confusion was due to robbers; it seems unlikely that when the tomb was sealed after the burial the rooms were left in a tidy well-ordered state. But among the tumble of boxes, furniture and chariots stood three great gilded wooden couches, apparently unmoved and undamaged.

These great couches stand high off the ground, held rigid by solid rectangular bases. They are gilded and could not have been used as real beds without suffering damage. Similar couches can be seen on the walls of other tombs in the Valley, and fragments have been found in the debris of robbed tombs. They surely played an important role in the posthumous activities of the king, possibly as means by which the royal mummy might travel to its heavenly destination. Each couch is inscribed simply with the words 'the Osiris Nebkheperure',

a designation which confirms that they were made for the use of the dead king, not in his life.

Two strange, but distinctly ritual, objects were found in the Burial Chamber. In early times they were associated with a funerary deity Imyut, 'he who is within bandages', but later, as here, with Anubis, the divine supervisor of mummification. They clearly possessed great magical power.

Other important and probably obligatory items found in the tomb included a set of magical bricks and an Osiris bed. The unbaked mud bricks, inscribed with magical spells, were placed in niches hidden in the four walls of the Burial Chamber. Each had a specified amulet fixed in it. The Osiris bed in the Treasury awaited the royal resurrection; it consisted of a frame almost two metres long, in the shape of Osiris, filled with Nile mud and planted with grain; the germination of the seed would mark the resurrection of the king as Osiris.

RITUAL COUCH OF ISIS-MEHTET

(CARTER 73, J.D'E. 62013,
HEIGHT 188 CM, LENGTH 208 CM, WIDTH 128 CM)

Two elongated cow figures form the two sides of this magnificent couch. The legs, back and front fit into holes in the plain, black-painted base. Between the bodies is fixed the mattress of the couch by hooks which fit into bronze staples on the inner flanks of the animal bodies. The cows carry on their heads horns and disks which closely resemble the regular headdress of the goddess Isis. The paneled footboard at the tail end carries amuletic protection in the form of *djed* and *tyet* signs for endurance and life. The animal tails swing round in almost complete circles. Apart from the base, the whole couch is covered with gesso-plaster and gilded. The trefoil decoration on the bodies is made of dark blue paste; the eyes are made of translucent quartz with painted details, and are outlined in blue glass. An inscription on the cross board of the mattress, contained within an elongated cartouche, purports to identify the deity represented by these cows. It reads: 'May the good god live, may he exist for ever, Lord of the Two Lands, who effects the kingship of Re the Osiris, King of Upper Egypt, Nebkheper(u)re, beloved of Isis-Mehtet, justified'.

Here there is some confusion. This divine name properly belongs to a lion-goddess, whereas there is a cow-deity called Mehturt often linked with Isis. The name Isis-Mehtet in the text, however, is determined by a hieroglyph showing a seated deity with cow-head. One may possibly ascribe some confusion to the ancient scribe who prepared the inscriptions. But it seems certain that a cow, not a lion, deity was intended.

RITUAL COUCH
OF AMMUT

(CARTER 137, J.D'E. 62012;
LENGTH 236 CM, WIDTH 126 CM,
HEIGHT 134 CM)

Among the objects which
specially caught the eyes of Carter
and Carnarvon when they entered
the Antechamber of Tutankhamun's
tomb were the three great gilded
couches with animal heads, lined up
head to tail against the wall opposite
the entrance. They were the first
complete examples to be found of a
kind that was known only from
representations in scenes in the tomb
of Sethos II, and from fragments
found in earlier excavated royal
tombs. Their function puzzled the
excavators, and has continued to
puzzle scholars. They were
undoubtedly ritual beds, and it is
possible that they were to assist and
protect the dead king in his journeys
through the underworld. The deity
for this couch is Ammut, the
'gobbler of the dead', as the
inscription on the rail between the
heads states; the king is 'beloved of
Ammut'. The 'gobbler' is usually
shown in scenes of judgement in the
Book of the Dead, waiting to eat the
hearts of those who fail to qualify
for the realm of Osiris. In vignettes
she usually has a crocodile head, lion
forequarters, and hippopotamus rear.
Here the heads are hippopotamus,
the bodies crocodile, and the back
legs lion.

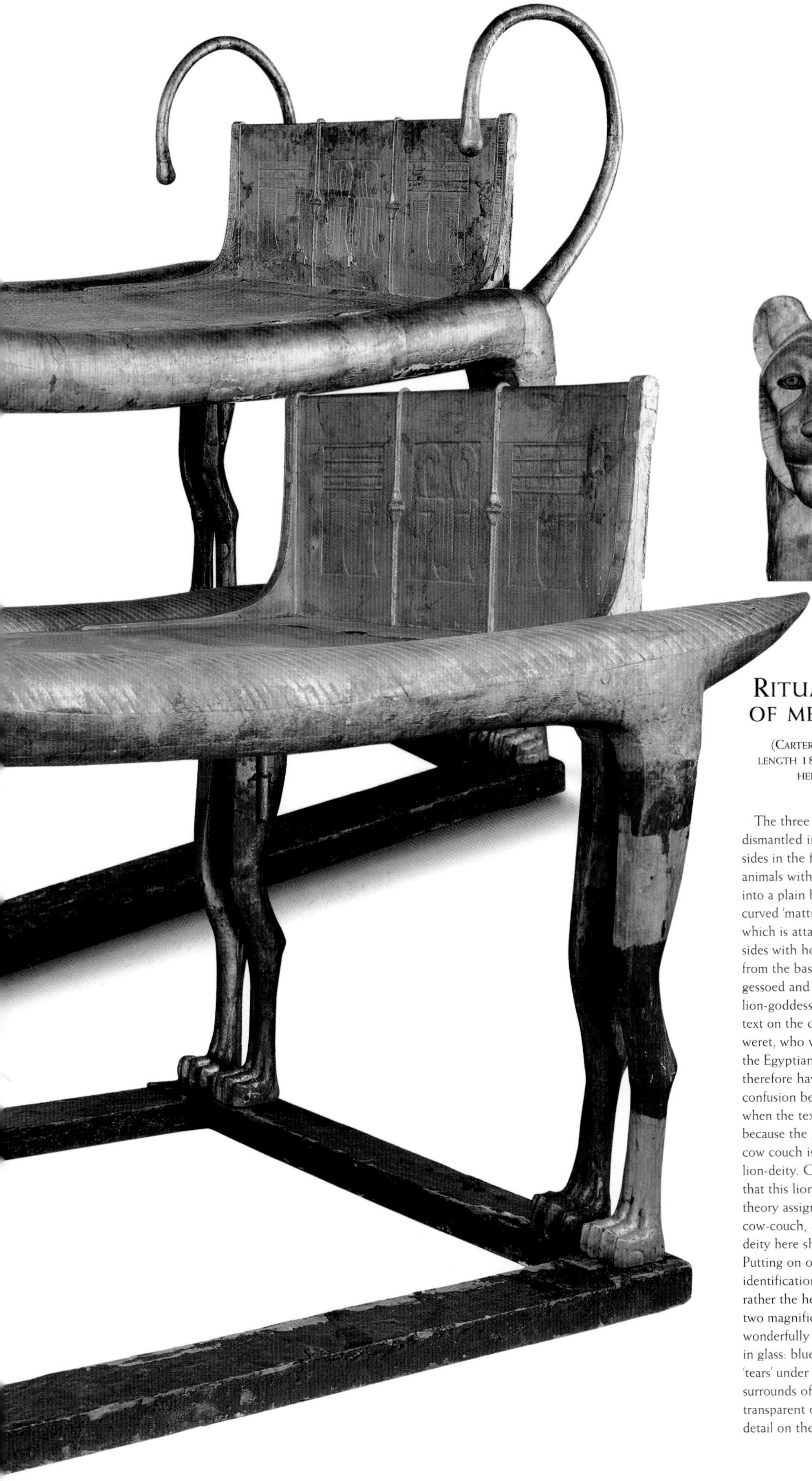

RITUAL COUCH OF MEHT-WERET

(CARTER 35, J.D'E. 62911;
LENGTH 181 CM, WIDTH 91 CM,
HEIGHT 156 CM)

The three ritual couches can be dismantled into four pieces: two sides in the form of elongated animals with long legs, which slot into a plain base, and a top, a curved 'mattress' with footboard, which is attached to the animal sides with hooks and staples. Apart from the bases they are all made of gessoed and gilded wood. This lion-goddess is identified from the text on the cross rail as Meht-weret, who was a cow-goddess in the Egyptian pantheon. There may therefore have been some confusion between the couches when the texts were added, because the goddess named on the cow couch is Isis-Mehtet, usually a lion-deity. Consequently it is likely that this lion couch should be in theory assigned the text on the cow-couch, and the protective deity here should be Isis-Mehtet. Putting on one side this matter of identification, one should consider rather the heads of the goddess – two magnificent lioness-heads, wonderfully lifelike. The details are in glass: blue for the nose and the 'tears' under the eyes, black for the surrounds of the eyes; the eyes are transparent quartz with painted detail on their reverses.

JAR LID WITH FLEDGLING AND EGGS

(Carter 620(1), J.d'E. 62072; width 13.4 cm)

A charming piece like this jar lid needs perhaps little explanation. It was found in the Annexe and probably belonged to one of the perfume vases found there or in the Antechamber, where fragments of the saucer were found. It consists of the flat jar lid with a saucer which here represents the nest. They are made of calcite, as are the four eggs in the nest. The little fledgling, however, is made of wood, painted in a light creamy brown color with details in black, including the chick's feathers. Its tongue is made of pink-stained ivory.

142

The fledgling has just emerged from its egg and stretches itself, trying out its useless wings. Is there here a reference to Amarna sentiments about nature as expressed in the great Aten hymn: 'The chick in the egg speaks in the shell; you give it air in it to make it live; you have brought it to completion so that it can break it – the egg; and it comes out of the shell to speak of its completion; and it walks on its two feet when it comes out of it'?

It is an indication of the fascination which scholars and members of the public have with the religious revolution of Akhenaten and its place in the history of monotheism, that connections and suggestions are sought in objects which may only be simple representations of charming subjects. So with this chick!

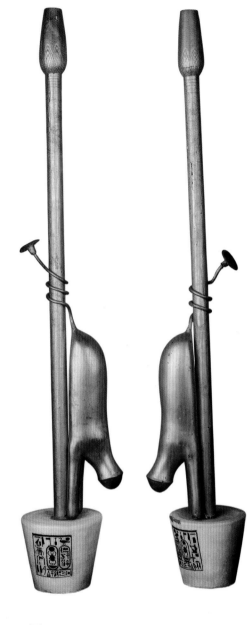

Two anubis emblems

(Carter 194 and 202, J.d'E. 61374, 61375; height 167 cm)

Almost a pair of modern sculptures. These two strange objects were placed in the north-west and south-west corners of the Burial Chamber, significantly placed, because they are associated with Anubis, the principal god of embalming. They are easier to describe than to explain. Each consists of a tall pole, the top in the form of a lotus bud. Hanging from this pole by a long gilded bronze tail terminating in an open papyrus flower is an animal skin, headless. The whole of this upper part is of gilded wood, apart from the tail. Each is fixed firmly in a calcite base like a flower pot, and inscribed: the left reads 'The Good God, Nebkheperure, son of Re, Tutankhamun, ruler in southern Heliopolis, given life like Re for ever and ever, beloved of Anubis who presides over the embalming booth', the right gives, Anubis (slightly differently written) the epithet 'who is in the place of embalming', and it omits 'like Re'. This emblem, or fetish, as it is sometimes described, was associated with Anubis, and an example has been found, dated to about 1950 BC, which has an actual animal skin stuffed with linen.

Figures of Anthropomorphic Deities

The Treasury contained many pieces of magical and ritual significance which have not been satisfactorily explained by scholars. Why were they placed in this room and not elsewhere? The explanation might simply be that this material had to be deposited somewhere, and room was not very plentiful in this tomb. It has always to be asked why, but often no profitable answer can be found.

There were in the Treasury twenty-two shrine-shaped black boxes with double doors, sealed when discovered. They contained figures of the king, of deities with animal attributes, and deities in human form. All the figures are made of wood; most are covered with gesso plaster and gilded; all were wrapped with marked and dated pieces of linen. Such markings were common in ancient Egypt, arranged no doubt by the royal housekeeper, just as in a great house of the nineteenth century. Some of the dates go back to the early years of Akhenaten's reign, but this need not necessarily imply that the figures so covered had been made and draped at that time.

The figures with human form make up a strange company. Some are of deities closely associated with the dead king and his protection: such are Isis and Nephthys, the divine mourners for the deceased. There are cosmic gods like Atum and Ptah; and Amsety, the Canopic genius identified with the deceased's liver. All these seem suitable for inclusion in the tomb. But there are others, like Menkaret, who holds a seated figure of the king on her head, and Mamu; such are little known, and probably unimportant, members of the vast company of Egyptian gods. Also puzzling is the presence of two black-painted figures of a young man holding a sistrum, thought possibly to be Ihy, a child of Hathor.

144 Upper part of a figure of the little-known deity Mamu: one of the pieces found in the Treasury. The god is shown mummiform with the Osirian beard. The sensitive face is post-Amarna in style.

145 The great creator god Ptah, the thinking deity, whose principal cult-center was in Memphis, pre-eminent among Egyptian cities. His skull cap here is made of blue faience, and he holds a bronze staff inlaid with gold.

FIGURE OF IHY

(CARTER 275A, J.D'E. 60732; HEIGHT 63.5 CM)

This dramatic, black-painted figure was stored in the Treasury in a shrine-shaped box containing in addition two gilded figures of the king wearing the red crown, and the two figures of the king in a reed boat, harpooning. By association it might seem that the king is again shown in this figure, which unfortunately is not identified by inscription. It has been thought to be the king as a boy, wearing the lock of youth; but more generally it is seen to be Ihy, the child of Hathor of Dendera and Horus of Edfu. Ihy is usually shown carrying a *menat*-necklace and a sistrum, and it is a

sistrum, here distinctively gilded, that he holds in his right hand. The sistrum is particularly associated with Hathor, and her distinctive head can be seen on the sistrum held by the young god; it is topped by a shrine-shaped section which in real examples held the metal rods and discs which produced the rather tuneless clattering noise of the shaken instrument. Ihy played a subordinate role in the ceremonies concerning the birth of the king as a royal and divine child. The eyes and brows of this figure are inlaid with gold.

FIGURE OF SHU

(CARTER 282A, J.D'E. 62735; HEIGHT 74 CM)

There is a small question of identification with this fine divine figure. In most of the other divine figures found in the Treasury of the tomb the texts on the bases describe Tutankhamun as being 'beloved of' the deities represented. In the case of this figure the text reads: 'Shu, Horus-strong-of-arm'. The king himself is often described as Horus-strong-of-arm, but here it appears that there is a linking of Shu with this form of Horus. It remains an unsolved problem. It seems to be Shu who is principally shown here. He was one of the most distinguished primeval gods of ancient Egypt, a member of the Ennead (company of nine gods) of Heliopolis, the son of Atum and consort of Tefnut. He is the god of air, and his function was to keep apart earth and sky. In this gilded wooden figure he is shown as a mummiform man with a headdress of two double feathers. He has an Osirian beard which, like the eyes and brows, is painted black.

FIGURE OF TA-TA

(CARTER 303A, J.D'E. 60741; HEIGHT 65 CM)

Like some other divine figures from the chests in the Burial Chamber, this figure poses a problem. It is a question of identification. A nice clear inscription in yellow paint on the base names the king: 'the good god, Nebkheperure, justified, beloved of Ta-Ta'. So was the god identified by Carter, presumably with the Egyptological backing of Alan Gardiner or James Henry Breasted, his textual advisers. Ta-Ta is written as if it were a god's name and, on the pattern of other similar texts on these divine figures, the king is 'beloved of' him. No easily identifiable god in the huge Egyptian pantheon carries such a name, and it must be suspected that Ta-Ta is the divine personification of the Two Lands, for *ta* is land in Egyptian, and the Two Lands are the South and the North. It would also explain why the figure wears the white crown of Upper Egypt. If this suggestion is correct then the god should be called Tawy, more correctly the Egyptian for Two Lands.

FIGURE OF PTAH

(CARTER 291A, J.D'E. 60739;
HEIGHT 60.2 CM)

Gods from the Memphis area were well represented among the gilded divine figures found in the Treasury. Here is Ptah, the most important Memphite god throughout the Dynastic Period. He was like Tatjenen, his predecessor and ostensible begetter, a creator god, and considered the patron deity of craftsmen. He is identified on the sloping end of his base as Ptah 'Lord of Truth'; the base itself takes the form of the hieroglyph for 'truth'. The base text also names Tutankhamun. This god is usually shown as a mummiform figure with no headdress, but a tightly fitting cap. Here the body is mummiform, but marked as if it were covered by a feathered garment. He also wears a broad bead collar. The figure is of gilded wood, the gold being of the purplish red kind, except on the face. The cap on the head is made of blue faience, and the eyes marked in blue glass. The straight beard is of gilded bronze. He holds a bronze *was*-scepter of authority incorporating the *ankh*-sign of life and *djed*-sign of endurance. In the Egyptian pantheon Ptah occupied a place among the handful of first-rank deities. He was specially venerated as a god of intellectual integrity, whose reputation never diminished over 3000 years.

Associated with his temple in Memphis was the ancient cult of the Apis bull, the living manifestation of the deity, which flourished especially in the last centuries of the Pharaonic Period.

FIGURE OF ATUM

(CARTER 290A, J.D'E. 60734;
HEIGHT 63 CM)

An inscription in yellow paint on the base of this divine figure identifies the deity as 'Atum, the living god'. It is one of the gilded wooden divine statuettes placed in black-painted chests in the Treasury. Atum was a real heavy-weight within the Egyptian pantheon. Here he is shown in a very simple form, unidentifiable by any external mark – crown or headdress, or particular items of divine regalia. He is shown mummiform, with a many-rowed broad bead collar; he has no beard. His eyes are emphasized with black paint. His name, Atum, might mean 'he who does not exist' or 'he who is complete'. The most acceptable – if indeterminate – rendering of the name is 'the undifferentiated one'. But the truth is that Atum was by no means an uncertain deity, but one who always occupied a primary place in the hierarchy of Egyptian gods. In a very late text in the temple of Edfu, Horus is addressed, 'You are Atum, the figure beautiful of face, who fashioned the body of the Ennead'. Atum was indeed the first of the company of nine gods of Heliopolis, the so-called Ennead. He, by himself, created Shu (air) and Tefnut (moisture), who in turn produced Geb (earth) and Nut (sky). This last pair then completed the company by producing Osiris and Isis, Seth and Nephthys. Atum, especially associated with the sun-god as Atum-Re, remained a supreme deity.

Figures of animal deities

The idea that the ancient Egyptians worshipped animal gods is one of those well-established myths which it may be impossible to dispel. It is true that many Egyptian gods were represented with animal forms, or with animal heads, and it is true that the existence of many mummified animals, particularly cats, baboons and dogs, but also bulls, falcons, snakes, small mammals, even insects, suggests a devotion to the creatures in question. Many gods were manifested as animals, or in some aspects shown in animal form. Even the great sun god at his daily birth at sunrise was shown as Khepri, the scarab beetle. The god Amun might be seen as a goose or a ram; Thoth, the scribe of the gods, could appear as an ibis or a baboon. The rationality behind these theophanies is hard to determine; in most cases, probably, the associations with animals go back to very early times, and their significance may even have been lost for the Egyptians by the Eighteenth Dynasty.

Some of the black-painted boxes in the Treasury contained figures of animal deities; the presence of some is hard to explain. Those of the Canopic genii are properly qualified. Sakhmet, the lioness-headed deity, is not particularly funerary, but may have been included as consort of Ptah, the great creator god. They were not, however, placed conjugally in the same box. The impressive Anubis jackal on a shrine, god of embalming, very properly guarded the Canopic shrine in the Treasury. Nearby was a gilded cow-head of Hathor, appearing from the West, as in some religious papyri – the West to which the deceased was to go. Others are less easily explained, just as the absence of some better known deities with funerary associations is strange. Why the black-painted goose of Amun in the Burial Chamber, or two serpent standards of the Xth Upper Egyptian nome (province) of Aphroditopolis in the Antechamber? One is drawn to the conclusion that much that was put into the tomb was there more by chance than by plan.

150 *The elegant, but threatening, jackal of Anubis, the god of embalming, placed to guard the intimate contents of the Canopic shrine in the Treasury.*

151 *The goose of Amun, a striking black-painted image with gilded beak, one of the sacred creatures placed in the Treasury, a mark of the rehabilitation of the pre-Amarna cults of Thebes.*

FIGURE OF SAKHMET

(CARTER 300A, J.D'E. 60794; HEIGHT 55.2 CM)

Sakhmet is the identificatory name written in yellow paint on the base of this figure, one of the many gilded divine figures found in black-painted, shrine-shaped chests in the Treasury. Sakhmet, 'the powerful one', was the divine consort of Ptah, and her principal shrine was in Memphis. She was, however, identified with other female deities, and her presence was particularly evident in the temple of the goddess Mut in Karnak, where many hundreds of statues of Sakhmet were set up in the reign of Amenophis III. Her presence in Tutankhamun's tomb has, more probably, a Memphite reference. She is here shown seated on a throne with a feathered pattern, and she herself wears an elegant, tight-fitting garment with a carefully marked floral pattern. Her nose is of black glass, and she carries a sun-disk on her head. The linen cloth draped over her in the shrine carried the name 'Herakhty in his name as Shu, who is in the Aten', the earlier form of the designation of the Aten in the reign of Akhenaten.

FIGURE OF DUAMUTEF

(CARTER 304B, J.D'E. 60728; HEIGHT 58 CM)

The four Canopic genii are represented among the gilded deities found in the Treasury. Purple or red tinted gold leaf was used for this figure; the markings for eyes and brows are in black paint. The base is also painted black. These Canopic genii, who were known as early as the Pyramid Texts of the Old Kingdom, were commonly shown as mummiform figures, and up to the Eighteenth Dynasty have human heads. Then three of the genii were given the heads of creatures, Amsety alone retaining a human head. Here Duamutef is jackal-headed, an identity which may have great antiquity. In the regular mummification process, in which the various internal organs were assigned to particular Canopic genii, Duamutef is generally thought to have care over the stomach of the deceased; but there is some evidence to suggest that his proper charge was the spleen. Neither the archaeological nor the pathological evidence is conclusive in this matter, as ancient dessicated entrails treated with unguents are not easily identified.

FIGURE OF QEBHSENUEF

(CARTER 304A, J.D'E. 60730;
HEIGHT 55.5 CM)

The black-painted base of this figure is uninscribed, but there is no doubt about its identification as the son of Horus, the Canopic genius Qebhsenuef. Here he is shown as a mummiform human body with a falcon head wearing a tripartite wig. It is remarkable how skillfully the Egyptian artist cobbled together such disparate parts to make a figure which seems perfectly natural, once you have come to terms with the idea of a bird-headed human body. The falcon-head has a black-painted top, a black glass beak, and elaborate eye markings in blue glass. Most of the evidence, textual and scientific, seems to agree that Qebhsenuef guarded the intestines, called *mekhtu* by the Egyptians, apparently a corruption of *imy-khet*, 'what is in the body'. In the hierarchy of divine personages in charge of the Canopic equipment of the dead, the goddess who took charge of Qebhsenuef was Selkis, the scorpion, and they are paired on the appropriate Canopic coffinette.

A PAIR OF NOME STANDARDS

(CARTER 37A, 38B, J.D'E. 60751, 60752; HEIGHT 81 CM, 68 CM)

Why would a king want a nome standard in his tomb? A nome was a province of ancient Egypt, 20 in the north and 22 in the south. Why two of the same nome? Certainly there would not have been room for the 42 standards in this small tomb. If, however, these standards should be taken as representatives for the whole series of nomes, why choose the Xth Upper Egyptian nome, called Wadjyt or Edjo, the Greek name of its capital being Aphroditopolis? These questions cannot reasonably be answered, and one is drawn to the conclusion that the standards were in the royal storerooms, and could be used to swell out the royal funerary equipment. But their existence in the tomb is still peculiar. Both take the form of a serpent curved over a typical standard support, with a feather attached to the curve of the snake. They are of gilded wood, beautifully and simply formed. The Aphroditopolite nome is in Middle Egypt, south of Asyut and north of Akhmim.

FIGURE OF NETJER-ANKH

(CARTER 283A, J.D'E. 60754; HEIGHT 56.5 CM)

This fine figure of an erect cobra was stored in the Treasury in a wooden shrine also containing the figures of two falcon deities, Sopdu (see next) and Gemehsu. It is very stylishly carved, with the detailed markings on the body delicately delineated. The cobra-figure itself is of wood, gilded, with just the eyes separately made: the surrounds are of bronze and the eyes of transparent quartz with details painted on the back. At the front top edge of the base is a short text in yellow paint: The Osiris, Nebkheperure, beloved of Netjer-ankh'. The divine serpent Netjer-ankh is not a well-known member of the Egyptian pantheon. It is found on some coffins of the Middle Kingdom dating to the Twelfth Dynasty, and a serpent so named can be seen in a part of the Book of what is in the Underworld in royal tombs in the Valley of the Kings. In this later context Netjer-ankh appears as a guardian of the entrance to one of the sections of the Underworld through which the dead king must pass.

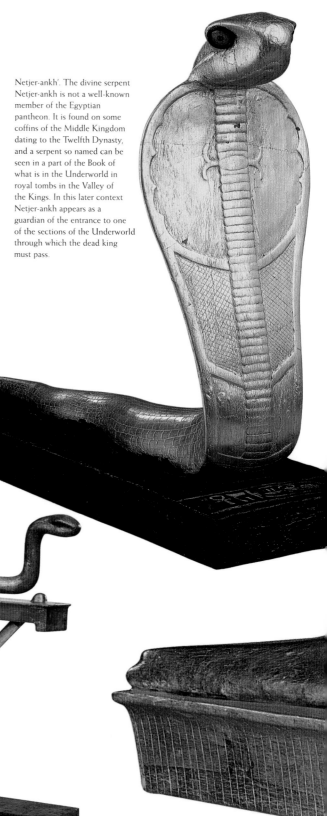

STANDARD WITH SOPDU

(Carter 283b, J.d'E. 60747; height 65.5 cm)

'Lord of the foreign countries' was an epithet given to the god Sopdu as early as the Old Kingdom, and throughout the dynastic period he was seen as exercising authority over desert areas beyond Egyptian frontiers. This image of a falcon with a feathered headdress could be considered a form of Horus of Nekhen (Hierakonpolis), the old Upper Egyptian capital; but here it is undoubtedly the Lower Egyptian deity of Saft el-Henna in the eastern Delta, for the text on the base gives the prenomen of Tutankhamun who is 'beloved of Sopdu'. This excellent representation of Sopdu, 'the sharp one', is of gilded wood with blue glass markings for the eyes and a black glass beak. The gilding has the ruddy tint of purple or red gold. This piece could be seen as another district sign, like those of Aphroditopolis described above, but it is more likely to be just a divine standard of a god protecting the king's interests in the East, and sporting the royal flail from its back.

THE ANUBIS SHRINE

(CARTER 261, J.D'E. 61444;
TOTAL HEIGHT 118 CM, TOTAL LENGTH 270 CM,
WIDTH 52 CM)

The first impressive object to be seen when the Treasury was entered on February 16, 1923 was the jackal-god Anubis, with threatening head, ears pricked high, body swathed in linen, paws outstretched on a gilded shrine, with four long carrying poles. It stood there as if it had just been set down by priestly bearers at the time of the funeral. Everyone who saw it was impressed. The Canopic shrine, with its exquisite figures, was seductive, but the Anubis was haunting. It is not possible to say whether it was so placed as guardian of all the precious and sacred things stored in the Treasury, but it certainly served that purpose. One can imagine the awe, even terror, felt by those ancient intruders who penetrated so far into the tomb. The sight of that head, black and threatening, illuminated by flickering rush-lights, may have deterred the robbers. Many of the boxes there remained sealed.

The black-painted figure of the jackal, noble in its attitude, is made more dramatic by the gilding on the ears and on the collar and scarf around its neck. Its eyes, of calcite and obsidian, are outlined in gold, and – a last subtle touch – its claws are made of silver, a rare metal in the tomb. A point of interest is that one of the linen items draped around the neck was dated to the seventh year of Akhenaten, just about when Tutankhamun was born.

The pylon-shaped shrine is of wood, plastered and gilded, its principal decorative motif consisting of pairs of *djed* and *tyet* signs, powerful amuletic symbols of endurance and life associated with the cult of Osiris. Several compartments in the body of the shrine held amuletic figures and pieces of jewelry, and a number of strange practical items possibly connected with the process of mummification. A scribe's palette inscribed for Meritaten, Tutankhamun's sister-in-law, was placed between the jackal's paws on the top of the shrine.

Amulets

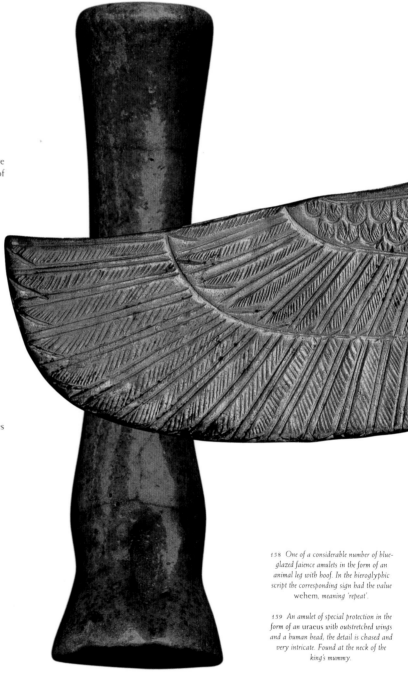

Ancient Egyptian religion was rich in symbolism, and the hieroglyphic script contained many signs with magical and amuletic power. It was not difficult therefore for the composers of texts and the makers of personal objects for life and for death to introduce elements charged with amuletic significance into what they wrote or what they designed. Amuletic forms were in consequence pervasive throughout Egyptian life and death.

Most of the pieces of jewelry found in Tutankhamun's tomb were designed to include the royal names and many amuletic emblems. There were also many single pieces of particular forms with religious meaning, and to these the term 'amulet' is generally assigned. They may represent a particular deity, an object connected with a particular deity, or one of more universal meaning. One sign that is usually thought to be amuletic is the *ankh*, the sign of life, but it is rarely found as an amulet on its own.

The most important amulets found in the tomb were those placed within the bandages of the king's mummy. Of the 150 objects recovered from the mummy, about twenty-five may be classified as amulets. Nearly all were placed around the neck, a part of the body clearly seen to be very vulnerable; here were very potent amulets – the *uraeus* serpent and the vulture, the two protective deities for the king; there were *djed*-pillars for stability, and *wadj*-scepters for renewal; there was a Thoth for wisdom and an Anubis for funerary protection. At the back of the head, very appropriately, was a small head-rest amulet, designed to support and protect the royal head. It was made of pure iron, a very rare material.

About thirty further amulets were found elsewhere in the tomb; their presence was scarcely needed, so well was the king protected otherwise.

158 One of a considerable number of blue-glazed faience amulets in the form of an animal leg with hoof. In the hieroglyphic script the corresponding sign had the value wehem, meaning 'repeat'.

159 An amulet of special protection in the form of an uraeus with outstretched wings and a human head; the detail is chased and very intricate. Found at the neck of the king's mummy.

Double *uraeus* amulet

(Carter 256,4G, J.d'E. 61856;
height 7 cm, width 6.5 cm)

Although no royal mummies in an intact condition had ever been found, enough information about the placing of jewelry and amuletic objects within the wrappings of non-royal persons existed to forewarn Howard Carter that he was likely to find splendid things on the body of Tutankhamun. He was not disappointed. The whole body from top to toe was enriched and protected by wonderful, mostly magical, objects; but no part was more protected than the royal neck. Here he found six layers of amuletic objects, each layer separated by many linen bandages. At the fifth layer he uncovered eight amuletic figures made of sheet gold, *uraei* and vultures. There can be no doubting the powerful protective role assigned to these creatures. They represented the gods of Upper and Lower Egypt specially charged with the safe-keeping of the king: Nekhbet, the vulture-goddess of Nekheb (Elkab), across the river from the ancient capital of Hierakonpolis, and Wadjyt, the cobra-goddess of Buto, deep in the marshes of the north-west Delta. The double *uraeus* of this piece possibly stands for both these goddesses, the Two Ladies, who sometimes 'confuse' their forms. They would know who they were.

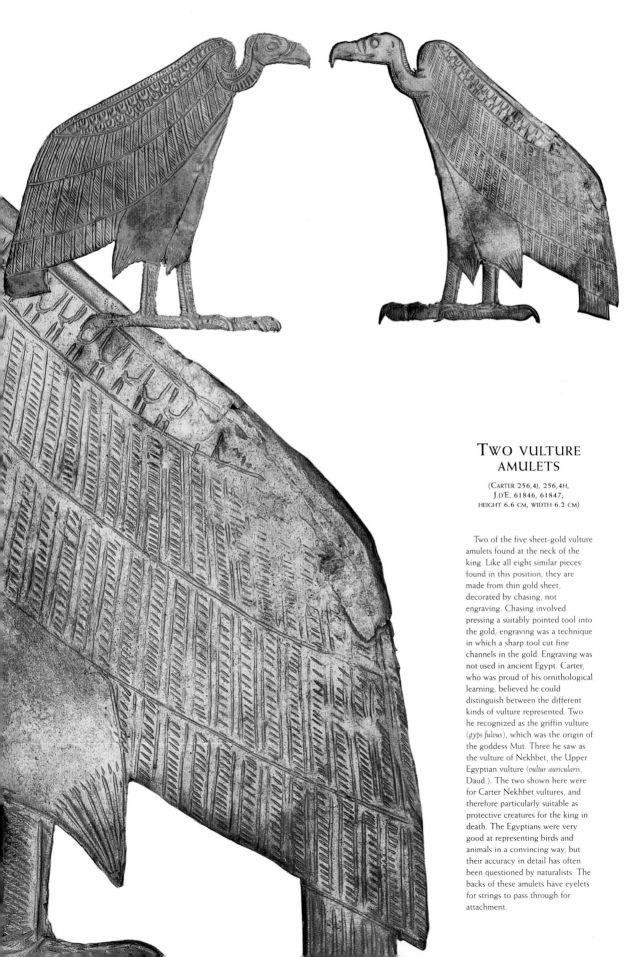

TWO VULTURE AMULETS

(CARTER 256,4J, 256,4H,
J.D'E. 61846, 61847;
HEIGHT 6.6 CM, WIDTH 6.2 CM)

Two of the five sheet-gold vulture
amulets found at the neck of the
king. Like all eight similar pieces
found in this position, they are
made from thin gold sheet,
decorated by chasing, not
engraving. Chasing involved
pressing a suitably pointed tool into
the gold; engraving was a technique
in which a sharp tool cut fine
channels in the gold. Engraving was
not used in ancient Egypt. Carter,
who was proud of his ornithological
learning, believed he could
distinguish between the different
kinds of vulture represented. Two
he recognized as the griffin vulture
(*gyps fulvus*), which was the origin of
the goddess Mut. Three he saw as
the vulture of Nekhbet, the Upper
Egyptian vulture (*vultur auricularis*,
Daud.). The two shown here were
for Carter Nekhbet vultures, and
therefore particularly suitable as
protective creatures for the king in
death. The Egyptians were very
good at representing birds and
animals in a convincing way, but
their accuracy in detail has often
been questioned by naturalists. The
backs of these amulets have eyelets
for strings to pass through for
attachment.

FIGURE OF WERET-HEKAU

(CARTER 108C, J.D'E. 61952;
HEIGHT OF FIGURE 14 CM)

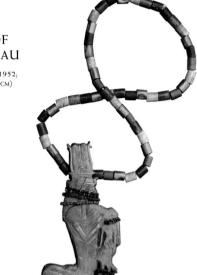

The wonderful golden shrine found in the Antechamber contained a stand for a small figure, parts of the ceremonial corselet, and a linen package containing this figure. It may not be precisely an amulet, but it was undoubtedly charged with magical force. Here is illustrated a well-known episode from mythology: the king is suckled by the goddess Isis; and here Isis appears in a transformation, a snake with human head, breasts and arms; she is Weret-hekau 'the great one of magic'. It is again extraordinary how acceptable the Egyptian artist has made an incident that should normally induce loathing. Weret-hekau has become a caring, nursing serpent with a female head wearing a queen's vulture headdress and a double feathered crown with horns. Tutankhamun is shown with distinctly Amarna-style physical characteristics, but not as a child; rather a grown king with the blue crown and a kilt with flowing streamers. The goddess has one arm around the king, and with her other hand she directs her breast to his mouth. The main figure is made of gilded wood strung on a necklace of simple beads of gold, carnelian, felspar and glass. Further strings of tiny beads surround the necks of the goddess and the king, and the feet of the king. The text on the base describes Tutankhamun as 'beloved of Weret-hekau'.

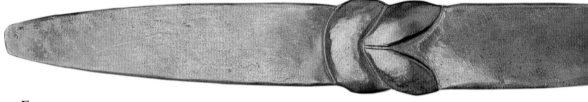

FAIENCE FIGURE OF THOTH

(CARTER 261G(2), J.D'E. 60743; HEIGHT 8 CM)

KNOT AMULET

(CARTER 256KKK, J.D'E. 61841; LENGTH 16 CM)

Compartments in the great Anubis shrine which guarded the entrance to the Treasury contained a very strange assortment of material. There were the important collection of pectoral jewels, pieces of cloth and clothing, a few *shabti*-figures, odds and ends tied up in small linen bundles, and some amulets and small divine figures – the forgotten contents of a drawer in a bureau. Among the amulets and divine figures was this little faience figure of the god Thoth in bright blue glaze with a few markings in manganese of wig striations and head details. The god is shown as a human figure with the head of the ibis, the most common animal form of this important deity. Thoth, the god of Hermopolis (Khmunu) in Middle Egypt, was a regular member of the great company of the gods, whose importance never waned. He can be considered the Head of the Divine Civil Service. He was the scribe of the gods and the patron deity of scribes. He also occurs among the gods and genii represented on coffins and Canopic equipment. His presence in the Anubis shrine cannot be explained, but perhaps no explanation is necessary. As a small sculpture it has merit in its simplicity, and in the fineness of the glaze.

Covering the thorax of Tutankhamun's mummy was a bewildering series of objects separated by much bandaging: Carter identified thirteen layers. In the seventh, among a number of other objects, were two strange pieces of solid gold, shaped as ties or knots. They were placed to the right and the left of the thorax, running parallel to the arms. Carter could offer no explanation; for him they were 'of unknown meaning', the judgement on many objects which are thought to be amulets. Sometimes they cannot be explained physically – what exactly was the *djed*-pillar, or the equally common *tyet*? In some cases meanings can be assigned through the use of the object in the hieroglyphic script in meaningful contexts. Sometimes an amulet has a form which is quite recognizable, but without identifiable meaning. This knot amulet falls into this last category. A slightly different knot-hieroglyph has the sound *tjes*, a root which can mean 'join, tie', and as a noun 'vertebra'. The amuletic possibilities of *tjes* immediately become apparent. An utterance in the Pyramid Texts declares of the king: 'the gods have fastened together your face for you, and Horus has given you his eye'.

PARTLY GILDED
DJED-AMULET

(Carter 620(21), J.D'E. 61780;
HEIGHT 8 CM)

Most of the conventional amulets found in Tutankhamun's tomb, apart from those concealed in the mummy wrappings, were retrieved from the Annexe, a kind of glorious junk-room into which a huge amount of material of all kinds was stuffed – much of it before the great pieces were placed in the Antechamber, otherwise it would have been inaccessible. There were boxes with fine objects, kiosks containing *shabti*-figures, boxes of food, jars of wine, boats, furniture and a great many odds and ends. There were some fine amulets, including this *djed*. It is made of blue glazed quartz frit, commonly called faience, and the terminal parts, top and bottom, and of the four horizontal bars, are embellished with gold foil. There are markings in manganese, including a cartouche containing the prenomen of the king, Nebkheperure. Stability or endurance can be granted to the deceased by or through the *djed*-pillar – the stability of a living person provided by the backbone, or in nature by the trunk of a tree. The origins of the *djed* go back to the earliest times, when Egyptian religion was concerned with many natural objects and phenomena. When it was incorporated in the Osiris cult, it was not explained.

GOLD
DJED-AMULET

(CARTER 256KK, J.D'E. 61778;
HEIGHT 9 CM)

It is not often that one finds an object placed precisely where it ought to be, especially an amulet. This gold *djed* is one of two which were found at the neck of Tutankhamun's mummy. Spell 155 of the Book of the Dead contains a comment on the short chapter (mentioned below): 'To be said over a gold *djed* embellished with sycomore bark, to be set on the neck of the deceased on the day of burial. He, on whose neck this amulet is set, will be a worthy spirit who will be in the kingdom of the dead on New Year's Day, like those in the following of Osiris. A thing a million times true.' So was Tutankhamun equipped, and this *djed*, symbol of endurance, is inscribed with words from Spell 155: 'Spoken (by) your limbs, to you, weary of heart [that is, dead]. Put yourself on your side that I may put water under you and bring to you a *djed* of gold, and that you may rejoice in it.' And so it was done. The so-called *djed*-pillar, shown being raised to an upright position in ritual scenes, was closely associated with the Osiris cult, and has sometimes been interpreted as a formalized representation of the god's backbone.

GOLDEN PAPYRUS COLUMN

(CARTER 620(72), J.D'E. 61857; HEIGHT 5.9 CM)

The papyrus column in the hieroglyphic script means 'be green, be fresh, be healthy'. It is therefore a very appropriate sign to be used as an amulet. In view of its meaning, the ideal color for it is green, as will be explained in the next entry. This example, however, is of gold; it is carefully marked with the details of the flower head, and of the leaves at the base of the stem. It carries the simple inscription 'the good god, Nebkheperure'. At the top there is a suspension ring. It was found among the miscellaneous objects in the Annexe. Spell 160 of the Book of the Dead concerns the 'giving of a papyrus column of green felspar'. It states: 'I possess a papyrus-column of green felspar which is not flawed, which the hand of Thoth supports, for he abhors imperfection. If it is intact then I shall be healthy; if it is undamaged then shall I be undamaged; if it is not hit, then shall I not be hit. It is what Thoth has said that joins your spine together.'

FAIENCE PAPYRUS COLUMN

(CARTER 261F(6), J.D'E. 61788; HEIGHT 8.5 CM)

The correct place for the papyrus column to be set was on the throat of the deceased person, and it should be made of green felspar. Spell 159 of the Book of the Dead is to be spoken over such a papyrus column 'with this spell written on it; it is to be placed on the neck of the dead person'. The spell itself is somewhat elusive: 'You who have come out of the god's house today; she whose voice is loud, goes around from the door of the Two Houses; she has taken the power of her father, who is advanced as Bull of the nursing goddess, and she accepts those followers of hers who perform great things for her'. A gold papyrus column inlaid with green felspar was found between two *djed*-columns on Tutankhamun's neck. This example, much more modest, is not made of green felspar, but of blue faience; the glaze could have been green, as that was possible in the Eighteenth Dynasty. The markings are carried out in manganese. It was found in the great Anubis shrine in the Treasury.

FAIENCE
WAS-SCEPTER

(Carter 620(15), J.d'E. 61787;
length 10.5 cm)

The *was*-scepter is not often
found as an amulet, but there can
be no doubting its significance and
power. It was a divine instrument,
carried by most gods, and
sometimes used by them to offer
life and endurance to a king in the
form of *ankh* and *djed* signs on the
end of a *was*. This example, which
comes from the Annexe, is made of
blue faience and has
Tutankhamun's prenomen written
on it in black glaze. An eye drawn
in black on the curved top of the
staff confirms that the top was
considered to be in the form of an
animal's head, the front forming a
long snout, and the top long ears.
A satisfactory identification of the
creature has never been made. It
has been thought to be a donkey,
also that it represents the head of
the turbulent god Seth; but as this
god's animal is likewise
unidentified, the problem remains
unsolved. The *was* has a forked
end, like other staves. Its
hieroglyphic meaning is 'dominion'
and it frequently occurs with other
signs like *djed* and *ankh* in
decorative groupings.

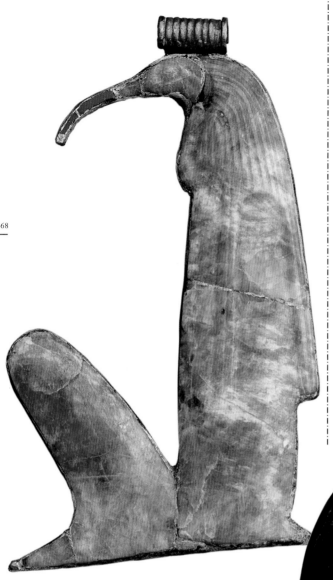

RESIN SCARAB WITH HERON

(CARTER 256Q, J.D'E. 61977; LENGTH 4.8 CM)

This unusual piece was found within Tutankhamun's mummy wrappings at about the level of his navel. It is a scarab made of resin, inlaid with a figure of a heron made up of lapis-lazuli and different colored glass. It is mounted on a gold plate inscribed with a text derived from Spell 29B of the Book of the Dead, which is for 'a heart amulet made of *sehret* stone'. This piece, however, is not a heart amulet, and it is certainly not made of *sehret* stone, which is thought to be hard and dark green. Such stones were commonly used for heart scarabs like the one mounted in the pectoral of a winged scarab with Isis and Nephthys (J. d'E. 61948).

The bird shown here is called *benu* in Egyptian, often translated as 'phoenix'. The *benu* is one of the forms in which the deceased can leave the tomb. Spell 13 of the Book of the Dead is one 'for going in and out of the West', and it includes the words 'I went in as a falcon, but I have come out as the *benu*'. In the spell on this base plate the king states: 'I am the *benu*, the *ba*-spirit of Re who guides the *bas* to the Underworld'.

FELSPAR THOTH AMULET

(CARTER 256,4A, J.D'E. 61863; HEIGHT 5.5 CM)

The fourth layer of objects around the neck of Tutankhamun's mummy contained, along with other amuletic objects, this figure of the god Thoth. It is the ibis-headed form of the god, shown with human body in squatting pose. It is backed by a gold plate to which it is cemented as thin pieces of green felspar. Felspar is a crystalline stone with a tendency to fracture, and it is clear that the craftsman who fitted in the pieces had some difficulty in achieving perfect joins. Nevertheless, the felspar shows some moulding of form, and details have been lightly incised. Thoth was very much a diplomatic deity, effecting reconciliation and acting as a go-between either in person or as a letter-writer. In the discussion of the papyrus column amulets above it was seen that he is mentioned in one of the appropriate spells of the Book of the Dead as being one who abhors imperfection. Felspar was the specified material for the papyrus column amulet.

GILDED HEART
WITH HERON

(CARTER 620(67), J.D'E. 61866;
LENGTH 5.8 CM)

This is a true heart amulet; it is shaped like a heart and it is properly associated with the *benu* bird. It comes from the miscellaneous material in the Annexe, and is made of gilded wood. One side is inscribed with the prenomen of Tutankhamun, the cartouche flanked by *heqa*-scepters of royal power and the feather of truth. The other side is inlaid with colored faience forming a figure of the *benu*. This bird is often considered the forerunner of the phoenix in classical mythology. In some forms of the Egyptian creation myth, the sun-god appears as the *benu*, perched on a reed growing out of the primordial mound. The classical phoenix was the fabulous bird rising from the ashes, promising a form of resurrection. The idea of rebirth is common to both myths, but it is misleading to think of the *benu* as the mythical ancestor of the classical phoenix.

RED GLASS *TYET* AMULET

(CARTER 46Y, J.D'E. 61833;
LENGTH 6.5 CM)

In the confused mass of objects left by the tomb robbers in the Antechamber, among a quantity of linen, was this amulet, called *tyet*. It incorporates an old magical idea connected with the goddess Isis, and there has been much debate about what it represents. Sometimes the ideas behind Egyptian signs wander or migrate over the centuries, and it is probable that any interpretation based on New Kingdom texts will be some way from the origins. This sign and its associated ideas are very old, and in its early form it looks not unlike the *ankh*, but with drooping side arms. It is generally thought to represent a folded cloth, but it has even been considered a form of the female genital organs. It is 'the knot of Isis' or the 'blood of Isis'; the former is more likely. According to the Book of the Dead it should be made of red jasper, and most examples are made of this stone or other red materials. This one is of red glass and it is inscribed 'the good god, Nebkheperure'.

FAIENCE *ANKH*

(CARTER 99A, J.D'E. 61790;
HEIGHT 10.8 CM)

This sharply molded figure of
the *ankh* was found along with
some cloth and a lump of bread in
the Antechamber. It is made of
bright blue faience with markings
in manganese. The prenomen of
Tutankhamun is written down the
stem of the piece. *Ankh* was the
Egyptian word for 'life', and gods
are often shown carrying it,
frequently offering it to the king.
The *ankh* was an important element
in the cult of the Aten during the
reign of Akhenaten, being shown
extended to the king and other
members of the royal family by the
rays decending from the divine
sun-disk. Although *ankh* was of
vital importance for the well-being
of everyone, it is surprising to find
how few actual *ankh* amulets can be
seen in collections of amulets,
compared with the large numbers
of *djed*-pillars, papyrus columns,
eyes of Horus and other magical
signs. In a sense, non-royal persons
received 'life' through the king;
it was the king who was charged
with 'life' directly by the gods.

FAIENCE *TYET* AMULET

(CARTER 620(18), J.D'E. 61828;
LENGTH 8.5 CM)

The markings on this *tyet* amulet
show very clearly why it is
thought to represent a folded
cloth, tied beneath the loop at the
top. It is not made of a red
material but of blue faience with
markings in manganese, including
the prenomen of Tutankhamun.
Spell 156 of the Book of the Dead
applies to the *tyet*: 'You possess
your blood, Isis; you possess your
power, Isis; you possess your
magic, Isis. The amulet is a
protection for this Great One,
which will drive off anyone who
would perform a criminal act
against him.' The text comments
further that this spell should be
spoken over the *tyet* amulet and
placed on the neck of the dead
person on the day of burial: 'For
the one for whom this is done,
the power of Isis will be the
protection of his body, and Horus,
the son of Isis, will rejoice over
him when he sees him'. There was
a *tyet* of red jasper placed on
Tutankhamun's neck.

Royal Figures

It is perhaps surprising that no stone sculptures of the king were found in Tutankhamun's tomb. Most contemporary private burials would include a votive figure in limestone, granite or quartzite, covered with ritual texts. Private tombs, however, incorporated burial chambers and offering chapels. Royal tombs had their chapels – funerary temples – far away from the Valley. The funerary temples of Amenophis III and Ramesses II, for example, were well populated with stone sculptures, many being colossal. It is not known with certainty whether Tutankhamun had a funerary temple, but two colossal quartzite statues of the king were found in the funerary temple of Ay and Horemheb at Medinet Habu. The assumption must be that a beginning at least was made on a temple.

In the tomb itself the principal images of the king were the two guardian figures in the Antechamber by the blocked entrance to the Burial Chamber. Partly draped in linen, with eyes dramatically outlined in gilded bronze and shiny black faces, they presented an awesome sight to the excavators. Similar figures, but ungilded, had been found by Giovanni Battista Belzoni in badly plundered tombs he had discovered in the Valley one hundred years earlier; their purpose had never been explained.

There were seven other gilded wooden figures of the king in the tomb, not all with the features of the young monarch. They were found in the black-painted shrine-shaped boxes in the Treasury. Four are quite remarkable, two showing statuettes of the king on the backs of leopards, and two showing the king in a papyrus skiff. Two simple striding figures show him wearing the red crown, and one with the white crown. Not all these figures may have been made as images of Tutankhamun, and some are distinctly modeled in the Amarna style.

172 and 173 The heads of the two guardian statues of Tutankhamun which stood on either side of the entrance to the Burial Chamber. They represent the king himself and his ka-spirit, his constant companion and double from the time of his birth. The ka is on the right. The color black implies regeneration.

GUARDIAN STATUE WITH *NEMES*

(CARTER 22, J.d'E. 60707;
HEIGHT 190 CM, WIDTH 56 CM)

Life-size wooden statues of
kings had been found by Giovanni
Battista Belzoni in tombs in the
Valley of the Kings which he had
opened in the early years of the
nineteenth century. Their function
was never made clear until
Tutankhamun's tomb was
discovered, and the excavators on
entering were confronted by the
two dramatic figures placed on
either side of the sealed entrance
to the Burial Chamber. They are
very similar, but not identical.
Both are made of wood,
constructed of a number of pieces,
plastered over and painted with
thick black paint – here and
elsewhere in the tomb black being
the color of regeneration. They
are gilded over the non-fleshy
parts – headdress, collar and
pectoral, arm-bands, bracelets,
staff and mace; the sandals are of
gilded bronze, as is the *uraeus* fixed
to the brow. The eyes are also
outlined in gilded bronze, and are
inlaid with crystalline limestone
and obsidian. This figure
represents the king himself,
wearing the *nemes* head cloth; the
text running down the middle of
the kilt reads: 'the good god to
whom one bows, the sovereign, of
whom one boasts, Nebkheperure,
son of Re, lord of diadems,
Tutankhamun, ruler in southern
Heliopolis, living for ever, like Re,
every day'.

GUARDIAN STATUE
WITH *AFNET*

(CARTER 29, J.D'E. 60708;
HEIGHT 190 CM, WIDTH 54 CM)

The text on the kilt of this pair to the preceding figure reads: 'the good god, to whom one bows, the sovereign of whom one boasts, the *ka* of Herakhty, the Osiris, King, Lord of the Two Lands, Nebkheperure, justified'. This, then, represents the *ka*-spirit of Tutankhamun, his ever-present companion and counterpart from birth. Here the *ka* joins the king himself in sharing the duties of guarding the Burial Chamber and its precious contents. The figure wears the *afnet* head cloth, but is otherwise scarcely to be distinguished from the other. They are noble pieces, sensitively carved, showing some influence of the art of the time of Akhenaten. The features are those of the young king. Some details of the decoration of the gilded parts are of great interest: they were first overlaid with linen, then layered with gesso-plaster before being gilded, the decoration first being carved on the plaster. The pendant hanging below the broad collar shows a winged scarab, a common theme on royal pectorals, representing rebirth. On the broad front of the kilt, an apron or long sporran-like piece is shown; it carries the text, and is flanked by chevron patterns and cobras hanging down on each side, with sun-disks on their heads. With staff and mace, this *ka*-figure and its fellow of the king himself stand ready to meet intruders.

ROYAL FIGURE WITH WHITE CROWN

(CARTER 296B, J.D'E. 62360;
HEIGHT 75.3 CM)

An inscription on the base in yellow paint identifies this statue as 'The Good God, Nebkheperure, justified', that is Tutankhamun. But there is no doubt that it does not look very much like him, and the bodily details are very distinctly in the Amarna style. It may well therefore have been made for Neferneferuaten, Tutankhamun's ephemeral predecessor, or even some other Amarna royal person, even Akhenaten himself. It was in one of the Treasury shrines along with one other piece, a remarkable figure of the little-known deity Menkaret, carrying a small figure of the king on her head. The present piece is more conventional in form. The king is shown stepping forward; he wears the white crown of Upper Egypt with gilded *uraeus*; the eyes are inlaid with crystalline limestone and obsidian, and surrounded with bronze outlines and eye-brows. A conventional broad collar lies on his chest and he wears a pleated kilt which dips down towards the back in a manner characteristic of the Amarna Period. In his right hand he holds the royal flail, and in his left a staff with a curved top, called an *awt*; it is in hieroglyphic writing sometimes replaced by the more familiar *heqa*-scepter, but it seems to be distinctive in its own right, even if its precise significance is not known.

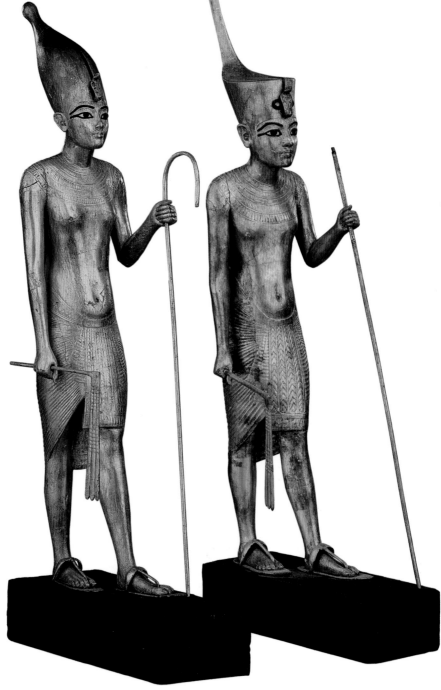

ROYAL FIGURE WITH RED CROWN

(CARTER 275D, J.D'E. 60713;
HEIGHT 59 CM)

The various figures of the king stored in black-painted shrine-shaped chests in the Treasury struck Howard Carter, with good reason, as showing Amarna influence. Although they represented traditional types of sculpture, they possessed 'a direct and spontaneous feeling for nature'; further, 'they show both energy and grace, in fact the divine and the human have been brought in familiar touch with one another'. Here speaks the artist in

Carter. Some of the gilded royal statues are thought to have been made for Neferneferuaten, Tutankhamun's predecessor.

This piece seems less likely to be a recycled image, although the body shows Amarna characteristics, such as the sagging belly, the forward-thrust head and a general softness of form. In other respects it displays the well-established features of Tutankhamun. It is one of five pieces, including two of the king

harpooning, which were found together in one shrine, all swathed in linen shrouds. The king here is shown in a familiar pose, with his left foot set forward, although not at full stride, as might be expected. He wears the red crown with a gilded bronze *uraeus* fitted to the brow. The eyes and eye-brows are inlaid with copper and the eyes themselves are of glass. The king stands with a plain long staff in his left hand, and the royal flail in the right.

THE KING ON
A LEOPARD

(CARTER 289A, J.D'E. 60715;
FULL HEIGHT 85.6 CM)

The two groups of king on leopard
differ in one small and one major
respect. The former lies in the staff
carried by the king: in the illustrated
example there is no handrest; in the
other there is a papyrus umbel
handrest, as in the case of the
guardian figures. The second
difference will be mentioned later.

In this group the leopard is shown
carrying a figure of the king, not the
king himself, on its back. Two-
dimensional similar figures are
depicted on the walls of other royal
tombs, but the significance, which
must be mythical, is not clear. The
whole of the group is made of wood,
the royal figure being covered with
gesso-plaster and gilded. The flail, the
staff, the *uraeus* on the brow, and the
sandals are all made of gilded bronze.
The eyes and their outlines are in
colored glass. The base of the statue
is painted black, as is the leopard,
which offers a sinister contrast to the
gilded figure. The effect is
emphasized by the gilded details on
the leopard's face and ears. There is a
litheness and strength in the animal's
figure, demonstrating the Egyptian
artist's remarkable ability to capture its
essential characteristics.

The major difference between the
two royal figures mentioned above is
that the two are designed according
to different schemes of proportion.
The illustrated example uses the
common canon used since the Old
Kingdom, while the other uses the
modified canon introduced during the
Amarna Period. The latter appears
more elongated than the former; it
has fairly prominent breasts and low,
broad hips; the effect is more
feminine than masculine. It has been
suggested that the second figure may
represent Nefertiti or
Neferneferuaten, rather than
Tutankhamun. Both figures were
surely made during the Amarna
Period, but their identity in the tomb,
and for the Egyptians – if not for
sceptical historians – was fixed by the
inscriptions on their bases; they name
Tutankhamun.

THE KING AS HARPOONER

(CARTER 275C, J.D'E. 60709;
HEIGHT 69.5 CM)

One of two similar pieces found with three other royal figures in one of the chests in the Treasury, this remarkable group is undoubtedly among the most sensitive, lively and aesthetically satisfying sculptures to have survived from ancient Egypt. It has a fluidity, grace and subtlety of carving which characterizes the best carvings in wood, as opposed to the more intractable stone. Unfortunately, wooden figures are subject to rot, termites and fire. One of the wonders of Tutankhamun's tomb is that its contents were spared such ravages, and most of the wooden pieces survived in a remarkable state of preservation. Carvings like this harpooner brilliantly demonstrate the supreme and subtle craftsmanship of the Egyptian woodcarvers.

The group shows the king in the act of throwing a harpoon. He wears the red crown of Lower Egypt, a beaded broad collar, a pleated kilt and apron, and sandals. He is shown poised at the point of delivery, his right leg slightly raised, elegantly balanced on a skiff, a light craft made of papyrus stems. The wooden figure of the king is lightly plastered to receive its gold-leaf finish. The harpoon, the *uraeus* on the royal brow, and the sandals are made of gilded bronze; the eyes, set in bronze sockets, are of glass and obsidian. In the left hand is a coil of rope made of bronze, which in reality should be attached to the harpoon. The skiff and its stand are of black painted wood, with gilded terminals.

An incident in the interminable struggle between the gods Horus and Seth for the inheritance of their father Osiris is depicted here. This myth in various forms can be traced back to the earliest historical times, when kings and even high officials are shown hunting the male hippopotamus, the embodiment of Seth, seen as the evil deity. Here the king is Horus; the hippopotamus must be imagined. The outcome is predictably a victory for Horus, although the power of Seth was not completely defeated thereby.

Royal Regalia

One of the most common, and for Egyptologists annoying, errors perpetrated by stage designers and film-makers involved with ancient Egyptian productions is to dress their casts in clothes which are specifically royal. The headdress with lappets (*nems*) is a particular candidate for misuse. Designers may be after authenticity, but what they produce is gross inaccuracy.

It would have been very convenient if the tomb of Tutankhamun had contained a set of royal crowns and headdresses. Then some ideas of what they were made of, and how they were made, could have been formed. Unfortunately none was found, apart from a fine linen cap with gold headband on the mummy: it might have been the *afnet*, or bag-wig, such as is shown on one of the guardian statues. The other statue wears the *nems*, the most common royal headdress, often thought to have been made of pleated linen.

180-181 *The 'palm' of a ceremonial fan, gilded and inlaid with the cartouches of Tutankhamun, flanked by vultures with protecting wings, and wearing the white (left) and red (right) crowns. The fan is crossed by a heqat scepter.*

181 *left The crook, together with the flail, is an instrument of royal authority.*

181 *right In the drawings are represented, from above, the red crown of Lower Egypt, the blue, or war, crown, and the white crown of Upper Egypt.*

Actual examples would have shown material and manufacture. So would the red and white crowns of Lower and Upper Egypt, and the blue crown, the so-called war crown.

Two examples of the royal ceremonial tail were found under the mummy. They were made of beadwork on linen, but were deeply embedded in the solidified resinous material at the bottom of the coffin; they have never been satisfactorily restored.

A fine royal diadem was found on the mummy beneath the mask; but the crook and flail held in golden hands on the mummy's chest were rotted away. Happily there were several sets of crook and flail found elsewhere in the tomb – the first examples ever found. The same is true of the ceremonial scepter found in the Annexe.

The fans also included in this chapter were used for the king, if not by the king, some on ceremonial occasions.

THE DIADEM

(CARTER 256,40, J.D'E. 60684;
DIAMETER 19 CM)

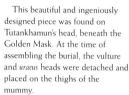

This beautiful and ingeniously
designed piece was found on
Tutankhamun's head, beneath the
Golden Mask. At the time of
assembling the burial, the vulture
and *uraeus* heads were detached and
placed on the thighs of the
mummy.

The principal element of the
diadem is a gold fillet fastened at
the back by a bow in the form of
lotus flowers. Some rigidity is
provided by the snaking body of
the *uraeus*, which arches from front
to back. Two long gold ribbons and
two substantial *uraei* hang down
from the back. Diadems formed
part of Egyptian royal insignia from
early times, and less elaborate but
beautifully crafted examples have
been found in minor royal burials
of the Middle Kingdom.

The principal decorative motif
consists of circular pieces of
carnelian set in gold with gold
central 'buttons'; these are found on
the main circlet and also on the
pendent ribbons and *uraei*. In all
places they are framed by block
borders of carnelian and blue glass.
The raised heads of the pendent
uraei are similarly inlaid. The
ribbons and pendent *uraei* are
attached to the circlet by hinges,
so that, as Carter pointed out,
they could move to fit over wigs
of different sizes.

Other parts of this versatile
diadem are adaptable. The vulture
and *uraeus* heads are removeable, as
already noted; they have grooves
on their backs which fit tongues on
the diadem. So designed, they
could be fitted onto other diadems,
crowns or headdresses – an
unusually economical arrangement.
Carter was particularly struck by
the workmanship of the vulture
head, noting the obsidian eyes and
the details of the wrinkling and
feathering. He confidently asserted
that it represented a form of the
bird known as 'the sociable vulture'.
The *uraeus* is equally well worked,
with finely fitted inlays, including
a blue glass tip to the head.

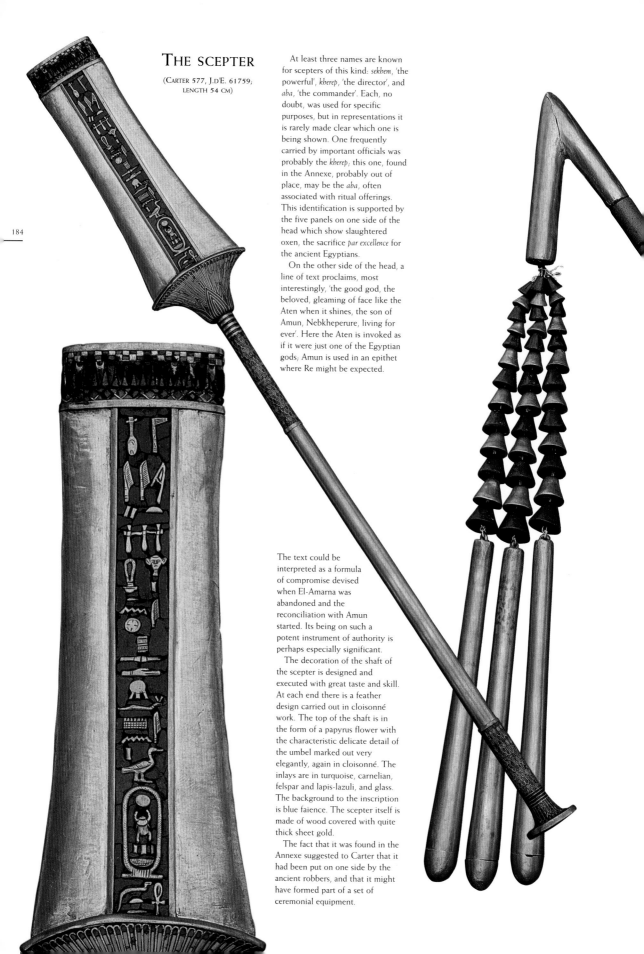

THE SCEPTER

(CARTER 577, J.D'E. 61759;
LENGTH 54 CM)

At least three names are known for scepters of this kind: *sekhem*, 'the powerful', *kherep*, 'the director', and *aba*, 'the commander'. Each, no doubt, was used for specific purposes, but in representations it is rarely made clear which one is being shown. One frequently carried by important officials was probably the *kherep*; this one, found in the Annexe, probably out of place, may be the *aba*, often associated with ritual offerings. This identification is supported by the five panels on one side of the head which show slaughtered oxen, the sacrifice *par excellence* for the ancient Egyptians.

On the other side of the head, a line of text proclaims, most interestingly, 'the good god, the beloved, gleaming of face like the Aten when it shines, the son of Amun, Nebkheperure, living for ever'. Here the Aten is invoked as if it were just one of the Egyptian gods; Amun is used in an epithet where Re might be expected.

The text could be interpreted as a formula of compromise devised when El-Amarna was abandoned and the reconciliation with Amun started. Its being on such a potent instrument of authority is perhaps especially significant.

The decoration of the shaft of the scepter is designed and executed with great taste and skill. At each end there is a feather design carried out in cloisonné work. The top of the shaft is in the form of a papyrus flower with the characteristic delicate detail of the umbel marked out very elegantly, again in cloisonné. The inlays are in turquoise, carnelian, felspar and lapis-lazuli, and glass. The background to the inscription is blue faience. The scepter itself is made of wood covered with quite thick sheet gold.

The fact that it was found in the Annexe suggested to Carter that it had been put on one side by the ancient robbers, and that it might have formed part of a set of ceremonial equipment.

FLAIL AND CROOK

(CARTER 269E, 44U,
J.d'E. 61760, 61762;
LENGTH OF EACH 33.5 CM)

These two instruments of royal authority are of great antiquity. They are chracteristically shown in later times as part of the regalia carried by Osiris, the god of the afterlife. It is wrong, however, to consider them as Osirian and carried by the living king in expectation of posthumous royalty. Osiris carries the crook and flail because he is a king, a divine king. He carries them because the Egyptian king carries them. The king carries them at the time of his coronation and at the occasions of renewal of royal power in the *sed*-festival. The flail and crook shown here seem to form a pair, not only by general similarity of form and construction, but also because they are of the same length, and would sit well together in the hands of the ruler. They were not, however, found together in the tomb; the flail was in the cartouche-shaped chest in the Treasury, which was intended for jewelry mostly; the crook was stored in a chest in the Antechamber. It is hard to believe that they do not belong together. It is also hard to avoid the conclusion that they may even have been held by Tutankhamun during his coronation in El-Amarna.

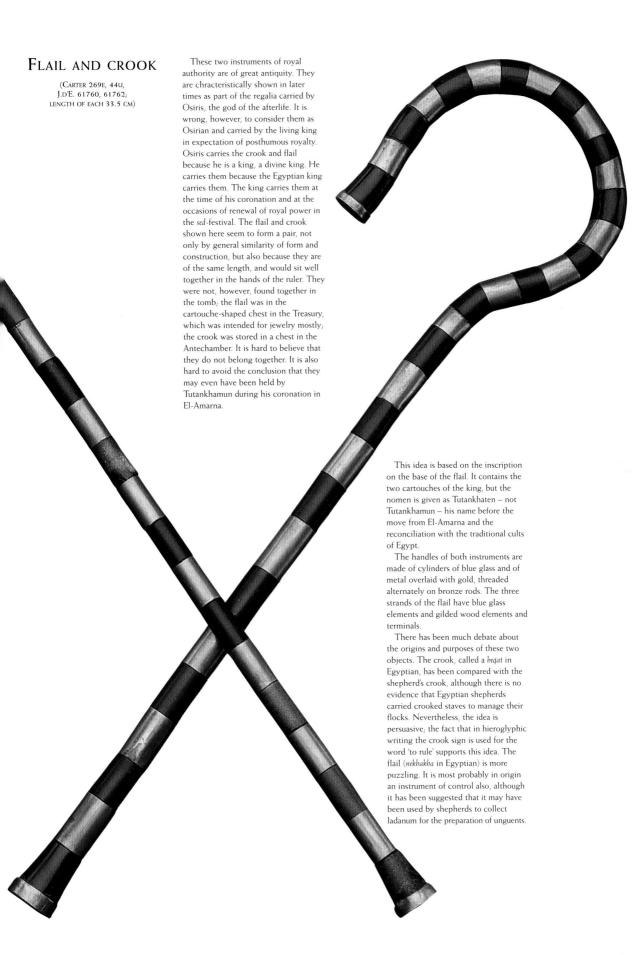

This idea is based on the inscription on the base of the flail. It contains the two cartouches of the king, but the nomen is given as Tutankhaten – not Tutankhamun – his name before the move from El-Amarna and the reconciliation with the traditional cults of Egypt.

The handles of both instruments are made of cylinders of blue glass and of metal overlaid with gold, threaded alternately on bronze rods. The three strands of the flail have blue glass elements and gilded wood elements and terminals.

There has been much debate about the origins and purposes of these two objects. The crook, called a *heqat* in Egyptian, has been compared with the shepherd's crook, although there is no evidence that Egyptian shepherds carried crooked staves to manage their flocks. Nevertheless, the idea is persuasive; the fact that in hieroglyphic writing the crook sign is used for the word 'to rule' supports this idea. The flail (*nekhakha* in Egyptian) is more puzzling. It is most probably in origin an instrument of control also, although it has been suggested that it may have been used by shepherds to collect ladanum for the preparation of unguents.

THE OSTRICH HUNT FAN

(CARTER 242, J.D'E. 62001; LENGTH 105.5 CM, WIDTH OF PALM 18.5 CM)

Fan-bearing was an important official function in ancient times, particularly in Egypt, where large fans were used also as sun shades. They were further marks of position and status. This fan, most splendid in appearance, is also, from its texts and scenes on the head or palm, very informative. It was found in the Burial Chamber, between the two innermost shrines; from the remains of its feathers it was clear that it had originally been fitted with thirty ostrich feathers, white and brown, alternately set.

What the fan shows in itself, the texts on the handle and the scenes on the palm confirm. The text on the handle states that the feathers were obtained by the king while hunting in the Eastern Desert of Heliopolis, that is not far from Memphis. The scenes illustrate the hunt. One side shows the king in his chariot at full gallop in the heat of the hunt. The two horses with feathered plumes and elaborate trappings pursue a pair of ostriches on the point of being brought down by the king's arrows. The royal hunting hound closes in on the stricken birds. The text on the other side describes the king as hunting as fiercely as Bastet (the cat deity of Bubastis), his horses being like bulls (in their strength). The scene on this side shows the aftermath of the chase: the king rides sedately in his chariot, holding back his horses, which seem to be straining at the bit. In front march two attendants weighed down with the bodies of the two dead ostriches.

The handle and the palm of the fan are made of wood covered with thin gold plate. The top of the handle is in the form of a lotus flower with down-turned petals. The scenes and texts are chased into the gold, with much of the detail produced by delicate punching.

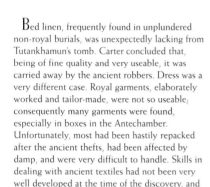

Dress and
Cosmetic Objects

Bed linen, frequently found in unplundered non-royal burials, was unexpectedly lacking from Tutankhamun's tomb. Carter concluded that, being of fine quality and very useable, it was carried away by the ancient robbers. Dress was a very different case. Royal garments, elaborately worked and tailor-made, were not so useable; consequently many garments were found, especially in boxes in the Antechamber. Unfortunately, most had been hastily repacked after the ancient thefts, had been affected by damp, and were very difficult to handle. Skills in dealing with ancient textiles had not been very well developed at the time of the discovery, and many pieces could not be rescued from their wretched state.

Nevertheless, the skilful fingers of Carter, Arthur Mace and Alfred Lucas had much success in recovering many recognizable pieces of clothing, mostly made of fine linen and embellished with delicate embroidery, elaborate beadwork and gold sequins. Tunics, loincloths, shirts, kilts, underclothes and caps, made up the bulk of what could be identified; there were two large garments, heavily embroidered, which Carter compared with the robe called a dalmatic, worn by priests on ceremonial occasions and kings at the time of their coronations. There were sashes and scarves, large numbers of gloves, and many pairs of sandals. The gloves and sandals were made of many materials, and often richly decorated; some were simple and 'everyday'. In total the tomb held a full wardrobe for life in the underworld, formal and casual.

The Egyptians had a huge repertoire of cosmetic containers, often finely designed. Those for a king were special, and many must have been plundered from the tomb, being of exquisite quality. Mirrors of precious metal have gone, but their elaborate cases were left. Several small quantities of galena and malachite for eye-paint were found, but only a few eye-paint containers; there were no combs, and the king's shaving equipment seems scanty; cosmetic spoons were unexpectedly lacking. Undoubtedly most of the missing cosmetic pieces were made of precious materials, and were prime targets for the ancient robbers.

188 A figure of Neferneferure, fifth daughter of Akhenaten and Nefertiti, and sister-in-law of Tutankhamun; from the lid of a cosmetic box found in the Antechamber. The inlays are of faience.

189 The central element of the back of the corselet of the king. A bird (probably a falcon) with scarab body, is flanked by uraei with the crowns of Upper and Lower Egypt. It holds ankh signs in its claws.

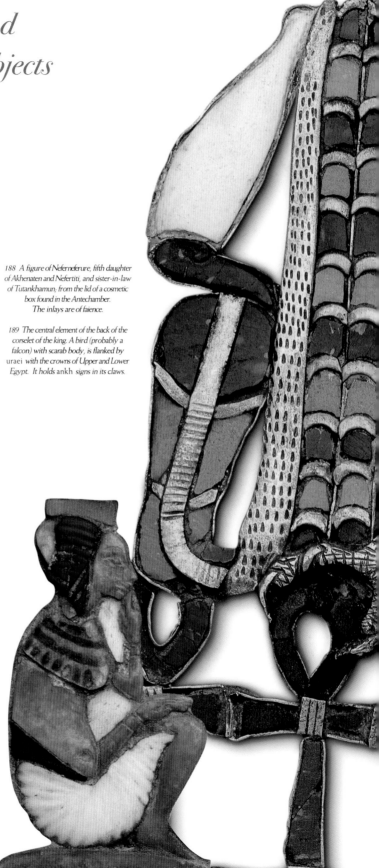

TUTANKHAMUN'S MANNEQUIN

(CARTER 116, J.D'E. 60722;
HEIGHT 73.5 CM)

Close to the golden shrine, tucked under the great ritual couches in the Antechamber, the excavators could see a most realistic face peering out from among the parts of chariots and boxes. It was this armless and legless figure, a torso painted white with a head painted brown, and with a gilded crown. Carter himself suggested that it was something upon which royal garments could be tried out, or fitted, a kind of tailor's

MIRROR CASE IN THE FORM OF *ANKH*

(CARTER 269B, J.D'E. 62349;
HEIGHT 27 CM)

This highly decorated and inscribed gilded wooden case was made for a mirror. One ancient Egyptian name for mirror was *ankh*, the word used for 'life', and this case has been made in the form of the *ankh*. The mirror which it originally contained would probably have been pear-shaped, a form of mirror first used in the New Kingdom. Mirrors played a part in funerary symbolism, and many early tomb stelae, especially of women, show mirrors in cases beneath the chair of the deceased. This case was surely made for Tutankhamun's burial, and it may be assumed that the mirror it contained would have been made of silver or gold; the container itself is lined with thin sheet silver. Robbers clearly took the mirror in antiquity. Most surviving mirrors from ancient Egypt were made of bronze, which when well polished would have a good reflective surface. The lid of this truly royal piece has in its central depression a form of Tutankhamun's prenomen on top of a lotus flower, and flanked by *uraei* with sun-disks. The inlays are of glass, apart from the sun-disks, which are carnelian. Long texts on the loop and handle of the case, on both sides, apply many epithets to the king. Among other things, he is 'image of Re' and 'pure egg of Khepri'.

dummy or mannequin. Nothing of the kind has otherwise ever been found from ancient Egypt. A scrutiny of the kinds of clothes worn by important people, as shown in paintings, reliefs and sculptures, makes it clear that many items were very carefully tailored, to fit not just well, but closely and neatly. The tomb of Tutankhamun itself produced an extraordinary amount of clothing of all kinds, much of which, sadly, was in a poor condition; but there was enough material in a reasonable state to demonstrate the range of items made for a king, and also the excellence of workmanship, not only in the making of garments, but in embroidering them in many different techniques.

THE ROYAL CORSELET

(Carter 54k, J.d'E. 62627;
height 40 cm, length 85 cm)

This rare object, of a kind known from representations on monuments, would have been worn by the king on ceremonial occasions. It was found in fragments in various parts of the Antechamber, including the gilded shrine, but enough has survived to give a fair idea of its original form. Carter's first reconstruction was, however, different from that shown here.

As now shown, there is a broad collar front and back, made up of rows of beads in glass made to look like tubular beads, the outermost row in each case having flower-shaped pendants of cloisonné work inlaid with semiprecious stones set in gold.

A pendent ornament shows Amon-Re presenting life and a long reign to Tutankhamun, who is supported by the god Atum and his divine consort Lusaas. Again the figures are made of cloisonné inlay of semiprecious stones and colored glass, including rare opaque white glass. The counterpoise ornament for the back is in the form of a rhomboidal pendant; in the center is a winged scarab with sun-disk, supported on each side by uraei wearing the crowns of Upper and Lower Egypt; from the coils of the uraei two ankh-signs of life hang. Eleven short strings of beads with floral terminals hang down from the base of this counterpoise.

The main part of the corselet, back and front, is made to represent the rishi, or feather decoration, found particularly on coffins. The individual elements are again inlaid with colored glass. In the present restoration, gold slide fasteners are placed along the edges of the body sections. It is altogether an extraordinary de luxe piece of armour, carried out spectacularly in gold and cloisonné work.

192

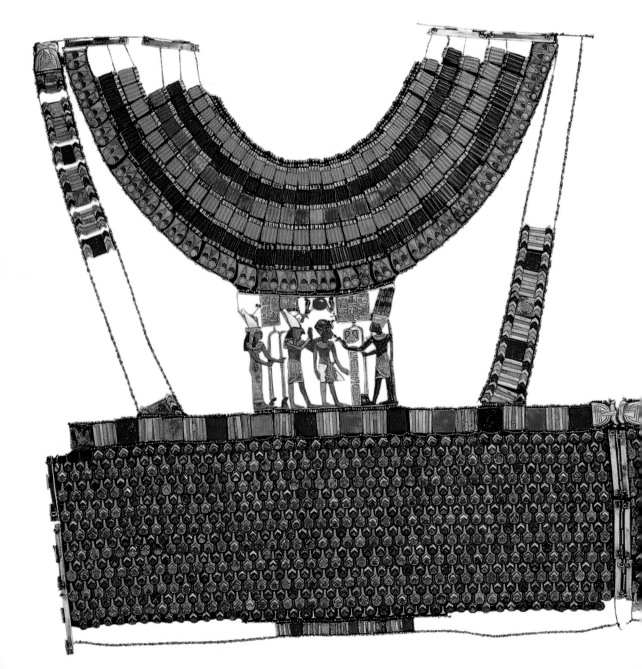

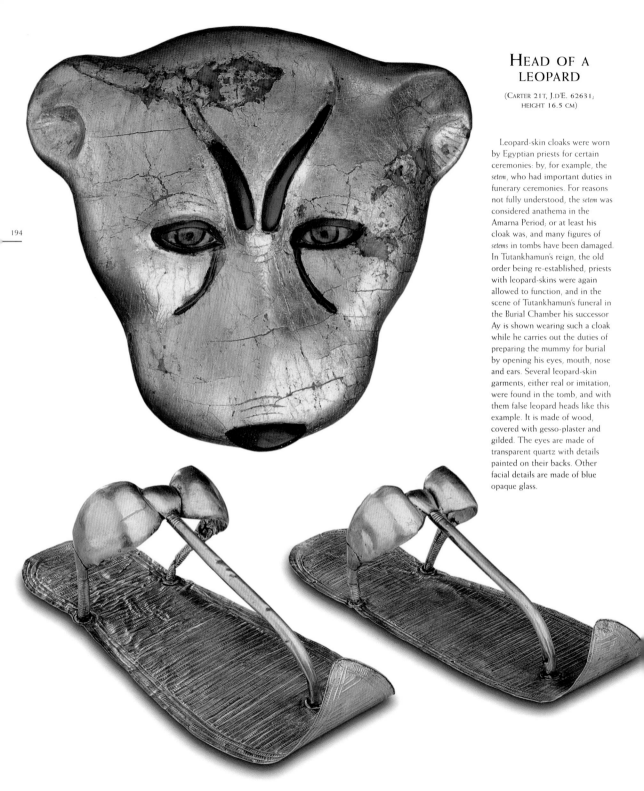

HEAD OF A LEOPARD

(CARTER 21T, J.D'E. 62631;
HEIGHT 16.5 CM)

Leopard-skin cloaks were worn by Egyptian priests for certain ceremonies: by, for example, the *setem*, who had important duties in funerary ceremonies. For reasons not fully understood, the *setem* was considered anathema in the Amarna Period, or at least his cloak was, and many figures of *setems* in tombs have been damaged. In Tutankhamun's reign, the old order being re-established, priests with leopard-skins were again allowed to function, and in the scene of Tutankhamun's funeral in the Burial Chamber his successor Ay is shown wearing such a cloak while he carries out the duties of preparing the mummy for burial by opening his eyes, mouth, nose and ears. Several leopard-skin garments, either real or imitation, were found in the tomb, and with them false leopard heads like this example. It is made of wood, covered with gesso-plaster and gilded. The eyes are made of transparent quartz with details painted on their backs. Other facial details are made of blue opaque glass.

PAIR OF GOLD SANDALS

(CARTER 256LL, J.D'E. 60680;
LENGTH 29.5 CM)

Of the many pairs of sandals found in the tomb of Tutankhamun, this pair is probably the only one which was never used in the king's lifetime. The two soles of the sandals are made of sheet gold, with the straps around the ankles and the 'thongs' passing between the big toes and second toes, also of gold. The soles turn up at the front, a feature still common in casual footwear in the Near East. The surfaces of the soles are striated to represent the weave of the material of which simple Egyptian sandals were made, usually papyrus leaves or rushes. The feet of the mummy were fully equipped with the gold that would help in the king's posthumous regeneration.

Each toe was individually wrapped in linen before gold sheaths were fitted, each one marked with nails and toe-joints. Some linen bandages were then applied before the sandals were fitted, the gold thongs adjusted, and finally the feet fully bandaged. In form, these sandals are very similar to those on the feet of the guardian statues.

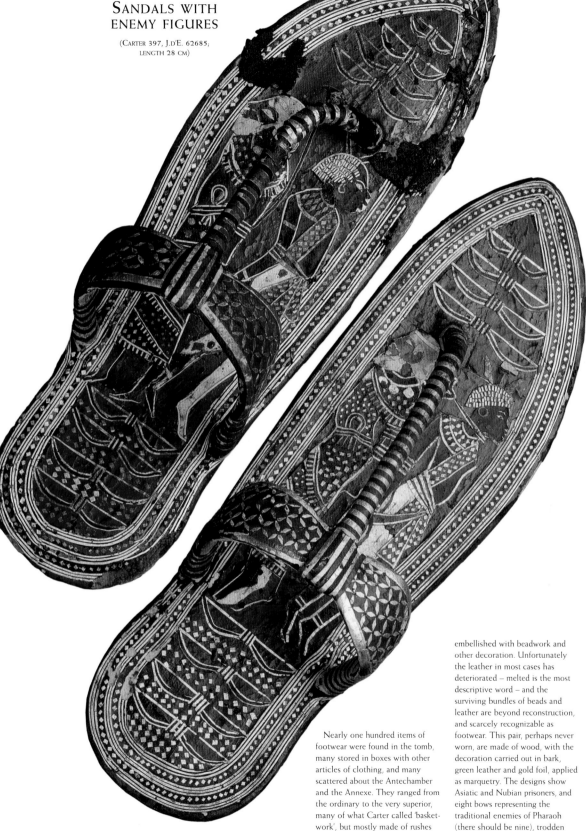

SANDALS WITH ENEMY FIGURES

(CARTER 397, J.D'E. 62685;
LENGTH 28 CM)

Nearly one hundred items of footwear were found in the tomb, many stored in boxes with other articles of clothing, and many scattered about the Antechamber and the Annexe. They ranged from the ordinary to the very superior, many of what Carter called 'basket-work', but mostly made of rushes and papyrus leaves. Some are made of leather, the best examples embellished with beadwork and other decoration. Unfortunately the leather in most cases has deteriorated – melted is the most descriptive word – and the surviving bundles of beads and leather are beyond reconstruction, and scarcely recognizable as footwear. This pair, perhaps never worn, are made of wood, with the decoration carried out in bark, green leather and gold foil, applied as marquetry. The designs show Asiatic and Nubian prisoners, and eight bows representing the traditional enemies of Pharaoh (there should be nine), trodden under the king's feet. The straps are of bark, decorated with gold leaf.

IVORY JEWEL BOX

(CARTER 54DDD, J.D'E. 61449;
HEIGHT 13.97 CM, WIDTH 16.8 CM)

Shape was often of greater importance to the Egyptian artist-craftsman than material. To put it another way, inspiration for a particular form would lead to the making of things in a material for which the form was not really suitable. In architecture it was common. In the case of this small box it turned out to be a success. It was found in the Antechamber in a large chest containing a miscellany of objects, made to the design of wooden boxes but here carried out most skillfully in ivory. The main panels of the top, sides and bottom are single pieces, which must have been difficult to obtain and cut, considering the structure of an elephant's tusk. The ivory is plain, the various sections being cemented together. Remarkably, it still opens and shuts well, without signs of warping. The knobs for closing, the caps on the feet, and the little hinges are made of gold, the hinges in particular being most precisely made. A panel under the front knob contains Tutankhamun's two cartouches and his Horus name, 'strong bull, Tut-mesut'. A hieratic docket on the lid describes its original contents: 'gold, rings for the funeral procession'. It was, as Carter described it, a jewel box. The back panel is decorated with an applied lotus capital column.

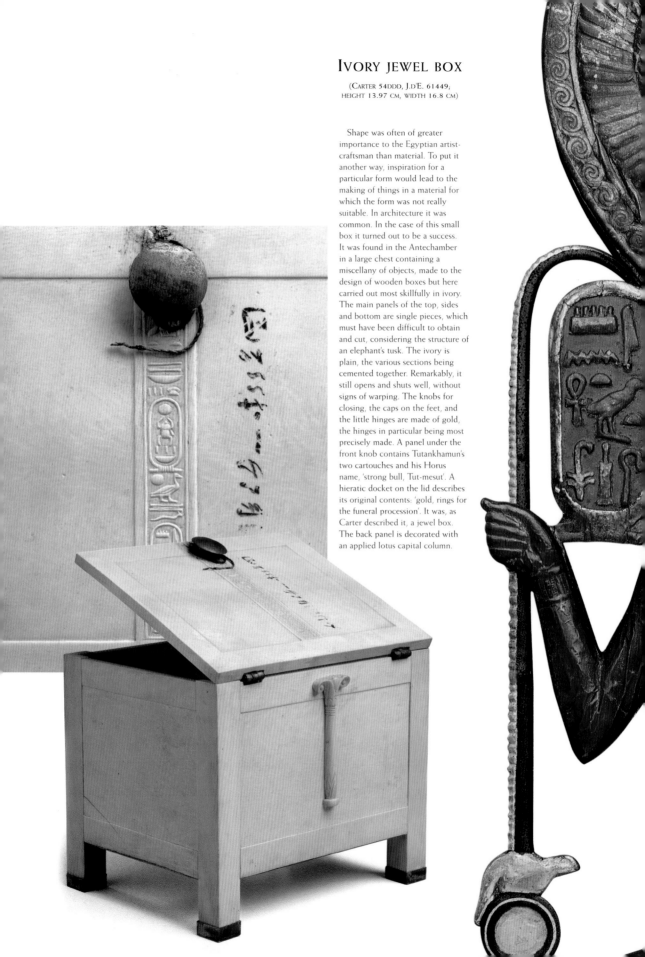

MIRROR CASE WITH KNEELING GOD

(CARTER 271C, D, J.D'E. 62348;
HEIGHT 26.8 CM, WIDTH 14.2 CM)

This mirror case is iconographically more interesting than the case in the form of an *ankh* described above. Both are fine examples of the woodworker's craft. This piece was found in a box of mixed material in the Treasury which, according to Carter, had lost most of its original contents and been repacked indiscriminately by the Necropolis guards who attempted to clear up the mess made by the tomb robbers. The mirror itself had been taken from the case; it was undoubtedly made of a precious metal, silver or gold, probably gold because the inner surfaces of the box are gilded. The mirror would have been pear-shaped. The principal feature of this case is the kneeling figure of the god Heh, whose duty it was to promote the long reign of the ruling king. His name means 'million', and he is here shown typically holding two notched palm branches terminating at their bases with tadpoles (which stand for a hundred thousand) over *shen*-signs of 'dominion'. Tutankhamun's cartouches are placed on each side of the god's head, and the upper part of the case has a formalized version of the king's prenomen, incorporating the figure of a flamboyant winged scarab. The gold leaf covering the box is of the purplish-red variety, except for the palm branches, tadpoles and *shen*-signs which are of bright, purer gold.

COSMETIC BOX

(CARTER 240BIS, J.D'E. 61496;
HEIGHT 16 CM, WIDTH 8.8 CM, DEPTH 4.3 CM)

An evil-smelling brown powder found in this box confirmed paradoxically that it was made to contain a scented cosmetic ointment. Carter states that its was found in the bottom of the great sarcophagus, but there is some evidence to suggest that it was placed between the two outermost shrines.

It is a spectacular example of the jeweler's art, its decoration full of symbolism. To begin with, it is by no means clear whether it was made for life or for death. The representations of the king in the cartouches on the front of the box show him as a child, with the side-lock of youth, the *uraeus* on the brow indicating that he was already king. The conclusion ought to be that the piece was made early in his reign; but it is also possible to see

some scholars, however, take the contents of the cartouches to be simply figures of the king squatting on a sign for 'festival', and, above, sun-disks with pendent *uraei*. On the other hand, cartouches are for royal names, and this is a royal piece.

The cartouches on the other side of the box show similar figures of the king without side-lock, wearing the blue crown; the face of one is black, which here may be a reference to regeneration. The inlays are of carnelian and colored glass.

Simpler chased designs on the sides of the box show the god of eternity squatting on a festival sign and holding palm branches notched with the promised years of Tutankhamun's reign. The king's names are shown in cartouche with some flamboyance.

The silver base of the box has on its underside a chased design of papyrus and poppy clumps with flying ducks, in form and detail reminiscent of palace paintings at El-Amarna.

the child not as the young king, but the king as the young Horus. Other interpretations seem possible.

The box is in the form of a double, two-sided, cartouche, its lids topped with double plumes with sun-disk. It is usually accepted that the figures and hieroglyphs in the four cartouches represent cryptic writings of the king's prenomen, Nebkheperure;

Jewelry

In spite of the great number of pieces of jewelry found in Tutankhamun's tomb, it is thought that what has survived gives an inadequate impression of what was available to a royal person in the Eighteenth Dynasty. All the items found on the mummy, and many of those found in the various boxes in the Antechamber and Treasury, including the great Anubis shrine, were funerary or religious. As for Tutankhamun's personal jewelry, the ancient robbers would surely have chosen to remove such pieces before considering the funerary jewels. One may be sure that his personal jewelry would have been miraculously designed, and made of the finest materials.

If the best has gone, what is one to say of the remainder? 'Not bad!' There are scarcely two pieces that are the same, and as a group they display a remarkable range of metal-working techniques, some of which were not rediscovered after post-classical times until the Renaissance. These ancient craftsmen could beat gold, make gold leaf of the finest quality, build up cloisons for

the reception of inlays, make gold wire, use solder, apply granulation. They could make scenes and designs by repoussé-work and by chasing, but not by engraving. The evidence that they could make cloisonné enamel is very slight, but their skills at inlaying glass were so good that in some cases enamelling has been surmised.

Technically some of the pieces are not of the highest quality of which the Egyptian craftsman was capable, in comparison, for example, with royal pieces of the Middle Kingdom. In design, however, one must marvel at the remarkable invention shown by the jewelry-makers. The pectorals present a range of pattern and use of divine symbolism which suggest that there were master jewelers at work in the ateliers of the royal establishments. Who designed? Who determined the designs? Who chose what was to be made? Who, again, supervised the craftsmen, workmen who had little status in the order of society? Yet even these lowly individuals must have derived much satisfaction from the production of such wonderful pieces.

200–201 *Pectoral ornament in the form of a falcon with sun-disk, outstretched wings and holding* ankh *and* shen *signs in its claws. The cloisonné inlays are of glass and semiprecious stones.*

Collars

COLLAR OF THE TWO LADIES

(CARTER 256NNN, J.D'E. 61875; WIDTH 48.7 CM)

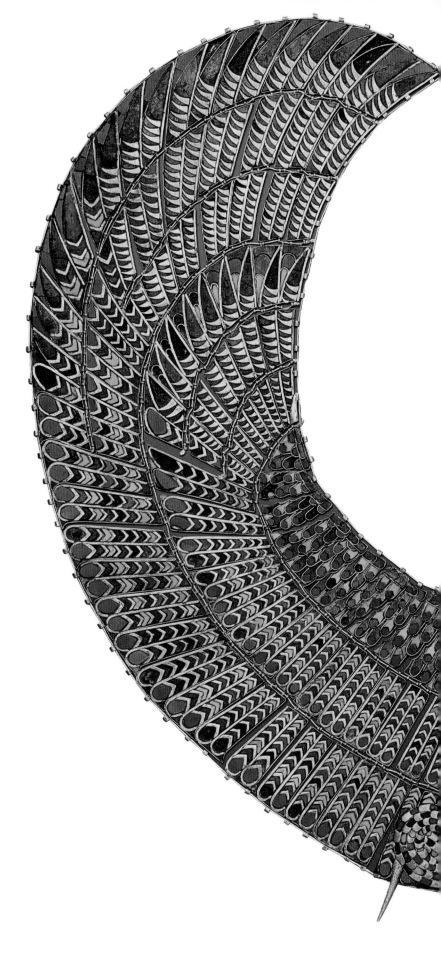

This most elaborate collar was one of three found within the wrappings of the king's mummy, lying on the breast. From paintings of collars on wooden coffins of the Middle Kingdom, this piece should be called 'the collar of the two ladies (the *Nebti* in Egyptian)'. The two ladies are the *uraeus* and the vulture, goddesses who protect the king as ruler of Lower and Upper Egypt – Wadjyt the cobra and Nekhbet the vulture. Here they are shown together with a single pair of outstretched wings; the vulture shows only one leg.

Technically this piece is a *tour de force*. Apart from the central figures of the two goddesses, it is composed of 171 separate gold plaques, strung together by threads which pass through tiny eyelets at the top and bottom of each plaque. The backs of the plaques are chased with feathering detail, and the fronts are inlaid in cloisons with tiny pieces of colored glass. Each piece of glass was individually cut to fit its appropriate cloison. Towards the tips of the wings there is less inlay and more gold. The whole collar is very flexible and lies easily over a surface which is not even.

The figures of the two goddesses are particularly well ornamented with colored inlays, red glass imitating carnelian, used to subtle effect. The vulture head is very carefully modeled with chased detail, the beak and the eye being made of obsidian, naturally occurring black glass. The folds of the cobra are strikingly inlaid with a checker pattern of gold and colored glass.

All properly designed collars and heavy necklaces are provided with a counterpoise, designed to hang down the back and hold the collar in position. In Egyptian it was called *menkhet*. The counterpoise of this collar is of a simple bell-shape with panels of colored glass. Gold wire attached it to the collar.

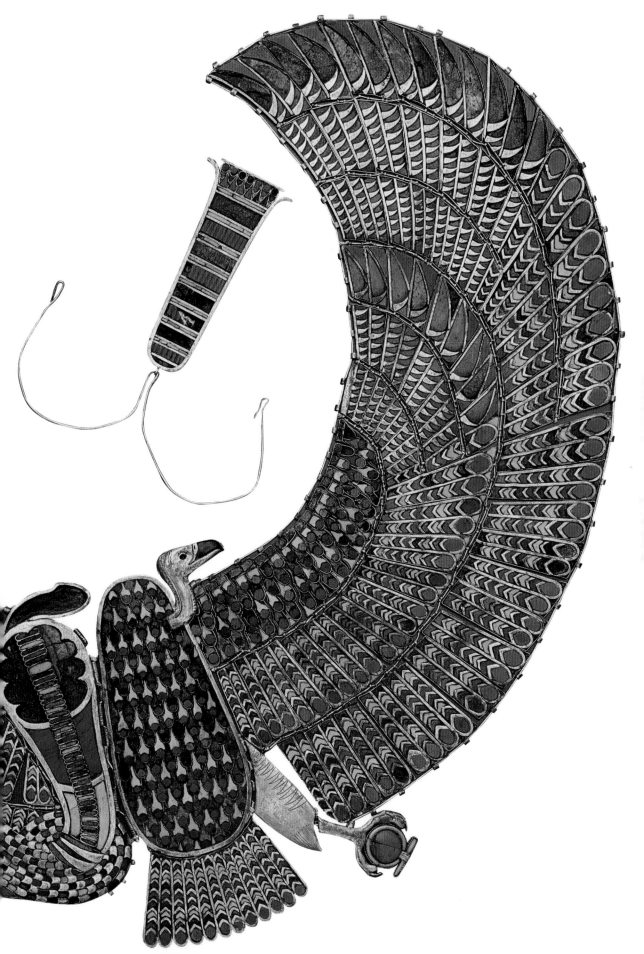

SHEET GOLD COLLAR

(CARTER 236G, J.D'E 61917;
WIDTH 33 CM)

More than one hundred items which can be called 'ornaments' were found on Tutankhamun's body. Not all of these can be described as jewels, but that term can be applied to many that fall into the common categories of jewels: collars, necklaces, bracelets, bangles, rings, circlets, pectorals. Others can more properly be classified as amulets – divine figures or objects associated with gods. Seventeen were placed in the area of the neck and upper thorax, and some of these have already been illustrated as amulets, among them some sheet gold figures of deities.

This piece, which represents a winged form of Wadjyt, the cobra goddess of the ancient northern capital of Buto, is not unlike some of these sheet gold amulets. What distinguishes it as a collar is the presence of a counterpoise attached to the points of the wings by gold wire. It also lay lower down than the neck, on the body's thorax. It was not robust enough for daily use.

The collar was cut to shape from a sheet of gold beaten to less than a millimeter thick. Ancient Egyptian goldsmiths learned in a very early period how to beat gold into thin sheets from small nuggets. There are several scenes in tombs of the Old Kingdom showing the beating of gold on an anvil with what appears to be a rounded stone. Gold sheet and foil were much employed to embellish furniture and funerary objects, and gold leaf was used to gild wood on a base of gesso plaster. Gold leaf was made to a thinness almost equal to modern gold leaf, but one gains the impression that gold foil and sheeting were preferred, because they were more opulent. The detail on this collar and counterpoise were marked out by chasing; the markings on the serpent figure itself are particularly well made.

FALCON-HEADED
BROAD COLLAR

(CARTER 256 AA(1), J.D'E. 61880;
WIDTH 36 CM)

Four collars of this kind were
found among the wrappings of the
king's mummy, in the region of the
legs, all folded and crushed. It
seemed a very casual way to treat
objects charged with magical power,
and presumably put on the body for
good funerary reasons. Fortunately,
their method of construction
allowed them to be folded without
difficulty, and it was not too difficult
for the excavators to restore them to
their proper shapes.

This kind of collar, the *usekh* or
broad collar, is regularly shown
being worn by important officials
and royalty, and in everyday life it
was commonly made up of rows of
small cylindrical beads of faience;
the outermost row might have beads
shaped like petals, as in the case of
the example illustrated here. The
terminals of such collars are in the
form of falcon's heads; consequently,
on early coffins this type is called
'collar of the falcon'.

The falcon here presumably
represents Horus, god of the living
king; but as such collars have been
found in non-royal burials, a specific
royal association may not be
appropriate.

There is a strange mixture of
simplicity and ostentation in the
design and construction of this collar.
It consists of eleven wedge-shaped
sections made of sheet gold; the nine
concentric rows of beads are
reproduced by sections of colored
glass, in red, pale blue and dark
blue, to represent carnelian,
turquoise and lapis-lazuli; the inlays
are ribbed to give them the
appearance of cylindrical beads. The
outermost row imitates drop beads
in the form of poppy petals. The
falcon head terminals, or shoulder
pieces, are made of gold with facial
markings in dark blue glass. The
menkhet, or counterpoise, is also of
gold inlaid with rows of ribbed glass
'cylindrical beads'.

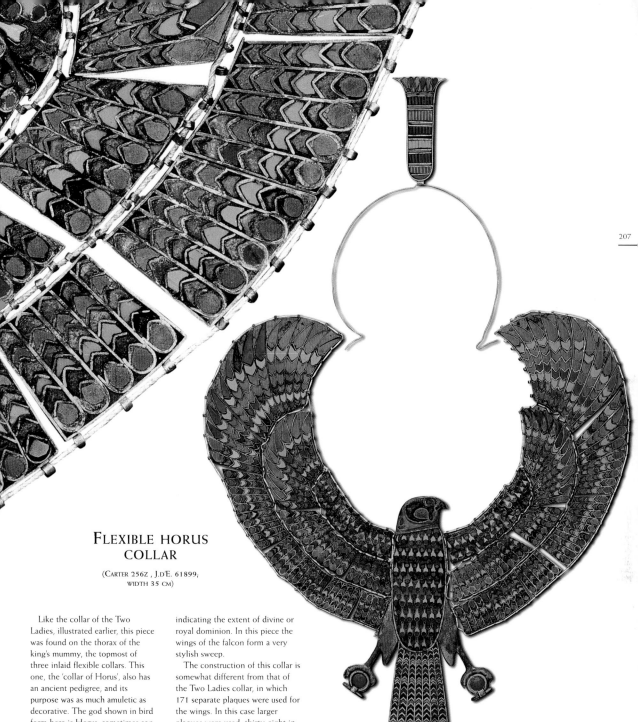

FLEXIBLE HORUS COLLAR

(CARTER 256Z , J.D'E. 61899;
WIDTH 35 CM)

Like the collar of the Two
Ladies, illustrated earlier, this piece
was found on the thorax of the
king's mummy, the topmost of
three inlaid flexible collars. This
one, the 'collar of Horus', also has
an ancient pedigree, and its
purpose was as much amuletic as
decorative. The god shown in bird
form here is Horus, sometimes son
of Osiris, also the divine
representative of royalty of whom
the king was the embodiment in
life. Here the falcon is displayed
frontally with its head turned to
one side in the usual Egyptian
manner; the legs are splayed out
and the claws hold *shen*-signs,
which are like circular cartouches.
The *shen* and the cartouche in
detailed representations are shown
as made of cord or rope, with a tie
at the bottom. Its meaning is not
absolutely established, but it is
generally thought to represent all
that the sun encompasses,

indicating the extent of divine or
royal dominion. In this piece the
wings of the falcon form a very
stylish sweep.

The construction of this collar is
somewhat different from that of
the Two Ladies collar, in which
171 separate plaques were used for
the wings. In this case larger
plaques were used, thirty-eight in
all, each marked on the reverse for
correct assembling and made up in
groups to form the 'districts' of the
wings. Throughout his life
Howard Carter was an eager and
careful student of birds – he
painted them with immense care
and skill – and he was always
punctilious in using the correct
ornithological terms when
describing birds. For this collar he
noted that the ancient craftsman
had distinguished the 'districts' of
the wings in order to reproduce
the different types of feather; he
specifies 'the primaries,

secondaries, coverts, lesser coverts
and so-called bastard wing'.

The glass inlays, individually cut
to fit the cloisons on the plaques,
stand for turquoise, red jasper or
carnelian and lapis-lazuli. The
feather pattern on the falcon's
body and the chevrons on the tail
produce a spectacular effect. The
menkhet counterpoise has ribbed
inlays of glass reproducing cylinder
beads.

Necklaces
with Pectorals
and Pendants

NECKLACE WITH
FALCON PENDANT

(CARTER 256uuu, J.D'E. 61891;
WIDTH OF PENDANT 9 CM,
LENGTH OF CHAIN 65 CM)

Deep within the bandages of the mummy were three necklaces with pendants, one on the chest and one to either side, on the left a winged scarab and this one on the right. According to Carter all showed signs of wear, used probably in life and perhaps holding special significance for the king.

Here the pendant is a falcon with outstretched wings circling round to enclose the head with sun-disk and *uraeus* above it. It is Re-Herakhty, the great risen sun. The head looks directly forward, which is unusual; this modest change from the usual iconography gives the piece a dramatic impact.

The disk of the sun is of carnelian, and the cloisonné inlays of the wings and tail are of colored glass. The body of the falcon is of open-work gold enclosing a greenish stone, possibly chalcedony.

Rings soldered to the tips of the wings secure the pendant to the chain of the necklace, which is made of wire woven by an ingenious technique much exploited, and possibly invented, by Egyptian jewelers. The two ends of the chain terminate with round carnelian beads which connect with the small counterpoise. This final element is another *tour de force* of the Egyptian craftsman: it is heart-shaped and

made of carnelian set inside an open-work gold 'cage', decorated with the king's prenomen, Nebkheperure, in a cartouche supported by *uraei* on either side.

Carter expressed the opinion – no doubt suggested by one of his helpers, like Alan Gardiner – that this necklace should be paired with the one with a lunar reference (J.d'E. 61897).

Mythologically the two could be linked to the two eyes – one the sun, one the moon – an idea with associations to Osiris and to Re: 'His right eye is the sun, his left is the moon', one necklace perhaps to be used in the morning, the other in the evening.

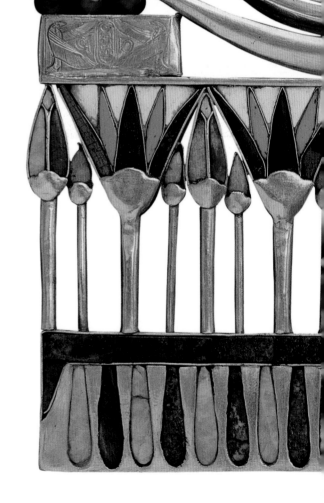

NECKLACE WITH MOON PECTORAL

(CARTER 269K, J.D'E. 61897;
LENGTH OF NECKLACE 23.5 CM, WIDTH OF PECTORAL 10.8 CM)

The design of this wonderfully decorative piece is full of symbolism, but the symbols are used so imaginatively and subtly that the religious and magical significance becomes secondary to the overall appearance. It was found in the cartouche-shaped box in the Treasury, and like others found with it shows signs of wear during the king's lifetime.

The pectoral's central element is the moon, shown as disk and crescent, in the night bark on its nocturnal journey. The bark sits above a grove of lotus flowers and buds growing out of a longitudinal element inlaid with lapis-lazuli, and representing the sky, from which droplets of moisture hang down, inlaid with felspar and lapis. The moon itself is made of electrum (a mixture of gold and silver) to distinguish it from the sun, which in most of this tomb's jewels is made of pure gold, or of inlaid carnelian. To the left and right of the bark are rectangular terminals for the bead strings of the necklace.

These terminals are chased with Tutankhamun's cartouches supported by winged *uraei*.

The pectoral is linked to the counterpoise by four rows of beads, round and barrel-shaped, and made of gold, lapis-lazuli, felspar, glass and a dark colored resin. Some of the gold spherical beads are soldered together to make spacers which hold the four rows together. Design again distinguishes the counterpoise, the main component of which is an open lotus flower, flanked by lotus buds, at the bases of which are poppies and two rosettes. Felspar and lapis-lazuli are used for the lotus inlays, with an imaginative touch of white calcite used for the tips of the buds. The poppies and rosettes are inlaid with carnelian. From a bar beneath the pendant lotus flower and buds hang nineteen tassels of gold and glass beads, joined in pairs at the ends with bell-shaped floral terminals. A clasp on the right side of the counterpoise is held in position by a retractable pin.

NECKLACE WITH PECTORAL OF TUTANKHAMUN WITH THE GODS OF MEMPHIS

(CARTER 267Q, J.D'E. 61941;
PECTORAL: HEIGHT 11.5 CM, WIDTH 14.1 CM;
COUNTERPOISE: HEIGHT 8.4 CM, WIDTH 7.8 CM;
LENGTH OF STRAPS 34.3 CM)

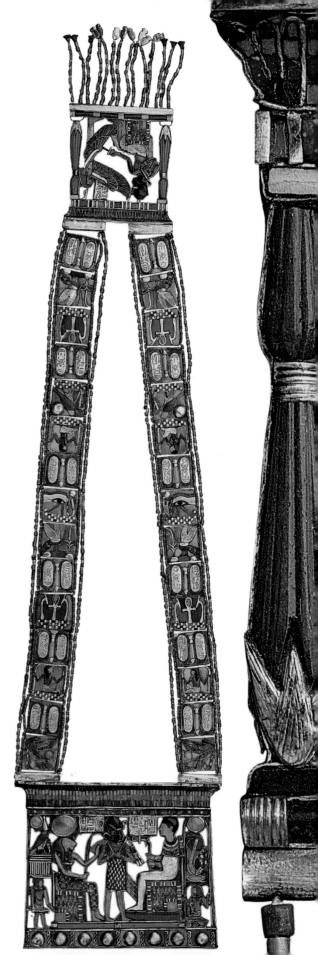

Among the pieces of jewelry found in the tomb, this piece is unusual in that both the pectoral and the counterpoise contain scenes showing the king with gods. It was found in pieces in the Treasury, the main pectoral in the ivory and ebony veneered chest, and the counterpoise and chains in the cartouche-shaped box.

It has been suggested that it was made either for, or to commemorate, the king's coronation. This important event would have been celebrated in Memphis, where the Court had moved from El-Amarna. In the pectoral scene Tutankhamun stands between the mummiform Ptah and lioness-headed Sakhmet, his divine consort, whose principal sanctuaries were in Memphis. The whole conception of the piece is spectacular and dramatic, and yet there are signs of indifferent craftsmanship in some details; also the gold is not of the finest quality.

The theme of the necklace is the king's reign and its infinite duration – a pathetic hope! In the pectoral scene the king holds his instruments of royalty, the crook and flail, and wears the blue crown and a short garment associated with coronation. His face and the crown are made of black glass, the color of regeneration. Ptah offers the king life, Sakhmet presents long reign. Behind Sakhmet stands the king's *ka*, or spirit figure, and behind Ptah kneels Heh, the god of eternity. In the border below is repeated the word for 'eternity'.

In the counterpoise scene, the king, no longer in coronation dress, is seated, receiving life from a winged figure of Ma'at, goddess of truth and order. Gold fishes of uncertain meaning and bell-shaped beads terminate the fourteen strings of beads hanging from the counterpoise. The straps of the necklace are composed of elaborately inlaid gold plaques containing the king's names, good wishes, protective amuletic signs and the motif of royal jubilee. The inlays and beads are mostly of variously colored glass, with a few elements in translucent quartz and calcite.

NECKLACE OF THE SUN RISING ON THE HORIZON

(CARTER 267G, J.D'E. 61896;
LENGTH OF STRAPS 50 CM,
WIDTH OF PECTORAL 11.8 CM)

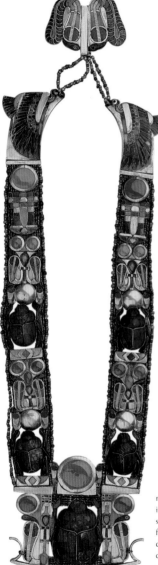

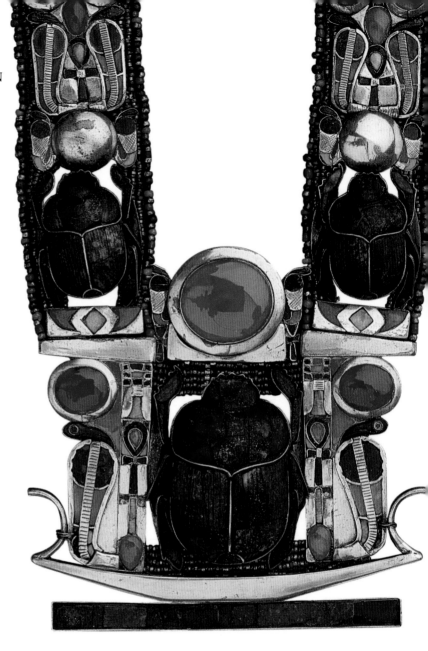

Symbolism in the details of this necklace concentrates on the sun in the early morning, rising as the scarab beetle, Khepri, pushing in front of it the sun, seen as the divine equivalent of the ball of dung pushed by the beetle in nature. The sun here sits in a dip in the hills – the horizon in the Eastern Desert. This is the central element of the pendant of this striking piece; it sits in the morning bark, supported by *uraei* and potent amulets.

The craftsmanship displayed in the making of this necklace is matched by the superior quality of the inlays: lapis-lazuli from distant Afghanistan, carnelian, felspar and turquoise from the Eastern Desert

and Sinai. Some of the beads which edge the elaborate straps are of colored glass, but this use of a less splendid material was dictated by practical considerations.

The decorated gold plaques which make up the straps continue the main theme of the pectoral: pairs of scarabs with golden suns flanked by *uraei*, pairs of *uraei* with carnelian suns, and double pairs of the *djed*-symbol for 'endurance', again topped by carnelian suns set in gold. The straps terminate with curved gold elements carrying cloisonné vultures, the embodiment of Nekhbet, protective goddess of the king as ruler of Upper Egypt.

Four short strings of gold and glass beads connect the main straps to the clasp of the necklace, which acts as a counterpoise, although one may doubt its efficacy as such in view of the great weight of the main piece. The clasp is of gold, formed in the shape of two *uraei*, inlaid with semiprecious stones and separated by a gold slide with which the piece can be opened.

The overall heaviness of the necklace is relieved remarkably by the ingenuity of the design and the clever use of color in the inlays. It is an opulent piece.

It was found in the Treasury, in the box veneered with ivory and ebony.

Necklace with Three Scarab Pectoral

(CARTER 256OOO, J.D'E. 61900; WIDTH OF PECTORAL 9 CM,
WIDTH OF CONTERPOISE 5.3 CM, LENGTH OF STRAPS 18.5 CM)

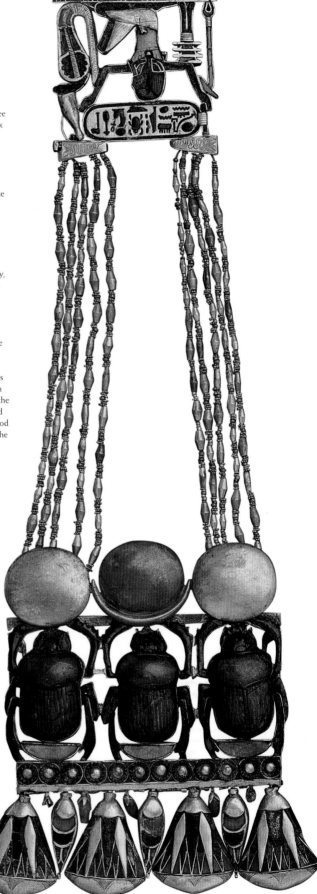

Placed around the neck of the king, this necklace occupied a prime position within the mummy wrappings. Iconographically it is one of the simplest of the many necklaces and pendants, most of which seem almost overloaded with symbolism. Here is restraint.

The principal elements in the design of the pectoral are three lapis-lazuli scarabs set in gold and surmounted by disks, the two outer ones being of gold and representing the sun. The central one is made of electrum and is therefore duller in color; it incorporates a crescent, and is the moon. Beneath each scarab is a basket-shaped sign inlaid with green felspar. There is in the grouping here something of the suggestion of the prenomen of Tutankhamun, which is usually written as a disk above a scarab, below which should be three small strokes indicating plurality and the basket-sign. Here the strokes are missing, but the idea of plurality is suggested by the tripling of the other elements. The bar towards the bottom of the pectoral is ornamented with twelve daisy flowers made of blue glass with gold

centers. From this bar hang four lotus flowers interspersed with three large lotus buds and, originally, six small buds, of which only three now remain. The inlays of the flowers and buds are of carnelian, felspar and blue glass.

Five strings of beads, mostly of gold but with a few spacers of blue glass, connect the pectoral to the counterpoise, to which they are attached by fasteners chased with figures of winged *uraei*. The openwork golden counterpoise is enlivened by a few glass inlays. The design shows a kneeling deity, possibly Heh, the god of millions of years, or Shu, god of the atmosphere, often shown supporting the sky. Here the god supports a long cartouche inlaid with the king's prenomen and title and epithet: 'The good god, Nebkheperure, chosen of Amon-Re'. In front of the kneeling god is an *uraeus* wearing the white crown of Upper Egypt, which here has the curled extension commonly found with the red crown; behind the god are the powerful amuletic signs, the *djed*-pillar and the *was*-scepter – endurance and power.

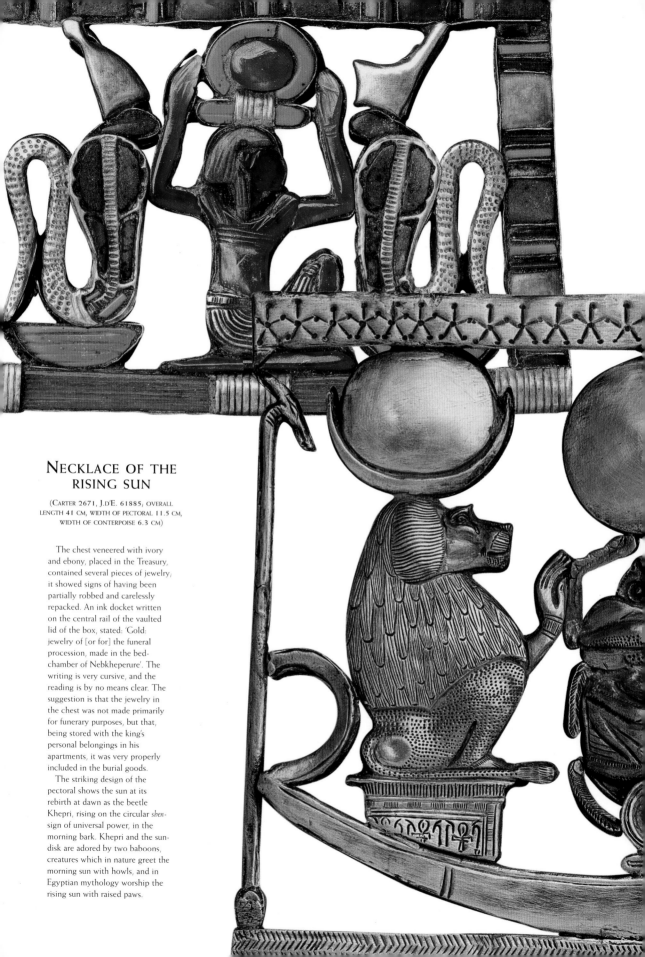

NECKLACE OF THE RISING SUN

(Carter 2671, J.d'E. 61885, overall
length 41 cm, width of pectoral 11.5 cm,
width of conterpoise 6.3 cm)

The chest veneered with ivory
and ebony, placed in the Treasury,
contained several pieces of jewelry;
it showed signs of having been
partially robbed and carelessly
repacked. An ink docket written
on the central rail of the vaulted
lid of the box, stated: 'Gold:
jewelry of [or for] the funeral
procession, made in the bed-
chamber of Nebkheperure'. The
writing is very cursive, and the
reading is by no means clear. The
suggestion is that the jewelry in
the chest was not made primarily
for funerary purposes, but that,
being stored with the king's
personal belongings in his
apartments, it was very properly
included in the burial goods.

The striking design of the
pectoral shows the sun at its
rebirth at dawn as the beetle
Khepri, rising on the circular *shen*-
sign of universal power, in the
morning bark. Khepri and the sun-
disk are adored by two baboons,
creatures which in nature greet the
morning sun with howls, and in
Egyptian mythology worship the
rising sun with raised paws.

The scene is bounded on each side by *was*-scepters of power, below by the waters of the Underworld, and above by the sky studded with stars. All the inlays are of semiprecious stones, set on a solid gold base which is worked with intricate detail on its reverse side. The little shrines on which the baboons sit carry repeated *ankh*-signs of life, supported by *was*-signs. The modeling of the baboons and the feathered markings of their 'capes' are exceptionally well worked.

The straps which connect the pectoral to the counterpoise are made up of eleven plaques on each side. The theme of decoration is long reign and jubilees. The workmanship is not as fine as on the pectoral, but the overall effect is good. The work on the counterpoise is also less precise and finished than that of the pectoral. A shrine shape contains a kneeling figure of the god of millions of years, Heh, supporting the *shen*-sign, and flanked by *uraei* wearing the crowns of Upper (left) and Lower (right) Egypt.

NECKLACE WITH WINGED SCARAB PECTORAL

(CARTER 256QQQ, J.D'E. 61887;
WIDTH OF PECTORAL 9.5 CM,
LENGTH OF CHAIN 42 CM)

Elegant and stylish are words which suitably describe this necklace. Some wear on it suggests that it was worn by the king in his lifetime, and one presumes that it was specially chosen to be worn by him in death. But how can one ever discover whether personal choice entered into the selection of jewels and other objects buried with a king in his mummy wrappings? It was the companion piece to the falcon pendant necklace found on the chest of the mummy (J.d'E. 61891), falcon to the right, scarab to the left: 'His right eye is the sun, his left is the moon'.

The motif of the pendant is Tutankhamun's prenomen, but with a lunar connotation. In simple hieroglyphs the prenomen is made up of sun-disk, scarab,

three strokes and a basket. Here the moon-disk with crescent replaces the sun, and, as is usual with this tomb's jewels, the disk is made of electrum, although the crescent is of gold. The scarab is provided with fine wings which sweep round to touch the horns of the moon's crescent. Lapis-lazuli inlays make up the body of the scarab, and the same stone with carnelian and pale green glass fill the cloisons of the wings. Three gold strokes for plurality separate the scarab from the basket, which is marked out with a central gold diamond and inlaid chevrons on each side. In the hieroglyphic script this kind of basket stands for 'festival'; a plain basket, or one with lines or a checkered design, is expected in the prenomen.

The gold chain which links the pectoral to the counterpoise probably replaces original straps consisting of five rows of beads, the points of fastening for which are very evident. Two carnelian beads separate the inlaid lotus terminals from the heart-shaped counterpoise, which consists of a carnelian core enclosed in a gold openwork cage which incorporates the royal prenomen supported by *uraei*.

NECKLACE WITH VULTURE PECTORAL

(CARTER 256PPP, J.D'E. 61892;
WIDTH OF VULTURE 11 CM,
LENGTH OF STRAPS 25.5 CM)

This necklace is, from a technical point of view, one of the most interesting jewels from the tomb. It was found on the mummy, suspended from the neck; its principal element, the pectoral pendant, is in the form of the vulture, the goddess Nekhbet, tutelary deity of Tutankhamun as King of Upper Egypt.

The design is simple: the vulture is shown with head turned to the left, and its spread wings turned down like a cloak in protective fashion; its legs are splayed out, and the talons hold *shen*-signs of universal power. The head of the bird is separately modeled and soldered to the body; its markings are delicately chased, the eye is of obsidian and the beak of lapis-lazuli. The point of special technical interest concerns the glass inlays of the body, the tail and some parts of the wings. The glass inlays on these parts show little depressions which may have been produced by air bubbles during the process of manufacture. If this is truly the case, these bubbles offer proof of the practice

of real enamelling which has not otherwise been found in ancient Egypt. In many of the pieces of jewelry from Tutankhamun's tomb a cloisonné technique with glass inlays has been observed. True cloisonné enamelling consists of filling the cloisons with powdered glass which is then fired in position; this results in inlays which completely fill, and are closely fixed in, their little gold enclosures. It has yet to be confirmed by close scientific examination that the technique was used in this case.

The back of the vulture, which is of solid gold, is carefully worked with chasing, and a pendant is shown hanging from the neck; it contains the royal prenomen.

The straps are made up of plaques of gold and lapis-lazuli, in the center of each of which is a circle of colored glass. The straps connect to the clasp, which is in the form of two resting falcons with heads lying on their backs; they are of gold inlaid with lapis, felspar, onyx, carnelian and green glass. A sliding fastener holds the two together.

NECKLACE WITH SCARAB COUNTERPOISE

(CARTER 101W, J.D'E. 61950;
WIDTH OF PECTORAL 8.5 CM,
LENGTH OF STRAPS 43 CM)

Much of the material found in the various storage boxes in the Antechamber consisted of jewels, the stringing of which had perished. Retrieving and restringing took a great deal of time, mostly carried out by Arthur Mace, a most meticulous archaeologist. This necklace Carter speaks of with some relief. It was found in its box lying flat upon the bottom, so that its shape and order could easily be determined: 'we were able to remove it bead by bead, and re-string it on the spot in its exact original order.' The beads are in three strands of blue glass and gold in droplet form, held in place by sets of three ball beads of gold fused to form spacers. The shrine-shaped pectoral is simple, made of gilded wood inlaid with a block border and a central inscription in glass. There are three lines of text beneath an extended heaven-sign: 'Good god, lord of the two lands, Nebkheperure, beloved of Osiris'. The scarab counterpoise also carries on its base Tutankhamun's prenomen flanked by the *heqat*-scepter of royal authority and the feather of truth and order.

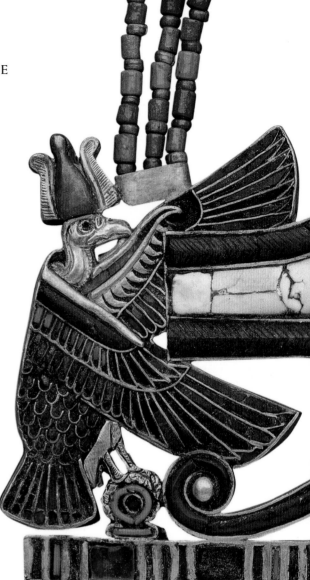

NECKLACE WITH INLAID *WEDJAT*

(CARTER 256VVV, J.D'E. 61901;
PENDANT: HEIGHT 5.7 CM, WIDTH 9.5 CM,
LENGTH OF CHAIN 33 CM)

Like some other of the jewels found on the royal body, this necklace shows signs of wear, and Carter considered it a piece worn by the king in his lifetime. The pendant is particularly handsome, a triumph of design and craftsmanship. It is of solid gold with much cloisonné inlay. The eye itself is inlaid with crystalline limestone and lapis-lazuli. It is flanked by the two royal protective goddesses, Edjo, the serpent of Buto in the Delta, and Nekhbet, the vulture of Elkab in Upper Egypt. Edjo here wears the red crown, and

Nekhbet the *atef*, in its form as white crown with side feathers. The inlays are of colored glass, carnelian and lapis-lazuli, and the *shen*-sign in the vulture's claws has a green stone which Carter compared with peridot, rarely used by the Egyptians. Three strings of small beads link the pendant to its counterpoise or *menkhet*, The beads are of variously colored glass with occasional thin gold spacers. The counterpoise consists of two *djed*-signs and one *tyet*-sign, all inlaid with glass, carnelian and lapis.

NECKLACE WITH FAIENCE *WEDJAT*

(CARTER 256RRR, J.D'E. 61951;
PENDANT: HEIGHT 6 CM, WIDTH 8.8 CM,
LENGTH OF CHAIN 29 CM)

One of the most powerful of the protective amulets used by the ancient Egyptians was the *wedjat*, the eye of Horus, stolen by Seth but restored by Thoth. There were several *wedjats* incorporated into the jewelry placed on Tutankhamun's mummy. This piece may seem strangely modest among the many gold jewels with which the deceased was loaded. The pendant itself is a *wedjat* made of blue faience; it incorporates the *uraeus*-serpent, royal protective symbol, and beneath the eye the *sa*-sign, also of protection. The text on the eye reads: 'Khepri, who is

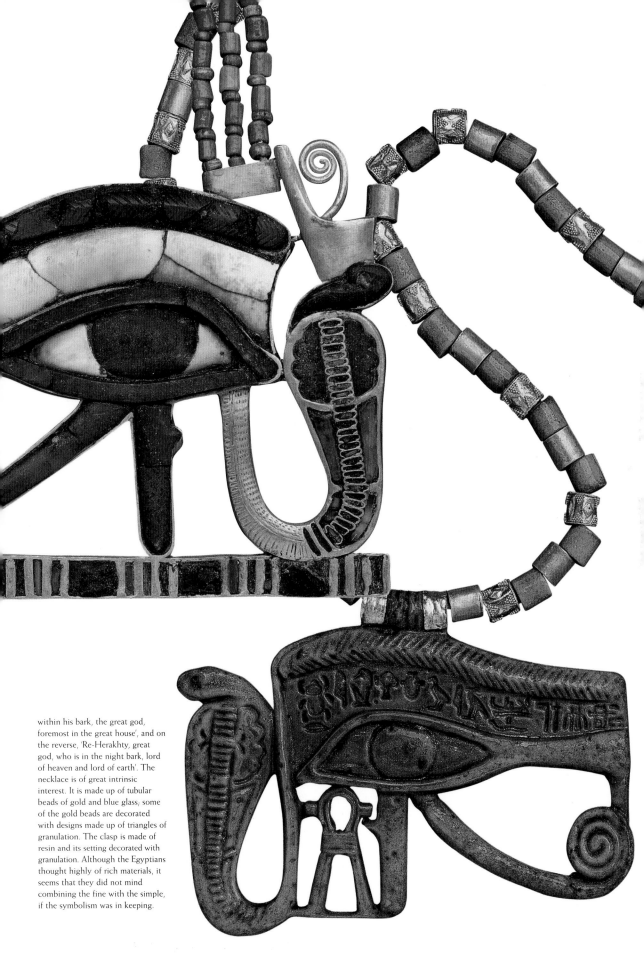

within his bark, the great god, foremost in the great house', and on the reverse, 'Re-Herakhty, great god, who is in the night bark, lord of heaven and lord of earth'. The necklace is of great intrinsic interest. It is made up of tubular beads of gold and blue glass; some of the gold beads are decorated with designs made up of triangles of granulation. The clasp is made of resin and its setting decorated with granulation. Although the Egyptians thought highly of rich materials, it seems that they did not mind combining the fine with the simple, if the symbolism was in keeping.

Pendants

PECTORAL OF ISIS AND NEPHTHYS

(Carter 2611, J.d'E. 61945;
height 12 cm, width 16.3 cm)

It surprised Carter and his colleagues to find compartments, little cupboards, in the great gilded pylon-shaped shrine on which rested the black-painted figure of the Anubis jackal, just inside the Treasury. The largest of these compartments contained eight pieces of jewelry, all pectorals, with no accompanying necklaces or counterpoises. It is difficult to understand what their purpose was, and why they were placed in this shrine. There were signs that the compartment had been disturbed, so its original contents may have been different from, or more numerous than, what was found. Carter took the view that all the pieces were funerary, and not for everyday use. Their designs all contain much symbolism, and they suggest a posthumous use for the rebirth or regeneration of the king. They vary greatly in workmanship and design, and in the preciousness of the materials used.

This kiosk-shaped pectoral is made of low quality gold, but its design is neat and effective. The main scene consists of a central

djed-pillar of endurance, surmounted by the sun-disk and flanked by the goddesses Nephthys (left) and Isis (right) with outstretched protective wings. These goddesses have many functions in relation to the dead king; they are among the Canopic deities, they have a more general protective role, and as principal mourners they are often shown as kites, the common scavenger birds of Egypt. In front of the goddesses are two cartouches containing Tutankhamun's names, from each of which hangs down an *uraeus* wearing a crown, the red on the left and the white (shown blue) on the right.

The top of the pectoral is in the form of a cornice, with a design representing palm fronds; beneath it is a frieze of flowers, hanging down. At the very top, at the right and left, are fittings to which the straps of a necklace could have been attached. There would have been four strings of beads on each side. These fittings are chased with winged *uraei*.

Apart from a little quartz, all the inlays are of colored glass.

PECTORAL OF A WINGED SCARAB WITH ISIS AND NEPHTHYS

(CARTER 261M, J.D'E. 61948;
HEIGHT 16.5 CM, WIDTH 24.4 CM)

Several features of this interesting piece point to the confused nature of this burial and its contents, and to the problems resulting from the further confusion created by the robbers, and by the necropolis guards in their attempts to tidy up the confusion.

When it was found in the Anubis shrine, this pectoral lacked the large stone scarab which now occupies the central position in the design.

It was later found in the cartouche-shaped chest, also in the Treasury. That the scarab and pectoral belong together is confirmed by the texts on both parts. The scarab, made of a hard green stone, is inscribed on its underside with Spell 30B of the Book of the Dead, in which the heart of the king is exhorted to act as a witness on behalf of the dead Tutankhamun before the divine conclave. It is what is called a heart scarab, found in royal and non-royal burials, and most usually placed on the mummy of the deceased close to the heart, which itself was left in the embalmed body. There were many scarabs among the jewels found on the king's mummy, but none bore this important heart text. Why, it may be asked, was this so?

Could this pectoral have been intended for the mummy and been overlooked? At least it was finally included in the tomb equipment, and placed not far from the Canopic chest containing the mummified remains of the other royal internal organs.

Set in the pectoral, the scarab is winged and supported by kneeling figures of Isis and Nephthys, who, in their texts, invoke Re on behalf of the heart. The top of the pectoral is in the shape of a winged sun-disk flanked by elaborately arranged *uraeus* serpents with sun-disks disposed among the coils. The fittings at the top suggest that the piece was made to have quadruple strings of beads as lateral chains.

All the cloisonné inlays are of colored glass, carefully cut and fitted. Particularly finely done are the inlaid dresses of the two goddesses, reproducing a very characteristic net pattern.

PECTORAL OF THE GODDESS NUT

(CARTER 261P1, J.d'E. 61944;
HEIGHT 12.6 CM, WIDTH 14.3 CM)

This unusual piece, which may not be a pectoral in the strictest sense, was also found in the Anubis shrine. It is itself shrine-shaped, but contrary to the common design of such pieces its suspension fittings are at the sides and not the top. This arrangement suggests that it may have been centrally placed in a belt or girdle which would have encircled the royal body.

A palm-frond cornice forms the top of the piece, and a block border runs around all four sides. The inlays here and elsewhere are of carnelian and colored glass. A solid gold plaque is the basis of this jewel, unlike most of the pectorals and other jewels from the tomb, which are of openwork. The result is to give it greater solidity, and the background is able to hold a substantial religious text. The central figure is the goddess Nut, the sky deity, described as 'great of power'. She stands with outstretched arms and wings which turn up at the tips to enclose cartouches containing the names of Tutankhamun. In the main text of eight lines Nut declares that she opens her arms over 'her son, the king Nebkheperure', and spreads her wings over 'all the beauty of Tutankhamun, ruler of Southern Heliopolis'. She does this, as Re does, 'in protection of these your limbs'.

The inscriptions are not without errors, some of which may be due to ancient alterations. It has been suggested that the names in the cartouches have been changed from those of Akhenaten, although the surviving traces are not very convincing. If this supposition is correct, it would follow that the piece was made early in Akhenaten's reign, when Nut and her text would not have been considered unsuitable. It would then also follow that it had been stored away in Thebes, waiting for better times, and was then recycled for Akhenaten's young successor.

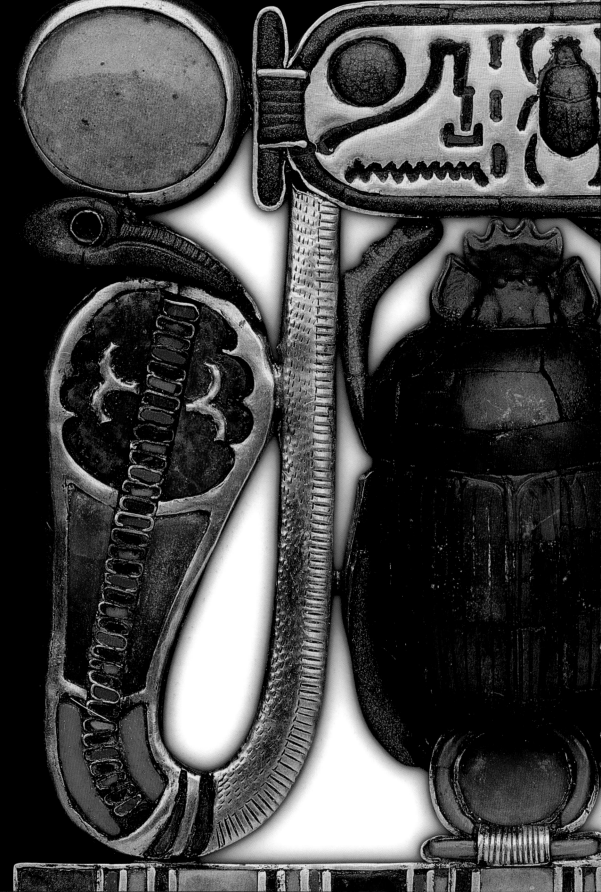

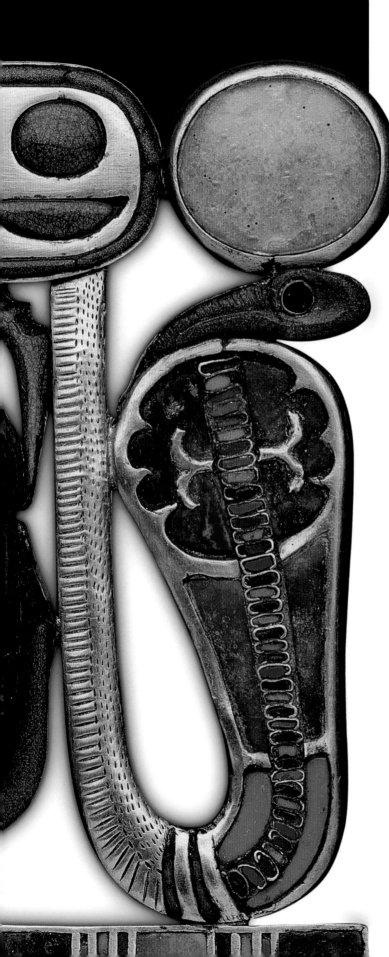

PECTORAL WITH SCARAB
SUPPORTED BY *URAEI*

(CARTER 267K, J.D'E. 61899;
HEIGHT 7.8 CM, WIDTH 8.7 CM)

This pectoral ornament, found in
the veneered jewel box in the
Treasury, is of exceptional quality in
terms of design, workmanship and
the use of materials. Its basis is good
quality gold.

The central element, as often, is
the scarab, to be identified with
Khepri, the sun at dawn. Here it is
carefully carved in the round in
lapis-lazuli, with detailed head
markings and wing striations. It
supports not the sun but a
cartouche, carefully formed and
inlaid with the prenomen of the
king, Nebkheperure, with the added
epithet 'Setep-en-Re', 'Chosen of
Re'. Between its back legs the beetle
holds the *shen*-sign, inlaid with
carnelian, the symbol of universal
power.

On either side of the scarab,
uraeus serpents hang down from the
cartouche. The bodies are in gold,
finely chased with linear markings;
but attention in both cases is drawn
to the head and the hood of the
cobra. Here there is craftsmanship
of superb quality on a very small
scale: the heads are in lapis-lazuli,
carved in high relief; the markings
on the hood, although stylized, are
exceptionally effective, the larger
inlays being in lapis and carnelian,
the rest in red, blue and greenish-
blue glass. The sun-disks are made
of carnelian in gold settings. At the
bottom of the pectoral is a block
border with glass and calcite inlays,
made with unusual precision.

The reverse of this piece also
warrants careful attention. It is the
solid gold base of the pectoral, but
it carries in molding and chasing the
same design as the front. The back
of the scarab is, in Carter's words,
'richly worked... showing complete
articulation of its legs and
underparts'. The prenomen in the
reverse cartouche is followed by
two different epithets: 'ruler of
Truth, image of Re'. On the back of
the two sun-disks are suspension
fastenings, each with three holes, in
which pieces of thread were found
at the time of discovery.

PECTORAL WITH SOLAR AND LUNAR EMBLEMS

(CARTER 267D, J.D'E. 61884;
HEIGHT CM 14.9; WIDTH CM 14.5)

Ancient Egyptian religion embraced a variety of ideas, developed over thousands of years; it was rich in symbolism, and the hieroglyphic script contained many signs which not only expressed concepts but also served as amuletic forms. The ingenuity of the Egyptian jewelry designer in exploiting this variety in the making of excellent products is fully exemplified by this colorful piece which is saturated with hidden and not-so-hidden meaning. It is the most spectacular of the jewels found in the chest in the Treasury which had been rifled and repacked. Why was a wonderful piece like this not stolen?

The central element, as so often, is a winged scarab, the body of which is formed from an unblemished, translucent chalcedony. It is in itself a solar symbol, the sun-god at dawn, Khepri, who is usually shown rolling the sun-disk in its front legs. Here there is a variation. The front legs support a golden bark, partly inlaid with turquoise, in which rides the left eye of Horus – the moon – flanked by uraei with sun-disks on their heads. Most striking is the disk of the moon with its crescent: the crescent is gold, but the disk is silver, and on it are soldered three tiny gold figures of the king flanked by ibis-headed Thoth and falcon-headed Re-Herakhty. Thoth and the king wear lunar disks and Re-Herakhty a sun-disk.

A little less overt symbolism can be found in the lower part of this pectoral. The back legs of the scarab are metamorphosed into vulture legs which characteristically hold shen-signs of authority, and also flowers: in the left an open lily, and in the right, a lotus and buds, both plants heraldically representing Upper Egypt. On each side the solar theme is resumed by erect uraei. At the bottom is a garland, serving as a kind of fringe, consisting of cornflowers, lotus and poppies. On the edge of the wings of the scarab on each side are six small loops, intended presumably to receive the cords of six strands of beads for suspension.

In addition to the materials already mentioned, the inlays are of lapis-lazuli, carnelian, calcite, obsidian and colored glass.

PENDANT WITH TUTANKHAMUN'S PRENOMEN

(CARTER 267A, J.D'E. 61886; HEIGHT 9 CM, WIDTH 10.5 CM)

Some of the most interesting, and less mythological, jewels found in Tutankhamun's tomb were discovered in the domed chest embellished with ivory and ebony veneers, and panels composed of many thousands of pieces of marquetry. It is a splendid box, which, according to its hieratic inscription, was filled with jewelry for the funeral, but from the king's apartments. The contents had been seriously disturbed by robbers who had penetrated as far as the Treasury. What they must have taken must have been exceptionally fine, or at least made of very valuable materials; for what was left behind made by itself a notable collection.

No two pieces of large-scale jewelry in the tomb were made to the same pattern, and even where motifs are repeated the details are varied, and the materials and execution often different. This pendant is a good example of fine design making much of a simple idea. The essence of the whole is Tutankhamun's prenomen, Nebkheperure, which makes up

the central element: the scarab (*kheper*) is made of a fine piece lapis-lazuli, and the three gold strokes below it indicate plurality (making *kheper* into *kheperu*). Between the forelegs of the beetle is the risen sun, a carnelian disk set in gold (*Re*), which in nature was the ball of mud and dung rolled forward by the beetle as food and protection for its eggs. Beneath the plural strokes is a basket shape inlaid with turquoise (*neb*).

What dramatizes this piece are the wings which are often added iconographically to the beetle form of Re (Khepri). Here they sweep around to form almost a complete circle, enveloping the royal name and offering it divine protection. The detailed decoration of the wings is carried out in cloisons filled with colored glass, lapis and carnelian inlays. The whole design has a gold backing with chased details of the front design on the reverse. Behind the sun-disk there is a tubular fitting through which could be threaded a gold chain or cord for suspension.

BA-BIRD PECTORAL

(CARTER 256B(2), J.D'E, 61903; WIDTH 33 CM)

Among the various trappings found on the outer surface of Tutankhamun's mummy was this pectoral in the form of a human-headed bird. It had been, like the whole of the surface, heavily anointed with resinous unguents which had solidified as a kind of carapace. Dextrously cleaned under the guidance of Arthur Lucas, Carter's invaluable chemical and conservation colleague, the various items were removed from the mummy; some had been seriously damaged by the unguents; on this bird the damage was limited to some of the inlays.

Here is a representation of the king's *ba*, a form of his spirit. The Egyptians conceived of the human spirit in two ways, which became active after death. There was the *ka*, sometimes erroneously called the 'double', which was associated with sustenance and potency. In the case of the king it was thought to have been formed at the same time as the royal person itself, and it remained in attendance on him throughout life and in the afterlife. The two great wooden guardian statues of

Tutankhamun which stood at the entrance to the Burial Chamber are often called *ka*-statues, because the royal *ka* is referred to in their inscriptions. The *ba*, on the other hand, was a mobile spirit, acting after the death of the person, enabling the deceased to move about and even to take different forms, and to leave and to enter the tomb. The presence of this pectoral figure on the royal body, unrestricted by the mummy bandages, provided the king with mobility – the ability to move as he willed as the *ba*.

The *ba* is shown as a human-headed falcon, and in this piece the wings, body and legs are those of a falcon. The head, turned to the left, is of gold with a wig of blue glass, somewhat discolored. A gold circlet with ribbons and a *uraeus* on the brow sits on the head. The face is remarkably sensitive; it has a short beard, quite different from the long, plaited, turned-up beard associated with Osiris. The inlays of the body and wings are all of glass, but only those in blue have remained in relatively good condition.

VULTURE PENDANT

(CARTER 267I, J.D'E. 61894; HEIGHT 14.1 CM, WIDTH 16.4 CM)

The form and position of the head of the vulture which forms the subject of this pectoral pendant are unusual. In most cases where the vulture is shown its head is turned to one side, following the general principle of confrontation in Egyptian art. Here, however, the head, which has been made separately of gold and soldered to the body of the bird, is modeled in the round; it is so positioned that when the piece lies on the chest, the face of the bird looks up towards the face of the wearer, in this case Tutankhamun. This attitude is quite appropriate, for this vulture is the goddess Nekhbet, Upper Egyptian tutelary deity of the king.

Nekhbet here wears a crown called an *atef*. In this case it takes the form of the Upper Egyptian white crown, the usual crown for Nekhbet, but with added ostrich feathers on the sides. The *atef* is particularly associated with Osiris, and with the dead king when he has posthumously become Osiris. On the walls of the Burial Chamber, in the scene in which Ay, Tutankhamun's successor, is shown opening the mouth of the mummified king, Tutankhamun wears this crown. In another of the

pectorals from the tomb (J.d'E. 61946) Nekhbet is again shown with the *atef*-crown; but Osiris in the same piece wears another form of the *atef*.

This pendant is made of gold and decorated as usual with cloisonné work. The vulture's head, as mentioned, is apparently cast gold, but the *atef*-crown is of lower grade electrum, with its side feathers inlaid with glass. The body and wings of the vulture are inlaid with lapis-lazuli, carnelian, and red and blue glass; the *shen*-signs in the bird's talons are inlaid with carnelian and pale blue glass. The reverse side of the piece is chased with details of the vulture's body and wings, and there are four rings for a suspension chain.

The pendant was found in the 'jewel' box in the Treasury.

233

Pectoral with Royal Prenomen and Lotus Fringe

(Carter 267n, J.d'E. 61890; height 12.5 cm, width 13 cm)

Some of the jewels found in Tutankhamun's tomb seem to have been made with particular religious or funerary ideas in mind. Some are essentially decorative, while still incorporating religious symbolism. Some were clearly made for burial purposes, to be included in the mummy wrappings; some showed signs of use before burial. Most display great inventiveness in the disposition of the various decorative and religious elements used in the designs. Some seem to have been designed when

the jeweler-craftsman had perhaps temporarily lost his inspiration.

This pectoral may be considered less successful than many others from the tomb. First impressions are good: it is large, and colorful in its display of semiprecious stones and colored glass; it contains enough amuletic references to keep the reflective mind busy. It is dramatic. But there are criticisms: the gold used for its basic form is of low quality; the workmanship of the inlays is not of the best, as can be seen in so many pieces. In the

design itself, the artist seems to have crammed in the *ankh*-signs and the eyes of Horus unnecessarily tightly, while the lateral *uraei* seem too big, dominating the central feature, which is the king's prenomen. In this royal name the central scarab, made of lapis-lazuli, with legs inlaid with the same stone, is provided with falcon wings inlaid with the same stone, and with carnelian and glass. These wings sweep round to touch the horns of the crescent moon, within which sits the lunar disk,

made of pale electrum. The theme of the transfiguration of the king, shown in the form of his name flying up to heaven, is strangely, but not uniquely, modified by the use of the moon instead of the sun; and the name itself is further diminished by the small plural strokes and basket which complete the prenomen.

At the bottom of the pectoral is a border or fringe of lotus flowers, interspersed with cornflowers and roundels, all inlaid with lapis-lazuli, carnelian and colored glass.

234

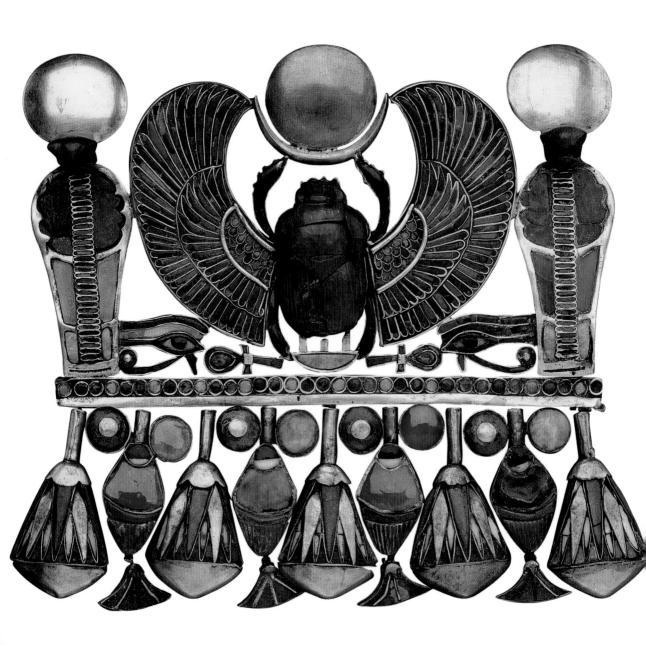

COUNTERPOISE WITH
A FIGURE OF ETERNITY

(CARTER 267E, J.D'E. 61898; HEIGHT 6.9 CM, WIDTH 8.2 CM)

The veneered jewel box in the Treasury contained four counterpoises which cannot easily be matched with any pendant to make up a complete necklace. There are two terminal bars on the top edge of this piece, one made to slide into a corresponding terminal on one side of a connecting necklace, the other with six perforations to take the threads of six strings of beads. None of the single pectorals found in the tomb has holes for six strings.

A figure of Heh, god of eternity or of millions of years, occupies the centre of the counterpoise. The attitude, with raised arms, is characteristic; the god is commonly shown with a sign for 'year' on his head. Here there is a large eye of Horus, the *wedjat*, a

symbol of wholeness and a strong protective amulet. The bare areas of Heh's body are inlaid with translucent calcite, set in a reddish paste which shows through the stone as a flesh-color. The wig is of blue faience, except for a small part showing beneath the right arm, which has been inlaid with calcite. Closely associated with Heh are the two side elements of the counterpoise; these are formalized palm fronds, notched to mark the years of the king's reign, and at their bottoms are small tadpole figures (*hefen*) on *shen*-signs. The tadpole in Egyptian numbering stood for one hundred thousand. Heh is often shown holding palm fronds similarly terminated. The theme here is clearly the everlasting reign of the Pharaoh.

The two great *uraei* which flank Heh are rather crudely made, apart from their solid glass heads, which are carefully modeled. The inlays of the sun-disks are carnelian, and those on the hoods of the cobras are glass and calcite. Behind Heh, inserted as if to fill up the space, is a *tyet*-sign, a powerful amulet often used decoratively, alternating with the *djed*-pillar; it is the Isis knot, often interpreted as the 'blood of Isis' and ideally made of red jasper when used as an amulet. Here it is inlaid with blue glass and calcite. The *tyet* offered protection and life.

A hinged lateral fitting of gold at the bottom is pierced to receive eighteen short strings of beads, some ending in fishes made of red and yellow gold, as in another counterpoise. These strings have never been restored.

PECTORAL OF THE WINGED VULTURE OF NUT

(CARTER 261P3, J.D'E. 61943;
HEIGHT 12.1 CM, WIDTH 17.2 CM)

A question can be raised about the king for whom this highly colorful and attractively designed pectoral was first made. The problem lies in the two cartouches containing the prenomen and name of Tutankhamun; both are written in reverse direction, and are wrongly placed according to the titles which go with them; the prenomen should be on the right, with the titles 'good ruler, lord of the two lands', and the name on the left with the title 'son of Re'. In the name cartouche, a sign has been omitted in the epithet '[ruler] in Southern Heliopolis'. It is likely, therefore, that the cartouches have been altered, and the job of replacement has been somewhat botched. It is thought that the original names in the cartouches were those of Akhenaten. If this were so, then such a piece would have been made early in that king's reign, when a depiction of the goddess Nut would have been acceptable. It may never have left Thebes, being recycled for Tutankhamun, his names inserted in the cartouches in place of those of Akhenaten. The pectoral was found in the Anubis pylon shrine in the Treasury.

Although the divine bird here shown, splendidly enriched with inlays of colored glass and carnelian in the *shen*-signs in her talons, is the vulture commonly recognized as the upper Egyptian royal protective goddess Nekhbet, the hieroglyphic signs above her humped back identify her as Nut, the sky goddess. She it is who traditionally envelops the dead king with her protective wings. This divine image therefore serves as a good example of how Egyptian iconography is to be understood not just by the forms shown, but also by the accompanying texts. Here it is specified that the vulture is Nut, not Nekhbet.

The shrine shape of the pectoral is framed on the sides and bottom by carefully inlaid block borders of colored glass; at the top is a formal cornice of palm fronds, and below it a frieze of pendent flowers. The fittings at each end at the top are perforated with three holes each to take strings of beads.

PECTORAL OF OSIRIS, ISIS AND NEPHTHYS

(CARTER 2610, J.D'E. 61946,
HEIGHT 15.5 CM, WIDTH 20 CM)

The possibilities of iconographic
confusion are well shown in this
pectoral, which is made of low
quality gold. It was found in the
Anubis shrine in the Treasury. It is
shrine-shaped with an inlaid cornice
at the top and a frieze of pendent
flowers. *Uraei* with carnelian sun-
disks descend from the two sides of
the cornice. Block borders of glass
inlay form the two sides and the
bottom.

The scene in the centre shows a
small mummiform figure with the
accoutrements of royalty, flanked by
a winged serpent and a vulture. Both
rest on baskets with a checker design
representing the weave of baskets;
both have their wings outstretched
to protect the mummiform figure. If
there were no inscriptions, the two
goddesses would be identified as
Wadjyt, the cobra deity, and
Nekhbet, the vulture deity. These
identifications are strengthened by the
red crown worn by the cobra, and
the white crown with feathers, worn
by the vulture. In the description of

Nekhbet in another pectoral,
where the same crown is worn, it is
usually called the *atef*.

In this pectoral, the small
mummiform figure is shown
wearing a rather different form of
the *atef*, one which is much more
commonly associated with Osiris.
Its white-crown form splays out at
the top and it carries a sun-disk;
furthermore, the crown in this form
incorporates curled ram's horns
which support the ostrich feathers
on each side. From its detailed
markings this *atef* seems to be made
in reality of some kind of
wickerwork, tied near the top. It is
very different from the simple *atef*
worn by the vulture. This
mummiform figure is described as
'lord of eternity, ruler of everlasting,
the good god, lord of the holy land'.
It could be Osiris, but it could also
be the king transformed into Osiris
after death. And this second
interpretation seems more likely, as
the two winged deities are by
inscription identified as Isis and
Nephthys. Isis (the vulture) 'gives
protection and life behind him like
Re', while Nephthys (the cobra)
'gives protection and life'.

Earrings

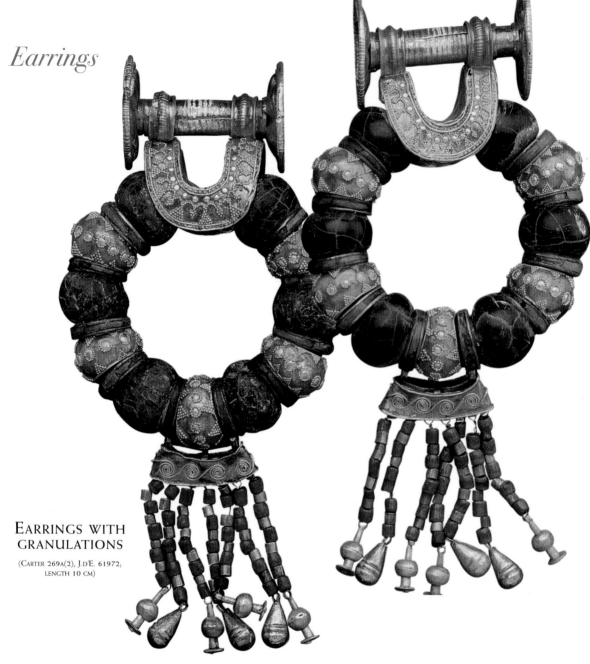

EARRINGS WITH GRANULATIONS

(CARTER 269A(2), J.D'E. 61972;
LENGTH 10 CM)

In this pair of earrings the daintiness and glowing colors of the following pair give way to a chunky, somber appearance which Carter found to be 'barbaric, but not unpleasing'.

The fastenings here are similar to those of the other sets of earrings and studs. A screw bar which passed through the pierced ear lobe fitted into a corresponding hollow tube. Both ends are covered by disk studs, here decorated with applied gold rosettes of gold wire and gold foil petals. All the main parts of the pieces are made of what is termed red, or purple, gold, the dramatic color achieved by the addition of small quantities of iron, in the form probably of iron pyrites, known as fool's gold.

These earrings are also notable technically for the lavish use of gold granulation, a jeweler's process used throughout Egyptian history. The precise method by which the granules were made is not known, and it is possible that they were just selected from the gold dust supplied to jewelers. They were fixed to the decorated surface by a process of colloidal hard-soldering, but it has not been possible to discover precisely what materials and technical method may have been used by the Egyptian craftsman to produce the result.

From the fastenings hang down gold hoops to which the main circlet of beads is linked. The hoops are decorated with formalized lotus flowers and buds linked by stems, all carried out in granulation. The beads are made of gold and resin, separated by disks of resin sandwiched between thin gold plates. The gold beads are embellished with granular designs of triangles and tiny gold bosses encircled by granulation. All the beads are cleverly graduated in thickness from inside to outside so that they sit neatly and tightly in a circle. Beneath the bead circles are wide bar beads decorated with wire scrolls, applied by the same process used for the granulation. The gold used for the scrolls and the granulation is not colored red. Seven strings of gold and glass beads complete these earrings, and they terminate in lotus seed heads in plain gold, and drop beads in red gold.

These earrings may not be 'barbaric', but they may show a foreign influence.

EARRINGS WITH DUCK HEADS

(CARTER 269A(1), J.D'E. 61969; LENGTH 10.9 CM)

Four pairs of earrings and a pair of ear-studs were found in the cartouche-shaped box which was stored in the Treasury. It is probable that all these jewels were used in Tutankhamun's early life, and had been put aside after he achieved puberty, or some other significant point in growing up. They were not, however, discarded completely, but stored to form part of his burial equipment.

This pair is the best designed of all the four, and it is distinguished not only by a superb use of the cloisonné technique, but also by some other technical aspects. The method for fastening the rings to the lobes of the ears was the same for all four pairs, and has been described above. In this case an additional subtle detail has been included. Disks of transparent quartz are fitted on both sides of the fasteners, and on the insides of the outer quartz disks are painted

241

tiny portraits of the king. These are flanked by the pendent *uraei* visible in the illustration.

The main element in the design takes the form of a bird with wonderfully formed and inlaid wings which sweep round to make a circle. The tiny cloisons are filled with intricately cut inlays of quartz, calcite, colored faience and glass. The head of the bird set in the middle of the wing's circle is anomalous. From the form of the wings, a falcon head is expected; the actual head is of a duck, and it is made, most rarely, of translucent

blue glass. The tail of the bird, equally finely inlaid with colored glass, is fringed at its bottom by a minutely worked gold frieze of tiny disks and a block border from which hangs a gold frame mounted with gold and blue glass beads arranged in a chevron pattern, and giving the appearance of pendent strings of beads. From these hang five *uraeus* heads.

In their balance, color, technical perfection and overall appearance, these earrings are among the most satisfying of surviving jewelry from ancient Egypt.

EARRINGS WITH PENDENT *URAEI*

(Carter 269a(5), J.d'E. 61968; length 7 cm)

A less ponderous fastening was used for this set of earrings. A circular fitment at the back was pushed through the pierced ear lobe and held in place by a cap. It is a less unwieldy arrangement than that of the ribbed tube, and probably more comfortable for a younger person to wear. There is no evidence to suggest that Tutankhamun wore earrings after childhood and early youth; but his ear lobes would have remained pierced, and it is not impossible that on certain grand occasions earrings were worn. The great Gold Mask found covering the head of the royal mummy shows pierced ears, but when it was first found these perforations were sealed with small covers of gold foil. The only supporting evidence for the wearing of such jewels by the mature king seems to be the representation of pierced ears on statues. Why would a great king like Ramesses II have himself shown with these

perforations if they had no function after puberty?

This pair of earrings, perhaps more correctly called ear-studs, are formed of circular gold plates set with carnelian bosses surrounded by four rings of inlay, each designed separately to represent different kinds of bead and decorative device. The materials are carnelian, calcite and light and dark blue glass. The gold is of the red variety used so spectacularly on one of the other pairs of earrings. The inlays are set in colored cement. The outer ring represents ribbed beads; the next ring has unidentified floral forms; the third is of simple glass and gold beads set alternately; the final, innermost, ring reproduces round gold beads. From this main circular element, in each case two rather large *uraei* hang down; they are of gold, with glass inlays, and heads in dark blue glass modeled in the round. Each *uraeus* is topped by a carnelian sun-disk set in gold.

EARRINGS WITH FIGURES OF THE KING

(Carter 268a(3), J.d'E. 61971; length 11.8 cm)

The use of somewhat inferior gold rather diminishes the spectacular effect undoubtedly intended for these earrings. The usual ribbed or screw tube fastenings are embellished with terminal bosses of gold inlaid with colored glass and carnelian, and also *uraei*; the inner *uraeus* of one earring is missing, and its companion on the other has a vulture head. Possibly each boss was originally fitted with two *uraei*, one with a vulture head.

242

The main element of the earring in each case is connected to the fastening by a falcon figure with outstretched wings made of gold inlaid with translucent quartz, through which can be seen details of the bird painted on the gold. The main ring is flanged and of gold with an outer edge marked as if granulated. The whole is surrounded by a ring of lenticular beads in gold, carnelian and blue glass.

The centre of each ring has a figure of Tutankhamun, flanked by two great *uraei* with sun-disks; this group stands on a *heb* or festival sign inlaid, like the *uraei*, with quartz and blue glass. The royal figure is carnelian; the king is shown wearing the blue crown, and he holds a crook of gold wire in his hand; there is a tiny gold *uraeus* on his brow.

From six of the gold lenticular beads hang strings of beads of carnelian and light and dark blue glass. Each pair of beads is separated from the next by four thin beads formed of tiny granules of gold fused together. Drop beads of gold, carnelian and light and dark blue glass serve as terminals for these strings.

While these pieces exhibit some weaknesses, such as the crude blocking out of the king's figure and the poor fitting of some of the inlays, special note must be made of the painting of the falcon details beneath the quartz inlays. Like the tiny royal portraits on the studs of the earrings with duck heads, such details are scarcely to be seen, and could hardly have been noticed when the earrings were being worn in life.

Bangles and Bracelets

BRACELET WITH SCARAB CLASP

(CARTER 269G, J.D'E. 62374;
LENGTH 15.8 CM,
HEIGHT OF SCARAB 6.6 CM)

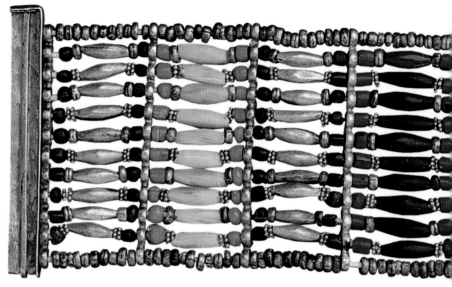

Two types of bracelet were found in Tutankhamun's tomb: the solid hoop-shaped kind with hinges and a pin fastening, and what Carter called the 'wrist-band' kind, composed of rows of beads separated and kept rigid at intervals by spacer beads, and with a large ornamental element at one end which, when the bracelet was worn, would appear as the centre-ornament.

Three bracelets were found in the cartouche-shaped box in the Treasury, which contained several other items of jewelry, like the earrings. All were thought to have been used by the king in his lifetime, and Carter was disappointed at not finding more in this box; it seems to have been used for many of the king's personal jewels. He supposed that the best pieces had been stolen in antiquity. Of the three bracelets, one was of the solid hoop form, and two of the wrist-band type, the one shown here and the other with a fine amethyst as the centre-ornament.

The principal feature of the centre-ornament of this bracelet is a scarab of lapis-lazuli. It is not carved from a single piece of stone but made up of a number of pieces fitted most carefully into gold cloisons fixed to a gold plate; the legs are also inlaid with the same stone. Between the back legs is held a basket shape inlaid with pale blue glass. The constituent parts of this centre-ornament look as if they

were intended to spell out the king's prenomen, Nebkheperure; but instead of the expected sun-disk between the front legs, there is a gold cartouche which contains the signs of the prenomen; the background of the cartouche is inlaid with blue glass.

Apart from the centre-ornament, the bracelet consists of ten rows of beads, the principal ones being barrel-shaped and made of gold,

electrum, blue glass, lapis-lazuli and calcite. Eight gold spacer beads give it rigidity, and there are small beads of blue glass and carnelian, and little granular beads in the form of rings. The bracelet is edged with gold beads, and finished with a fastening in gold which slides into a corresponding fitting on the side of the scarab – a simple but ingenious method of securing the bracelet when worn.

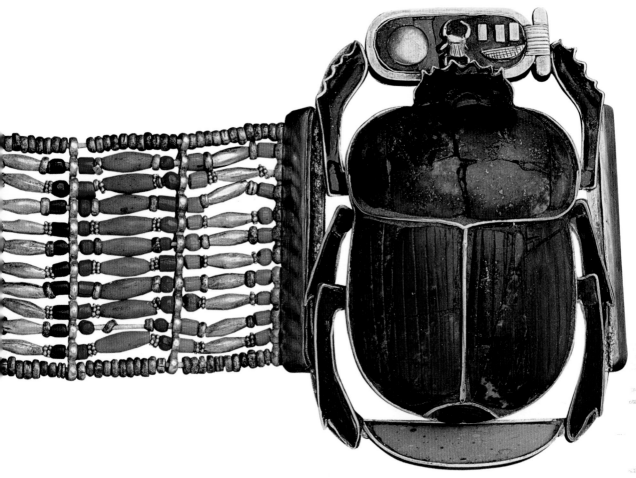

BRACELET WITH THREE SCARABS

(CARTER 256YY J.D'E. 62362;
LENGHT 17.6 CM, HEIGHT 4.3 CM)

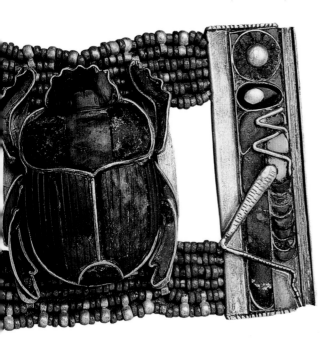

Tutankhamun appears to have had a predilection for bracelets. Apart from those found in boxes, there were numerous examples found within the mummy wrappings. The largest number, not surprisingly, were found on his two arms, seven on the right and six on the left, in each case filling the space between wrist and elbow. Although many of these bracelets incorporated in their designs religious or amuletic signs, like the *wedjat* or sacred eye of Horus, the *uraeus*, scarab and vulture, they were not, it seems, designed specifically for funerary use. Carter believed, with much good reason, that they were all used by Tutankhamun in his lifetime. From their crammed disposition on his arms, he was clearly determined to have as many as possible with him for use in his after-life.

This bracelet, which was on the king's left arm, combines in its design balance, amuletic protection, a wonderful use of color, and an imaginative touch in the clasp which held it closed.

There is here no centre-ornament as such; the whole length of the piece is embellished with decorative elements, spaced out in pairs. Firstly there are three scarabs in lapis-lazuli, the parts set in cloisons of gold, the scarab being not only the embodiment of the sun-god at dawn, Khepri, but also a symbol of general regeneration. Between the scarabs are very decorative groups of signs: at the bottom of the basket is the hieroglyph often used for simple graphic purposes, but also meaning 'lord' or 'all' – as it may do here; it is inlaid with pale blue glass. On each basket stand the *nefer*-sign and an *uraeus*, the former meaning 'goodness' or 'beauty', the latter being a powerful royal protective symbol. At the top of each group is a sun-disk set in gold; the inlays are of carnelian and colored glass. This decorative group admirably exemplifies the capacity of Egyptian symbolism and the hieroglyphic script to be used graphically, with elegance and meaning.

Six rows of tiny gold and glass beads form the upper and lower borders of the bracelet. The sliding clasp is unusually decorated with the figure of a grasshopper or locust and a rosette.

BRACELET WITH LAPIS-LAZULI CENTRE-PIECE

(CARTER 256DDD, J.D'E. 62370; LENGTH 16 CM, HEIGHT 4.2 CM)

Of the thirteen bracelets found on Tutankhamun's arms beneath the mummy wrappings, most included religious or magical amuletic signs, but a few seem devoid of meaningful decoration. Most of the bracelets showed signs of having been worn in the king's lifetime. This bracelet is one of those decorative pieces, and as such it is rare not only in the context of this

royal burial, but also in Egyptian jewelry generally. The Egyptians liked to have their jewels invested with magical power. The central element of this jewel is a disk of lapis-lazuli flecked, as is so often the case, with brown markings. The setting is gold and decorated with two principal circular bands of design carried out in fine granulation. The outer band has triangular arrangements of granules while the inner has granules arranged around central bosses. The same decoration occurs on the side bars, to which ten strings of beads are attached. The beads are of gold, barrel-shaped and separated by little disks. It is a very flexible bracelet, and was held in place by a sliding bar.

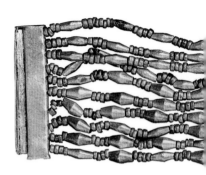

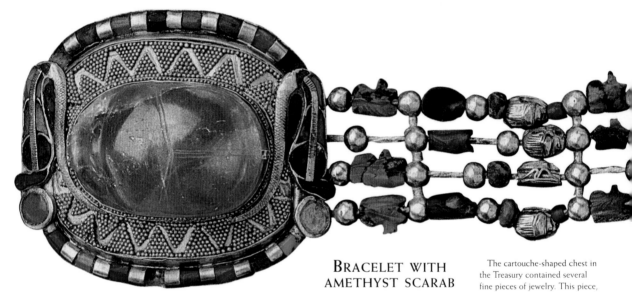

BRACELET WITH AMETHYST SCARAB

(CARTER 269M, J.D'E. 62380; LENGTH 18 CM, HEIGHT 3.5 CM)

The cartouche-shaped chest in the Treasury contained several fine pieces of jewelry. This piece, in its general design being rather similar to some of the bracelets found on Tutankhamun's arms, was included in this chest. It bears signs of having been worn in the king's lifetime. The main element in the design is the amethyst scarab, lightly marked

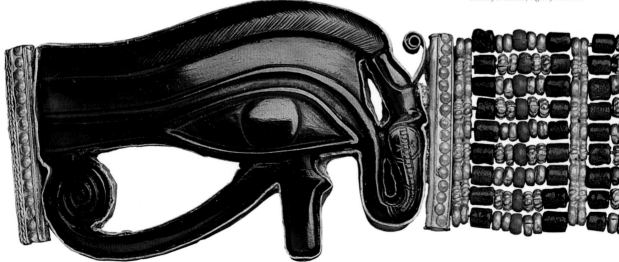

with detail, as is common with scarabs of this hard stone. It is placed in an oval setting decorated with gold granules arranged in a pattern of little triangles. The outer rim is bordered by gold and hard stone ring beads, and each end has an erect *uraeus* with carnelian sundisks. The back plate of this centre-piece is chased with the king's prenomen; he is 'the good god, lord of the lands, lord of achievement'. The 'strap' of the bracelet consists of four strings of beads, of gold, carnelian, lapis-lazuli and jasper, in the form of tiny *wedjat*-eyes, scarabs and spheroids. The gold scarabs are in some cases inscribed with the king's prenomen. There are eight gold spacer beads.

BRACELET WITH *WEDJAT*

(CARTER 25600, J.D'E. 62372; LENGTH 16.2 CM, HEIGHT 3.5 CM)

The central element of this flexible bracelet from the left arm of the mummy is the powerful *wedjat*-eye, associated particularly with the falcon-god Horus, and also with Osiris. Its name means 'that which is complete or healthy', a description of it when restored after it had been stolen by Seth. This *wedjat* is made of a flawless piece of carnelian, set in a gold cloison fixed to a back plate of gold. Emerging from the eye on the right side is an *uraeus* wearing the double crown of Upper and Lower Egypt.

An inscription chased on the plate reads: 'lord of the two lands, image of Re, Nebkheperure, ruler of all that is in order, given life like Re for ever and ever'. The 'strap' of the bracelet consists of nine rows of beads made of glass of several colors and thin gold granulated beads. At six places the rows are held together by long gold spacers which are made to look like thin gold granulated beads.

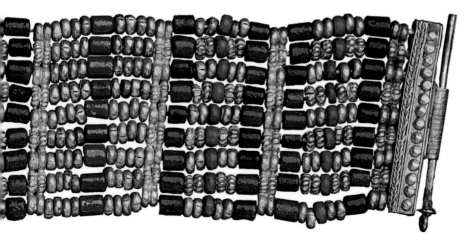

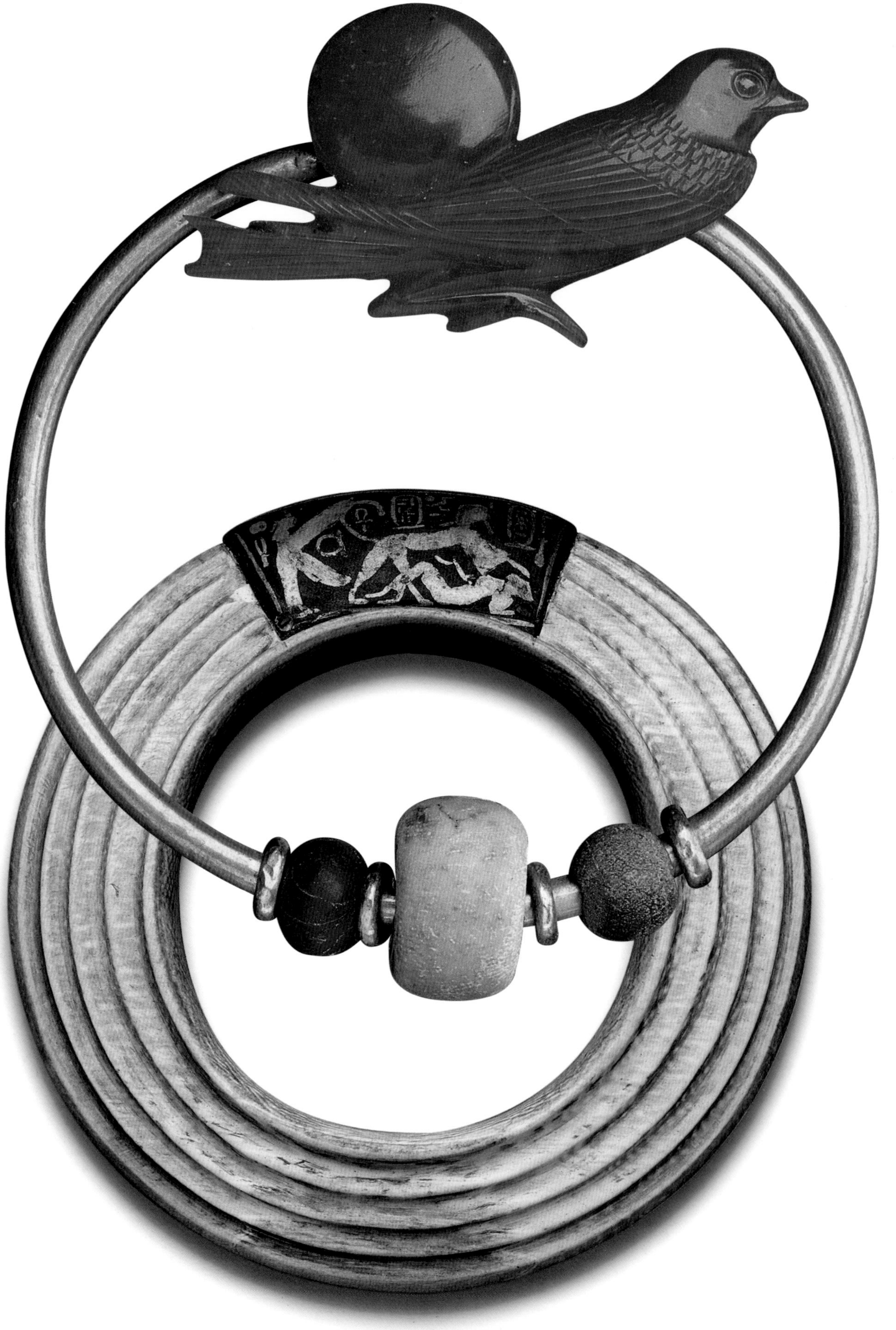

BANGLE WITH A BIRD

(CARTER 256UU, J.D'E. 62384; DIAMETER 5.2 CM)

What is the bird on this bangle? Many Egyptologists would identify it with the bird, apparently the swallow, used in the word for 'great', *wer*, on the basis of the shape of the tail. The position of the feet, however, is not what is expected. Carter, with his special avian knowledge, considered it to be the swift, and he supported his identification by the presence of the sun-disk on the bird's back. He noted that swifts nested in holes in the western cliffs by the Nile, and emerged at dawn, making a great noise, similarly returning at dusk to roost. Unfortunately the Egyptians were not as precise as one would like in depicting birds and other creatures, and on lexicographical grounds the *ment*-bird is the swallow. Its significance on this bangle, therefore, remains elusive, although some association might be made with Spell 86 of the Book of the Dead: 'Spell to be transformed into a swallow', which Carter mentions. The bird is made of carnelian, the beads of blue glass and quartz. This piece was found in the wrappings of the mummy, by its left elbow.

BANGLE WITH A MINIATURE SCENE

(CARTER 620(43), J.D'E. 62405; DIAMETER 8.5 CM)

There is some dispute about the nature of these objects – are they armlets or anklets? The difficulty of slipping fixed circles of some not very robust material over the foot and up to the ankle offers a strong objection to their being anklets. A number of such objects were found scattered on the floor of the Annexe, many being quite plain. This one, made of ivory, is more elaborate. It is ribbed, and has inlaid on both sides small plates made of copper or bronze.

On one side (not visible) the prenomen of Tutankhamun is inscribed in cartouche in fine gold wire. On the other side, also in gold, is a small-scale scene: the king as a lion mauls an enemy lying prone on the ground. A standing figure of a goddess, probably Isis, holds out protective wings towards the scene and to two cartouches containing the names of the king. There is a *shen*-sign of dominion between the wings.

BRACELET WITH SCARAB

(CARTER 269N, J.D'E. 62360; DIAMETER 5.4 CM)

Another piece from the cartouche-shaped box, this fixed bracelet is one of the finest and most substantial jewels from Tutankhamun's tomb. Its principal embellishment is a scarab, standing clear of its base. It is made of gold with the body of the scarab composed of pieces of lapis-lazuli, skillfully fitted together within gold cloisons. Each side is enriched with false beads of gold, lapis, quartz, turquoise and carnelian, with a border simulating granular work. On

the bend of the bracelet at each end is a charming design of a central mandrake fruit flanked by poppy flowers, with gold rosettes between the stems. The mandrake fruits are made of translucent quartz, their backs painted green; the poppy flowers are of carnelian. The bracelet itself is made of solid gold, and it has a hinge on one side and a fastening device on the other, both held together by gold pins. This piece is quite small and it has been suggested that it was worn by the king when a child.

Rings

DOUBLE RING WITH THOTH

(CARTER 4C, J.D'E. 62437;
DIAMETER 2.2 CM)

In one of the repacked boxes in the Antechamber the excavators found a piece of linen wrapped around eight gold rings. Carter believed that this little bundle represented part of the intended theft on the second occasion when the tomb was broken into. This ring is of solid gold, a double ring with two bezels decorated with divine figures. The left bezel has a figure of a baboon squatting on a shrine; it

LAPIS-LAZULI DOUBLE RING

(CARTER 256FF1, J.D'E. 62431; DIAMETER 2.3 CM)

In the course of unwrapping the mummy Carter uncovered two groups of finger rings, not on the king's fingers but placed near the wrists, five over the right wrist and eight by the left. These were mostly of semiprecious stones – chalcedony and turquoise – one of gold, one of resin and this one of lapis-lazuli. It is a double ring with a double bezel shaped like cartouches. In the right cartouche a figure of the king kneels offering milk or some other liquid to the deity in the other cartouche. The king is identified by his prenomen, written a little enigmatically: at the top is the sun-disk, below a winged scarab and the royal figure, which itself could be taken as part of the written name, shown kneeling on a basket which is regularly a component of Tutankhamun's prenomen; plural strokes are missing. The god receiving the offering is Amon-Re; he is shown seated on a throne wearing his feathered headdress, and holding the *was*-scepter and *ankh*.

wears a moon-disk on its head. The right bezel has an ibis-headed deity, carrying a *was*-scepter of power, and also wearing a moon-disk on its head. Both are forms of Thoth, the principal god of Khmun, or Hermopolis, who was a moon deity as well as the god of scribes and writing. The moon-disks are duller in color than the rest of the gold, and so too is the baboon's 'cape'; electrum was probably used for these details. The figures are placed in cartouche-shaped frames, and the backgrounds are in blue glass.

RING WITH AMON-RE

(CARTER 44F, J.D'E. 62451; DIAMETER 2 CM)

Another of the rings found in the linen bundle in the Antechamber. Carter reconstructed the scene: one of the robbers, having helped himself to a collection of gold rings, wrapped them in a piece of linen taken from the tomb equipment. When he was caught the bundle was confiscated and tossed into the box where they were ultimately found. If this reconstruction is true, it says much for the integrity of the Necropolis guards, who might easily have slipped them into the folds of a garment. The story of their survival may not, however, have been as Carter surmised. This ring is very heavy, and of solid gold, with a bezel shaped like a cartouche. Inside, carefully chased, is a figure of god, named as Amon-Re. He is seated on a throne, the characteristic feather pattern of the side of which is rendered by small punch marks. He is shown wearing his usual cap with double feather and disk, and a streamer at the back; in his left hand he holds the *was*-scepter, and in his right, the *ankh*.

RING WITH THE SUN BARK

(CARTER 44G, J.D'E. 62450;
DIAMETER 2 CM)

The heavy gold rings found in
the tomb have often been
described as signets. Strictly
speaking, a signet ring carries on
its bezel a name or device which
can be used for identificatory
purposes. You seal a letter with a
signet, and the recipient
recognizes the impression. You
seal a door or a box with a seal to
give the sealing an authority.
Egyptians used signets to seal
letters and other documents, and
the signet might well take the
form of a scarab set in a ring, or a
solid ring with an inscription cut
into the bezel. Many of the rings
found in the tomb could have
been used as signets, but none
seems specially designed for use as
a signet. This solid gold ring, for
example – one of those from the
robber's bundle – would produce
an impression if it were applied to
a mud sealing, but it is not
primarily to be considered a
signet. The design on the bezel is
religious/magical. It shows a bark
holding a sun-disk with two
baboons on either side, standing
and raising their paws in adoration,
greeting the sun at dawn. The
background is blue glass.

TRIPLE RING WITH FIGURED BEZEL

(CARTER 265FF5, J.D'E. 62428;
DIAMETER WITH FIGURES 2.6 CM)

An intricate and carefully crafted
bezel distinguishes this ring, one of
those found by the right wrist of
the mummy. The ring itself is not
simple; it has a triple shank made of
resin and covered with gold foil.
Each end of the shank is made to
represent a posy of flowers
consisting of a central papyrus in
felspar, flanked by two red poppies
in carnelian. The three parts of the
shank are bound around with gold
wire, and the three together are
bound with more wire just below
the posies. The bezel itself is at its

RING WITH
SCARAB BEZEL

(CARTER 256VV3, J.D'E. 62439;
DIAMETER 2.2 CM)

Of the fine rings found in Tutankhamun's tomb, eight were found in the cloth bundle, probably abandoned by, or taken from, the tomb robbers, and most of the rest on the mummy of the king. Over twenty non-functional rings in faience with a variety of non-royal designs were also found in the Annexe. The fact that most of the rings found on the mummy were not on fingers, but placed near the hands, suggests that there was no room to put more on fingers when they were to be covered with gold finger-stalls.

Unlike the bracelets, which could be stacked all the way up the arms to the elbows, the rings had to be placed near the hands. This ring comes from the group of eight found by the left wrist. Its bezel turns on a spindle, the hoop of the ring being of solid gold with wire wrapped round each end. The bezel is a lapis-lazuli scarab; its body is simply marked with head and wing details, and on the base are just three hieroglyphic signs: the *ankh*, 'life', flanked by two *nefer*-signs, meaning 'good, beautiful'.

base cartouche-shaped. On the base sits a lapis-lazuli scarab with an *atef*-crown on its head; in front of the head is a gold bark with the moon riding in it. At the other end of the bezel, behind the scarab, is a falcon, probably the god Re-Herakhty, rising with open wings protecting the scarab. The craftsman could scarcely have crammed in more symbolism in such a small area. On the underside of the bezel the king's prenomen is lightly inscribed, identifying this as undoubtedly a personal possession.

Other Jeweled Objects

GOLD BUCKLE OF THE KING AND QUEEN

(J.d'E. 61987; LENGTH 9 CM, HEIGHT 9 CM)

Openwork plaques of this kind are often called buckles, although there is no satisfactory evidence to show that this was their actual purpose. Not all openwork pieces look like buckles, and it might be better to think of them as attachments for belts or other items of formal dress or equipment. They are not, as has sometimes been suggested, decorative elements from chariots.

Four openwork plaques were found in a box in the Antechamber; three others come from unidentified

places in the tomb, and all are illustrated here. This example is particularly elaborate in its design, which is carried out by repoussé work, with details in chasing, and in parts richly embellished with gold granulation. The gold has the reddish-purple sheen found on many other pieces from the tomb.

The central scene shows Tutankhamun and Ankhesenamun (named in cartouches) within an elaborate kiosk which has a double cornice topped by a frieze of *uraei* with disks, and above this a winged

sun-disk. The king sits casually on a throne, his feet on a footstool. He wears elaborate dress and the *atef-*crown, usually associated with Osiris and the dead king. The king is not dead here; he is approached by Ankhesenamun who presents a bouquet, and gently touches the king. The scene is closely similar to one on the back of the gilded shrine. In both cases the queen wears a feathered headdress, but on the shrine the king wears the blue crown. Elaborate floral arrangements flank the royal pair.

Beneath the kiosk, and symbolically under the feet of the king, are shown two prone foreign captives, an Asiatic and a Nubian. Two identical scenes occupy the ends of this piece, set at right angles to the main scene. The king is shown as a sphinx with human arms holding up in front of him a figure of Ma'at, goddess of truth and order, holding the *ankh*-sign of life, and squatting on a basket. There is a pendent *uraeus* and sun-disk above the sphinx's head, and over his back is a protective vulture holding an ostrich-feather fan.

GOLD PLAQUE WITH A BULL ATTACKED

(CARTER 44A, J.D'E. 61983;
LENGTH 8.5 CM, HEIGHT 6 CM)

A number of the gold plaques, some of which look like buckles, carry scenes of hunting or of animals attacking other animals. This piece has such a scene. It is one of the four found in the Antechamber. The central depiction, disagreeable as it is, again demonstrates the Egyptian ability to convey the movement of animals in a most lively and life-like manner. The tendency to make non-human representations more fluid can be found in tomb scenes in Thebes in the mid-Eighteenth Dynasty; the Amarna tendency in art promoted it further. The theme here is of a bull attacked by wild animals – a fairly common theme in Egyptian and Western Asiatic art. The unfortunate bull is attacked by a leopard from above, and by a lion from below. Desert plants fill the open spaces. In the two end sections, ibexes graze on plants. Much of the detail is again carried out skillfully in granulation.

GOLD PLAQUE WITH HUNTING SCENE

(CARTER 50TT, J.D'E. 61985; LENGTH 8 CM, HEIGHT 3.2 CM)

This piece of gold openwork – not a buckle, but a plaque of some kind – was found in a box in the Antechamber containing a large amount of clothing and textiles. It scarcely belonged there in the first place, and may have been part of a group found elsewhere in the same room. It seems to be complete in itself, and shows a violent scene of hunting, with two dogs attacking an ibex on the left and a bull on the right. The setting seems not quite to be the desert, because elaborate and unnaturalistic plants occur within the scene. Much of the detail is marked out by granulation, and this technique is used to particularly good effect in delineating the heads of the hunting dogs. There is great movement in the depiction of the interweaving of the animals, not the static idea of Egyptian art, which is here completely confounded. The top and bottom borders are filled with rosettes. The gold is of the purplish-red kind.

257

PLAQUE OF THE KING IN HIS CHARIOT

(J.D'E. 87847; HEIGHT 6.7 CM, WIDTH 8.5 CM)

Where this plaque or buckle was found is not known. It probably strayed in antiquity from the group of similar pieces found in the Antechamber. The principal motif is the king in his chariot returning from campaign. Two captives run ahead of the horses, an Asiatic and a Nubian – it was a wide-ranging campaign! The king's hound runs with the horses, and the king is offered 'life' by the vulture Nekhbet above, and 'protection' by the winged *uraeus* Wadjyt behind him. In the space below, a variant of the common heraldic device symbolizing the union of the Two Lands includes bound figures of kneeling captives, the usual Asiatic (on the Lower Egyptian side) and Nubian (on the Upper Egyptian side). The text on a panel before the horses' heads is too worn to be read; that between the wings of the *uraeus* contains Tutankhamun's prenomen; and that behind the wheel of the chariot wishes 'all life and protection be behind him like Re for ever'. The gold again has the purplish-red color.

GOLD MUMMY BAND

(CARTER 256B, J.D'E. 60673;
WIDTH 4.9 CM)

When the lid of the innermost coffin was raised, Carter, his assistants and the visitors invited to attend that most important occasion saw for the first time the mummy of a dead king, wrapped and ornamented for burial. It was an awesome sight, but also one which certainly filled the excavators with foreboding at the task that lay ahead. Everything apart from the mask had been liberally anointed with unguents which had set hard. Still much could be seen or detected of the surface trappings, and it was evident that the king's body was very richly equipped. What then seemed promising would turn out to be spectacular when removed and cleaned of the hardened unguents.

From the *ba*-bird on the royal chest, straps of gold and beads were disposed over the lower part of the body as if they were holding the linen wrappings in place. Carter noted that some of these straps had been made originally for what was expected to be a smaller body, and then later adapted to fit Tutankhamun's somewhat larger mummy. The main strap, running down the body, had two lines with texts in which Nut and Geb, the deities of sky and earth, address the body. From this central strap ran at right angles transverse straps with single lines of text in which the king is declared to be 'revered before' the four Canopic genii and Anubis, the god of embalming. The part shown here incorporates two separate transverse straps: the upper section, containing the cartouche with Tutankhamun's name, belongs to the right side of the body and comes from the text in which the king is 'revered before Amsety'.

The lower section belongs to an individual strap, in the text of which some of the epithets usually applied to Osiris are applied to Anubis: 'lord of the Holy Land, Foremost in the West'; it continues, 'may he grant that the lord of the Two Lands, Nebkheperure, should be the first [or unique] at the head of...'; the precise meaning is uncertain because some of the text is lost.

The signs in the text are inlaid with colored glass.

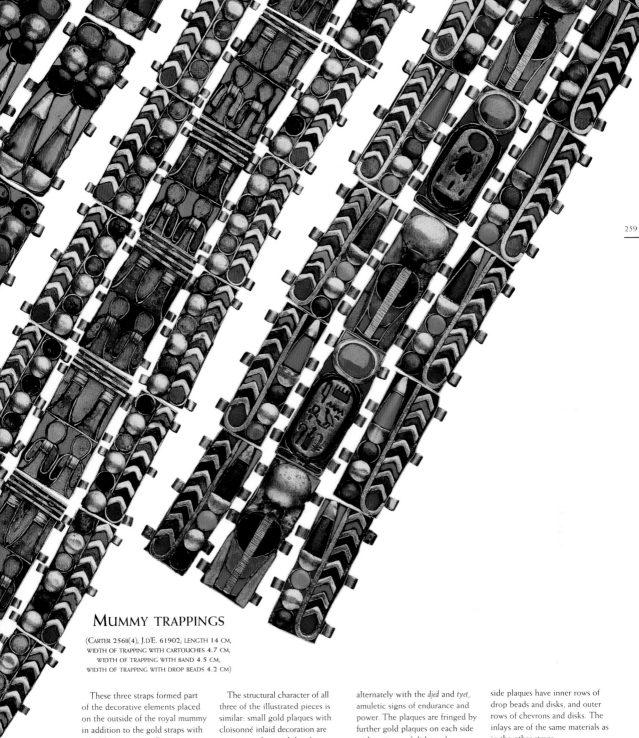

Mummy trappings

(Carter 256b(4), J.d'E. 61902; length 14 cm,
width of trapping with cartouches 4.7 cm,
width of trapping with band 4.5 cm,
width of trapping with drop beads 4.2 cm)

These three straps formed part of the decorative elements placed on the outside of the royal mummy in addition to the gold straps with inlaid funerary texts. Carter describes them as being placed 'along the sides of the mummy from the shoulders to the feet', arranged in festoons attached to the transverse trappings, as seen in the previously illustrated gold band. They are not, strictly speaking, jewelry, but they were made by the techniques of jewelry, and their spectacular appearance is comparable with the decorative straps of many of the pectoral necklaces from the tomb.

The structural character of all three of the illustrated pieces is similar: small gold plaques with cloisonné inlaid decoration are strung together, with beads separating and edging them. The left-hand strap consists of two rows of plaques side by side, with a simple repeated design of drop-beads and disks. The disks are not necessarily sun-disks, because some are inlaid with dark blue glass, the rest with transparent quartz set in reddish paste which gives them a pinkish tinge. Other inlays are in light blue glass and quartz.

The central strap has a single row of gold plaques decorated alternately with the *djed* and *tyet*, amuletic signs of endurance and power. The plaques are fringed by further gold plaques on each side with patterns of disks and chevrons. The inlays are again of dark and light blue glass, transparent quartz and carnelian.

The right-hand strap has the most elaborate scheme of decoration. The central row of gold plaques has *uraei* alternating with the names of the king, both prenomen and main name, or nomen. Each *uraeus* and cartouche is topped by a sun-disk, solid gold in the case of the *uraei*, and inlaid carnelian for the cartouches. The side plaques have inner rows of drop beads and disks, and outer rows of chevrons and disks. The inlays are of the same materials as in the other straps.

On the reverse of these straps are remains of religious texts, including the invocation of the heart from the Book of the Dead. Where royal cartouches occur, the names within, although mostly defaced, can clearly be read as those of Tutankhamun's ephemeral predecessor, Neferneferuaten. These straps therefore provide further evidence of a certain economical recycling of old funerary equipment for this burial.

260 A pair of gilded wooden sistra with bronze snake-shaped bars and disks which made a tinkling sound when shaken. This is a simple, functional pair.

261 left, left photograph A gilded wooden staff with a hand-rest in the shape of an open papyrus umbel. The decoration of this flower and at the top of the staff is in colored glass.

261 left, center photograph This staff is made of a hollow gold tube, topped by a small figure of Tutankhamun, whose name is written in tiny signs on the front of the belt of his kilt.

261 left, right photograph Elaborate wooden staff with a bent top of the kind carried by officials. It is lavishly decorated with gilding, applied gold spirals and zones of geometrical designs.

261 right Ivory scribe's palette with six colors found between the paws of the Anubis jackal in the Treasury. It carries the name of Meritaten, a sister of Ankhesenamun.

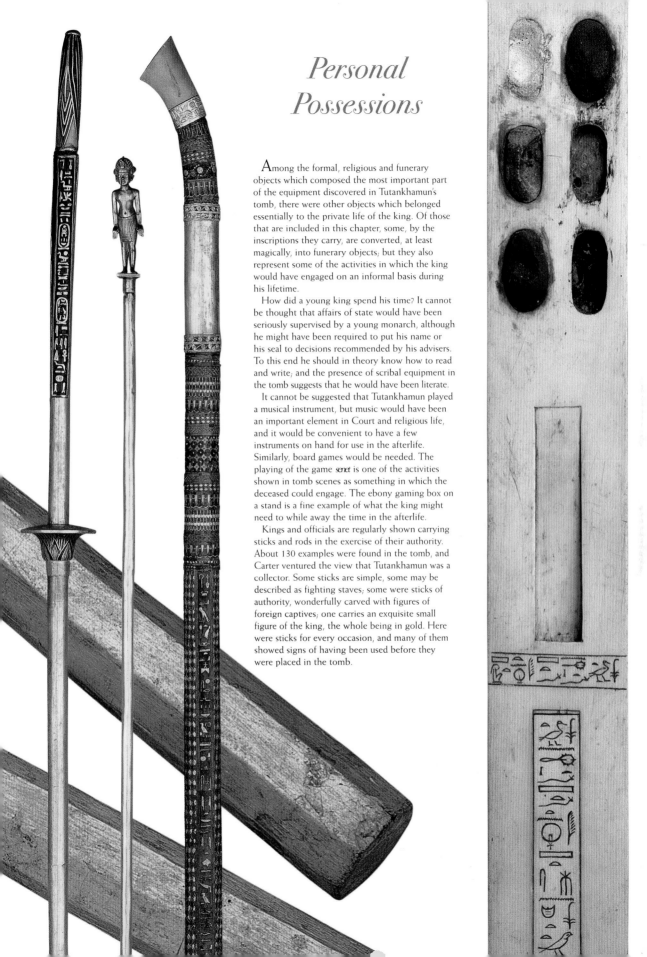

Personal Possessions

Among the formal, religious and funerary objects which composed the most important part of the equipment discovered in Tutankhamun's tomb, there were other objects which belonged essentially to the private life of the king. Of those that are included in this chapter, some, by the inscriptions they carry, are converted, at least magically, into funerary objects; but they also represent some of the activities in which the king would have engaged on an informal basis during his lifetime.

How did a young king spend his time? It cannot be thought that affairs of state would have been seriously supervised by a young monarch, although he might have been required to put his name or his seal to decisions recommended by his advisers. To this end he should in theory know how to read and write; and the presence of scribal equipment in the tomb suggests that he would have been literate.

It cannot be suggested that Tutankhamun played a musical instrument, but music would have been an important element in Court and religious life, and it would be convenient to have a few instruments on hand for use in the afterlife. Similarly, board games would be needed. The playing of the game *senet* is one of the activities shown in tomb scenes as something in which the deceased could engage. The ebony gaming box on a stand is a fine example of what the king might need to while away the time in the afterlife.

Kings and officials are regularly shown carrying sticks and rods in the exercise of their authority. About 130 examples were found in the tomb, and Carter ventured the view that Tutankhamun was a collector. Some sticks are simple, some may be described as fighting staves; some were sticks of authority, wonderfully carved with figures of foreign captives; one carries an exquisite small figure of the king, the whole being in gold. Here were sticks for every occasion, and many of them showed signs of having been used before they were placed in the tomb.

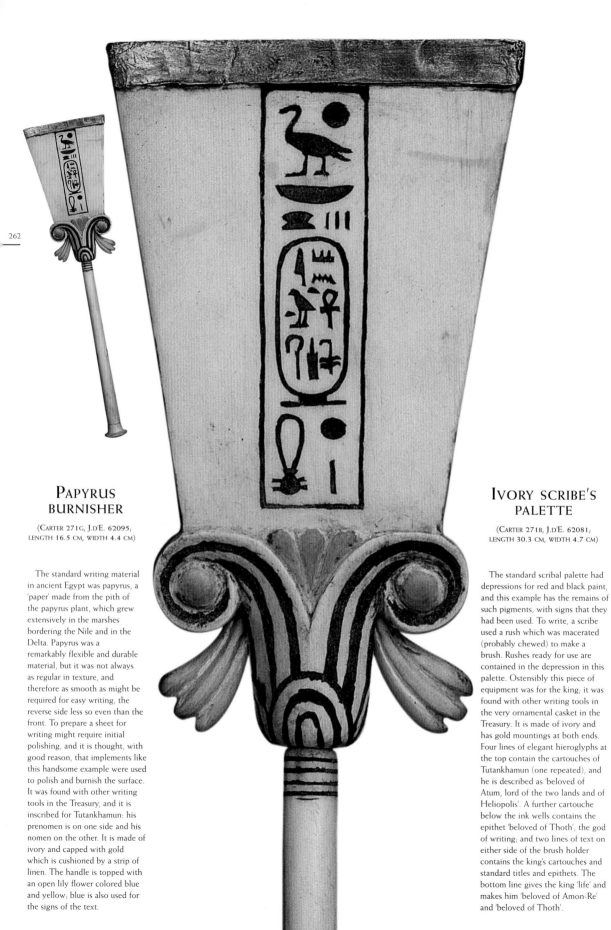

PAPYRUS BURNISHER

(CARTER 271G, J.D'E. 62095;
LENGTH 16.5 CM, WIDTH 4.4 CM)

The standard writing material in ancient Egypt was papyrus, a 'paper' made from the pith of the papyrus plant, which grew extensively in the marshes bordering the Nile and in the Delta. Papyrus was a remarkably flexible and durable material, but it was not always as regular in texture, and therefore as smooth as might be required for easy writing, the reverse side less so even than the front. To prepare a sheet for writing might require initial polishing, and it is thought, with good reason, that implements like this handsome example were used to polish and burnish the surface. It was found with other writing tools in the Treasury, and it is inscribed for Tutankhamun: his prenomen is on one side and his nomen on the other. It is made of ivory and capped with gold which is cushioned by a strip of linen. The handle is topped with an open lily flower colored blue and yellow; blue is also used for the signs of the text.

IVORY SCRIBE'S PALETTE

(CARTER 271B, J.D'E. 62081;
LENGTH 30.3 CM, WIDTH 4.7 CM)

The standard scribal palette had depressions for red and black paint, and this example has the remains of such pigments, with signs that they had been used. To write, a scribe used a rush which was macerated (probably chewed) to make a brush. Rushes ready for use are contained in the depression in this palette. Ostensibly this piece of equipment was for the king; it was found with other writing tools in the very ornamental casket in the Treasury. It is made of ivory and has gold mountings at both ends. Four lines of elegant hieroglyphs at the top contain the cartouches of Tutankhamun (one repeated), and he is described as 'beloved of Atum, lord of the two lands and of Heliopolis'. A further cartouche below the ink wells contains the epithet 'beloved of Thoth', the god of writing; and two lines of text on either side of the brush holder contains the king's cartouches and standard titles and epithets. The bottom line gives the king 'life' and makes him 'beloved of Amon-Re' and 'beloved of Thoth'.

GILDED BRUSH HOLDER

(CARTER 271E1, J.D'E. 62094;
LENGTH 30 CM)

In the hieroglyphic script the word for 'write' and cognates used a sign which represented a scribal kit – a palette, a bag of spare ink, and a tube to hold the brushes; these components were linked with a cord or strap, and scribes were often shown with their equipment slung over their shoulders. The ordinary palette had space for rush brushes, but a specially made holder would complete a good 'desk' set. This brush holder, found with the other items of the writing kit already described, is an especially elaborate example. It is shaped like a column with a palm tree capital. The abacus forms the lid and it pivots to open. It could be kept shut by having a string wound round the two little knobs on top and side of the tube. The top knobs and little base plate are made of ivory and the tube is of gilded wood, encrusted with zones of decoration with inlays of carnelian, obsidian and glass. The king's two cartouches are included in the central zone.

GILDED SCRIBAL PALETTE

(CARTER 171E2, J.D'E. 62080;
LENGTH 30.3 CM, WIDTH 4.3 CM)

This gilded wooden palette, the same size as the last and from the same box, is especially interesting because in the formal royal titulary at the top the king's name is given as Tutankhaten, the name he bore before he moved from El-Amarna. The epithet given is 'beloved of Thoth, lord of the god's word'. Carter was of the opinion that both palettes had been used, and that this one would have been the one the king used in his early reign. The question must be raised whether Tutankhamun knew how to read and write hieroglyphics or the hieratic script. The evidence for royal literacy is very slight, and it might be thought that someone in the king's position could have got through the affairs of state relying on advisers and secretaries. On the other hand, an ability to read and write was considered such an advantage in ancient Egypt that every effort might have been made to ensure that the heir to the throne obtained at least the basic competence to deal with written documents.

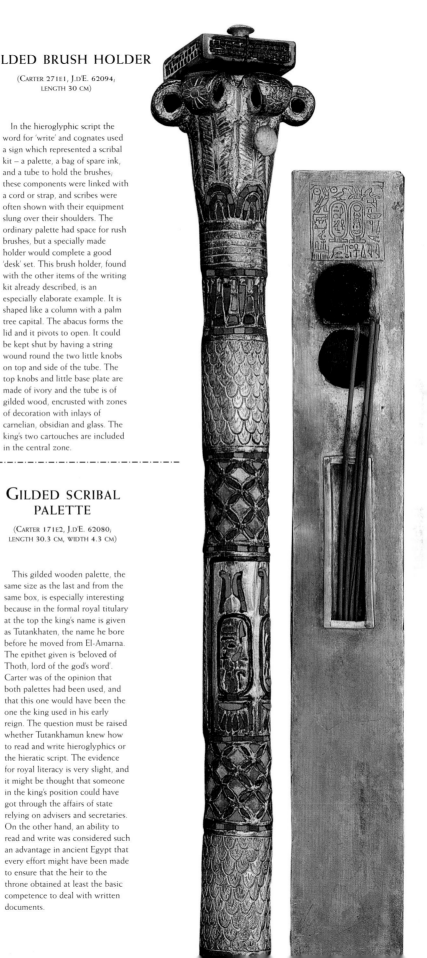

GAMING BOX
ON A STAND

(CARTER 345 (BOX), 383 (DRAWER),
580 (STAND), J.D'E. 62058;
BOX: LENGTH 44.6 CM, WIDTH 14.3 CM,
HEIGHT 8.1 CM;
STAND: LENGTH 55 CM, WIDTH 17.5 CM,
HEIGHT 20.2 CM)

One of the most satisfying
examples of the ancient cabinet-
maker's craft, this piece of semi-
recreational furniture was found in
several pieces in the Annexe. The
box is made of some ordinary
wood, veneered with ebony, and
marked out top and bottom with
playing squares of ivory. The stand
and sledge are of ebony, most
tastefully embellished with gold
on the 'drums' beneath the lion
paws and the braces which
strengthen the joints. The lion
claws are ivory. Inscriptions in
yellow paint along both sides, and
at the end where the drawer enters
the box, contain very full titularies
of Tutankhamun, with many
epithets, including the unusual
'beloved of all the gods, may he be
healthy for ever', a significant
variant of 'may he live for ever'.
Board games were much played in
ancient Egypt, and one in
particular, *senet*, was seen to be
played in the afterlife. In the
preliminaries of Spell 17 of the
Book of the Dead playing at *senet* is
listed as an activity which would
be beneficial to the deceased, and
in some tombs of the New
Kingdom the deceased and his
wife are shown playing.

DECORATED GAMING BOX

(CARTER 593, J.D'E. 62059;
LENGTH 27.5 CM, WIDTH 9 CM,
HEIGHT 5.8 CM)

The playing pieces belonging to the ebony gaming box described above were not found, and Carter deduced that they might have been made of gold, and therefore convenient things to be 'pocketed' by thieves. Ivory gaming pieces were found which may have belonged to this less distinguished box, also found in the Annexe. It has interesting features, and when new was probably a very attractive object. It is made of an ordinary soft wood embellished with ivory. On both sides are plaques carrying floral designs, lightly scored and stained in part with black and red color. The playing surfaces are covered with ivory, divided into squares by a material Carter described as stucco, then covered with gold foil.

There are two drawers fitted with ivory plates and little ebony bolts which engage in gold staples. Like the previous box, this one could be used for two different games. One employed the full surface marked out with 30 squares; this is *senet*. The other side is marked out for a game formerly known as *tjau*; this view is now thought to be incorrect. At one end are three rows of four squares each, with the central row extended by eight more squares. There remains much debate about how these two games were played.

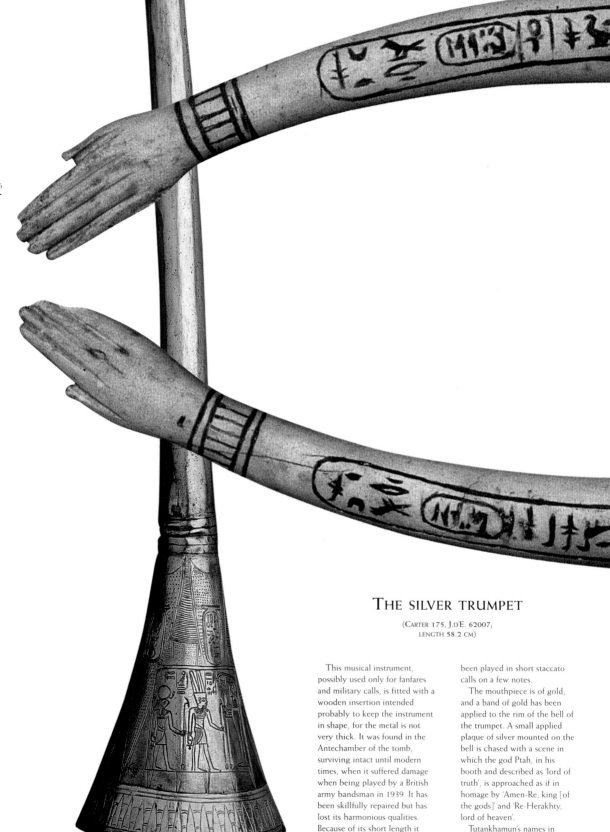

THE SILVER TRUMPET

(CARTER 175, J.D'E. 62007;
LENGTH 58.2 CM)

This musical instrument, possibly used only for fanfares and military calls, is fitted with a wooden insertion intended probably to keep the instrument in shape, for the metal is not very thick. It was found in the Antechamber of the tomb, surviving intact until modern times, when it suffered damage when being played by a British army bandsman in 1939. It has been skillfully repaired but has lost its harmonious qualities. Because of its short length it could never have had a great range of notes, and may have been played in short staccato calls on a few notes.

The mouthpiece is of gold, and a band of gold has been applied to the rim of the bell of the trumpet. A small applied plaque of silver mounted on the bell is chased with a scene in which the god Ptah, in his booth and described as 'lord of truth', is approached as if in homage by 'Amen-Re, king [of the gods]' and 'Re-Herakhty, lord of heaven'.

Tutankhamun's names in cartouches are also inscribed higher up the bell.

CLAPPERS OF TIYE AND MERITATEN

(CARTER 620(13), J.D'E. 62064;
LENGTH 15.7 CM)

Rhythm is an important ingredient in oriental music, and, as far as one can judge, perhaps as important as melody in ancient Egypt. Groups of musicians are shown with various stringed instruments and kinds of flute; drums, castenets and tambourines were used for rhythm, along with hand-clapping. Many sets of ivory clappers have been found, often shaped to follow the curve of an elephant's tusk; they end in carved hands. It is not thought that they could have been robust enough to stand much clapping together, and they may have been rattled rather than struck together.

This pair, found in the Annexe and made of ivory is of unusual interest because of its inscriptions. They read like extended cartouches, stating 'the king's great wife Tiye, may she live, the king's daughter Meritaten'. Tiye's name is enclosed in a further cartouche. The presence of these clappers in Tutankhamun's tomb remains unexplained, but they are scarcely 'heirlooms', as is sometimes claimed.

THE BRONZE TRUMPET

(CARTER 50GG, J.D'E. 62008;
LENGTH 49.4 CM)

'It was probably the most thrilling experience I shall have as a trumpet player'. So said a modern instrumentalist of the first rank. But it was 'not exactly melodious'. This instrument, almost 10 centimeters shorter than the silver trumpet, has an even smaller range of possible notes. The bronze is in part overlaid with gold, and the mouth is formed of a cylindrical sleeve with a silver ring at the end, fixed to the tube of the trumpet. The wooden insert is painted at the bell-end to represent a lotus flower.

The bell has on the outside an inscribed panel in which Tutankhamun is shown wearing the blue crown and carrying a hooked scepter, the crook of royal authority. He stands before a booth containing the mummiform figure of Ptah 'the Great One, south-of-his-wall, lord of truth, creator of all that is'. The king is offered 'life' by Amon-Re 'king of all the gods', who is supported by Re-Herakhty 'the good god, lord of gold'.

DECORATED STAFF

(CARTER 227A, J.D'E. 61756;
LENGTH 108 CM)

Stick contests, friendly and passionate, are still very common in Upper Egyptian villages, and there are few countrymen who do not carry a sturdy staff which may be turned to several purposes. Stick 'games' are shown occasionally in tomb scenes, and it is evident that sticks were important personal possessions. Carter thought that Tutankhamun must have collected sticks as a hobby, so many examples were found in the tomb. Many are simple, but others are of unusual shapes, embellished with figures in the round and decorated in such elaborate ways that they could scarcely be used for anything very active.

This stick, for example, would stand very little rough use. It is curved at one end in a manner of sticks sometimes held by officials and even soldiers. The end is shod with a gold ferrule.

The bands of decoration, of great variety and intricacy, are in addition to gold – the predictable material – made up of marquetry carried out, not in various woods but in different colored barks and even the iridescent wings of beetles.

STAFF WITH INVOCATION OF AMUN

(CARTER 204, J.D'E. 61667; LENGTH 145 CM)

This staff was found along with a large number of others in the Antechamber, many among the litter of chariot parts. Their variety is considerable, and some are most elaborately decorated with gold incrustation and inlays.

This example is relatively simple, but gorgeously simple. It is completely covered with gold foil, with just a little tasteful decoration at its top and beneath the hand-hold, in inlaid glass. There is also a text in gold against a blue glass background which states 'the good god, son of Amun, King of Upper and Lower Egypt, lord of the two lands, Nebkheperure, son of Re, of his body, his beloved, lord of diadems, Tutankhamun [ruler in] southern [Heliopolis], beloved of Amun, given life for ever and ever'.

In all cases where the name Amun occurs, it has replaced Aten. Presumably it was a stick made early in the reign, and 'corrected' for the burial.

STAFF WITH GOLD FIGURE OF KING

(CARTER 235A, J.D'E. 61665; LENGTH 131 CM
HEIGHT OF FIGURE 9 CM)

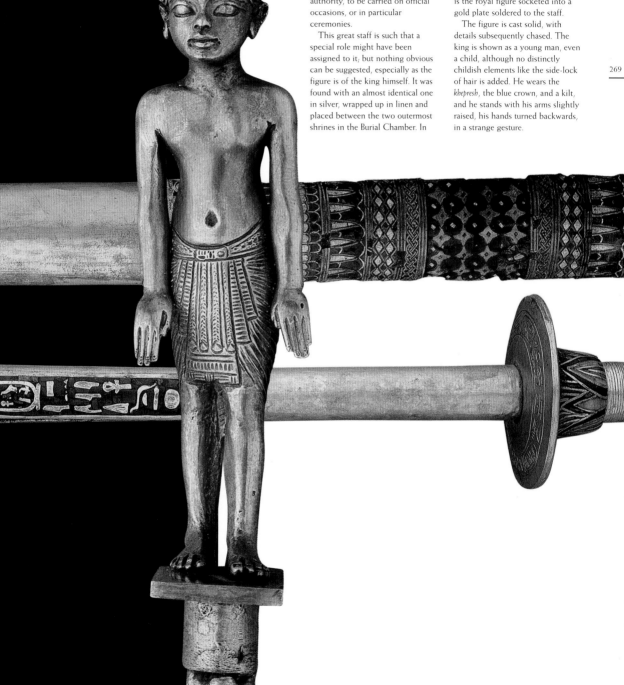

Many of the staves found in the tomb were just instruments of authority, to be carried on official occasions, or in particular ceremonies.

This great staff is such that a special role might have been assigned to it; but nothing obvious can be suggested, especially as the figure is of the king himself. It was found with an almost identical one in silver, wrapped up in linen and placed between the two outermost shrines in the Burial Chamber. In this case the shaft is tubular, of gold and hollow throughout. At the top is the royal figure socketed into a gold plate soldered to the staff.

The figure is cast solid, with details subsequently chased. The king is shown as a young man, even a child, although no distinctly childish elements like the side-lock of hair is added. He wears the *khepresh*, the blue crown, and a kilt, and he stands with his arms slightly raised, his hands turned backwards, in a strange gesture.

STICK WITH A LIBYAN CAPTIVE

(CARTER 100A, J.D'E. 61734;
LENGTH 109 CM)

The three sticks with handles shaped in the form of bound captives were found in a long box in the Antechamber of Tutankhamun's tomb, along with bows, bow-cases and other long objects.

The sticks illustrated here all carry Tutankhamun's prenomen, and may therefore be confidently assigned to his reign. But it must be doubted that he ever saw foreign captives brought before him in triumph by a victorious general, although his commander-in-chief, Horemheb, may have started the campaign to regain those parts of the Egyptian region of influence which had been lost in the reign of Akhenaten. Libya at this time posed little threat, but that did not prevent the inclusion of a Libyan prisoner on one of the sticks. The Libyan is almost entirely gilded, apart from his feet and hands which have been added in ebony. The head, although on such a small scale, is wonderfully realized, with much significant detail. At the other end of the stick there is a blue glass ferrule.

STICK WITH A NUBIAN CAPTIVE

(CARTER 48B, J.D'E. 61735;
LENGTH 102 CM)

271

This stick is almost identical to the last, except that a Nubian replaces the Libyan as part of the handle.

Sticks with figures like those found in the tomb are unknown from elsewhere, and no special idea for their function can be offered. Undoubtedly they offer humiliation to Pharaoh's traditional enemies.

Nubia was the land most closely linked to Egypt; the Nile was their common river, and from the earliest times trade and warfare distinguished relations between the two. Nubia was Kush, and Kush could scarcely be mentioned without the adjective 'vile'. The Nubian depicted on this stick was distinctly black, and the blackest of woods, ebony, was used to fashion the ungilded parts – feet, hands and head. The last is very finely carved, with characteristic features of the black inhabitants of Nubia, and the tight curly hair. A blue glass ferrule ends the stick.

STICK WITH ASIATIC AND NUBIAN CAPTIVE

(CARTER 50UU, J.D'E. 61732;
LENGTH 104 CM)

Egypt in antiquity was not easily invaded, protected by the sea and the deserts. In its isolation it was a privileged land, and for many centuries it escaped the turmoil and destruction brought about by the movements of peoples which affected Asia Minor in particular. For almost a millennium historic Egypt had no serious enemies, and it did not seek to extend its rule over neighbouring countries. Yet the Nubians to the south, the Libyans to the west, and the Asiatics (not always differentiated by race) to the east were seen to be the traditional enemies, potential if not active. Consequently in the depiction of the myth of royal power images of these peoples were used with predictable regularity, being destroyed, dragged as prisoners, or, as here on the handle of a stick, bound and crushed by the royal hand.

The stick is gilded, the figures of the Asiatic and the Nubian are carved in the round to make the handle. The exposed body areas of the Nubian are inlaid in ebony, and those of the Asiatic in ivory.

Weapons

One of the major royal images of the New Kingdom was the king as warrior. He was the gallant champion of his country; nobody was braver or stronger.

After the rather pacific Amarna interlude the warlike image was revived for Tutankhamun: as warrior king he is best seen in the miniature paintings of foreign campaigns and hunting on the painted box found in the Antechamber. There is, however, no reason to believe that the young king himself took part in Asiatic or Nubian campaigns, but he may well have joined in the hunt in his chariot.

Nevertheless, the king had to be properly equipped, and in his tomb were placed many

272–273 Part of the decoration on the inside of the body of Tutankhamun's chariot. The figures here represent bound captives, Nubians and Asiatics; they are carved on a base of gesso-plaster and then gilded.

weapons, some of which were of small size, some fully capable of being used effectively, some designed for hunting, not battle, and some for ceremonial purposes. Most spectacular were the chariots: two very grand and probably ceremonial, one not so grand but still highly decorated, and three of lighter construction, probably for everyday use. The king in his chariot is usually shown drawing a bow, and bows were lavishly provided. There were fourteen of the ordinary kind, known as 'self' bows, and about thirty composite bows of complicated structure; several hundreds of arrows and arrowheads were also found, as well as quivers and bow cases, one of them most elaborately decorated.

The throw sticks or boomerangs found in the tomb are mostly of ceremonial kinds, too grand for use in the hunting field. So too are the so-called openwork shields, which could scarcely have withstood a powerful blow. The *khepesh* swords, used more like clubs than cutting weapons, were of Asiatic design, as were the composite bows mentioned above. Asia contributed much to the arsenal available to the Egyptians. Asia, and most probably the Hittites, provided the iron used for one of the two daggers found on Tutankhamun's body. The iron dagger is not now seen as so wonderful a piece as the golden dagger, but the use of iron on such a scale in Egypt at this date is unique, and this dagger would have been more wonderful to the Egyptians than the gold.

State chariot

(Carter 120, J.d'E. 61989; width of body 105 cm,
depth 46 cm, diameter of wheels 90 cm,
length of axle 216 cm, length of pole 250 cm)

274

Of the four chariots found in the Antechamber, dismantled and in disarray, were two which were designated state chariots by Carter. There has been some confusion about which he described as 'the first', and which 'the second'. A careful comparison of notes, descriptions and photographs establishes that the one illustrated here is Carter's first state chariot. It is lavishly gilded and would have made a gorgeous sight when driven about in the bright Egyptian sunlight.

The most striking part is the body, within which the king would have stood. The framework is constructed of artificially bent wood with thin wood sidings covered with gesso-plaster and gilding. The floor is of leather thong mesh originally covered with an animal skin, possibly leopard, mat and several layers of linen cloth. The decoration of the outside of the body is mostly of a running scroll pattern, with a central panel containing the prenomen, name and Horus name of the king; above, a winged sun-disk, and at the sides *uraei* with the crowns and heraldic plants of Upper and Lower Egypt; beneath, a panel with lily flower decoration.

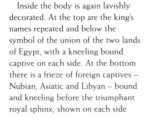

Inside the body is again lavishly decorated. At the top are the king's names repeated and below the symbol of the union of the two lands of Egypt, with a kneeling bound captive on each side. At the bottom there is a frieze of foreign captives – Nubian, Asiatic and Libyan – bound and kneeling before the triumphant royal sphinx, shown on each side

and trampling further enemies. This frieze is bold and fluid in conception, and executed with great liveliness.

The six-spoked wheels are ingeniously made of artificially bent wood, the 'tires' made of leather. Gilding, lavishly applied, somewhat restricts the discovery of precise details of construction.

The pole of the chariot and the yoke which rested on the necks of the two chariot horses are also made of artificially bent wood and gilded.

The terminals of the yoke are carved in the forms of an Asiatic and a Nubian captive.

Beneath the chariot is shown the head of the domestic god Bes.

OPENWORK SHIELD
WITH SEATED KING

(CARTER 488B, J.D'E. 61578; HEIGHT 74 CM, WIDTH 50 CM)

The coronation and reign of Tutankhamun provide the theme for the openwork scene on this shield. It has suffered some damage, but elements of the whole design can be reconstructed without much uncertainty. The gilding here is not of red gold.

The king is shown seated on an elaborate throne, the space between the legs filled with the heraldic device signifying the union of Upper and Lower Egypt, as can be seen in the so-called ecclesiastical throne from the tomb, though it is partly torn away. The king wears a ceremonial dress with 'cape' and broad collar; he holds the crook and the flail of royal authority, and on his head is a circlet of *uraeus*-serpents and the red crown with flying streamers. The tip of the crown and of its curled extension are broken away, as are the wings of the sun-disk set in the top of the curve of the shield.

Also broken away is one of two notched palm branches which closely flanked the king; the one on

the right is complete, and shows at its bottom the tadpole, indicating one hundred thousand, and the *shen*-sign. These palm branches signify long reign for the king. The tadpole and *shen* are all that is left of the second palm branch. Two ostrich-feather fans form the outer limits of the scene, and between the right-hand fan and the palm branch is a panel with a text: 'His Majesty appears within Thebes, upon the platform for foretelling the wonders of the possessor of power, Nebkheperure, given life'.

The king is therefore shown at the time of coronation with all the promise of his reign lying ahead. The scene is placed on a large basket-sign here indicating 'festival', below which two plovers with trapped wings and raised hand-shaped claws offer adoration, and pray for children and a long life for the king. These are the *rekhyt*-birds, standing for the common people of Egypt, trapped but loyal.

OPENWORK SHIELD
WITH KING AS SPHINX

(CARTER 379A, J.D'E. 61577; HEIGHT 89 CM, WIDTH 54 CM)

Four functional shields were found in the Annexe of the tomb; these were solid, with animal skins covering the wood. There were also four non-functional openwork shields which Carter considered to be ceremonial. Whether this identification is correct or not – they would certainly not have served a useful purpose in battle – they have the shape of shields, and the scenes on some of them are distinctly bellicose.

This example is full of warlike symbolism, vaunting the royal power, and the text on the right confirms this purpose. Here the king is shown as a sphinx in active role, trampling two prone enemies beneath his paws. Usually one

Asiatic and one Nubian would be expected as the representatives of conquered nations; but the two here have black bodies, and seem to be Nubian, although they wear Egyptian-style kilts, which are gilded. Across the bottom of the shield runs an extended sign for 'foreign country'. The sphinx is shown very formally, with upraised tail and carefully placed paws. The royal head wears the *nemes*-headdress, and the double crown of Upper and Lower Egypt.

The panel in front of the sphinx identifies him as Tutankhamun, and describes him as 'the good god, who tramples the foreign lands and smites the great ones of all foreign lands, possessor of power like the

son of Nut, valiant like Monthu, visiting Thebes'. Monthu, the old Theban god, whose shrine was preeminent in Thebes before the advent of Amun, was seen as a war-god, and is often shown as a falcon hovering over the king in battle. Here a falcon behind the head of the sphinx holds the *shen*-sign of universal power in its talons; it is alighting on, or hovering over, an ostrich-feather fan. The falcon is not named, but it is reasonable to identify him as Monthu. In the circle of the shield at the top is the winged sun-disk, manifestation of Horus of Behdet.

The gilding on this shield is carried out in red gold, which gives the piece a somewhat angry aspect.

276

OPENWORK SHIELD WITH THE KING SLAYING LIONS

(CARTER 379B, J.D'E. 61576;
HEIGHT 88 CM, WIDTH 55 CM)

The scene in this openwork shield shows Tutankhamun as the destructive king in pursuit of the safety of his realm. The central feature is a figure of the king himself leaning forward to grasp two lions by their tails. In his right hand he wields aloft a *khepesh* sword with which he will smite and kill the lions, which symbolize the enemies of Egypt. A panel of text in front of the king's head expresses his prowess; 'the good god, strong of arm, powerful of heart, like Monthu visiting Thebes… who fights lions and smites wild cattle…' It is the traditional image of a warlike king, but here it is lions he smites, not Asiatics and Nubians. He is shown wearing the Nubian wig and, perhaps surprisingly, an *atef*-crown. The winged sun-disk in the curve at the top of the shield is Horus of Behdet, protective deity and one with whom the king may be identified. Behind the king's raised arm is perched the vulture goddess Nekhbet, also with wings outstretched in protection. She wears the white crown of Upper Egypt and has the royal flail emerging from her back. She is raised high on a basket on top of a clump of papyrus plants which properly stands for the North, the Delta, the realm of Nekhbet's fellow protective deity, the cobra Wadjyt.

GILDED MACE

(CARTER 233, J.D'E. 61623;
LENGTH 82 CM)

One of the earliest royal images from Dynastic Egypt occurs on a small ivory tablet from the tomb of Den, a First Dynasty king, at Abydos. It shows the king standing astride a fallen enemy, and on the point of wielding a mace with a pear-shaped head to crush the wretched man's skull. The text says 'first occasion of smiting the East'. The enemy is the traditional Asiatic, and the scene was to become traditional also – the king grabbing his fallen enemy by the hair and delivering the *coup de grâce*. It is found as late as Roman times, especially on the pylons of temples. The two guardian statues of Tutankhamun in the Antechamber of his tomb show him holding his mace at the ready. They are of gilded wood, just like this example. It is one of a pair found between the two outermost shrines in the Burial Chamber.

MODEL THROW-STICK

(CARTER 54D, J.D'E. 61615A;
LENGTH 40.5 CM)

The great variety of sticks, throw-sticks and clubs in the tomb demonstrates the range of possible weapons used in battle and for sport by the ancient Egyptians. There can be little doubt that the majority of these angled pieces of wood were obtained by choosing naturally bent pieces of wood, which could be further shaped to produce the desired result. Many may have been used as simple clubs, the bent shapes making them more effective than straight sticks.

The many ritual or ceremonial copies of throw-sticks and boomerangs mostly take the gently curved shape of the examples illustrated here. Two very similar ones were found in a chest in the Antechamber, and at first Carter believed that they were made from electrum. This is not the case; they are of wood overlaid with gesso-plaster and then gilded, in this case with red gold. Both ends are tipped with blue faience, one shaped and marked as a lotus flower. The king's name is inscribed on the shaft.

CEREMONIAL THROW-STICK

(CARTER 620(5), J.D'E. 61612;
LENGTH 50.5 CM)

Large numbers of real throw-sticks and boomerangs were found in the Annexe. Studies have shown that some at least of these weapons had the ability to return when thrown, but many were in a sense disposable, until possible later retrieval.

Throw-sticks were much used in the sport of fowling; they are often shown used by tomb-owners in the ritual activity of bird-hunting in the marshes. Some of the throw-sticks found on the floor of the Annexe were never intended for actual use, like this handsome example.

It is a simple baton of ivory, the tusk shape allowing such a form to be made with ease. Each end has a gold foil cap, and the shaft has a series of zones of elaborate decoration mostly made of a variety of colored barks, skillfully applied. A finely formed hieroglyphic text on the ivory gives the short titulary 'the good god, lord of the two lands, Nebkheperure, living for ever'.

CEREMONIAL SICKLE

(CARTER 561, J.D'E. 61264;
LENGTH 27 CM)

The sickle was the implement commonly used for the cutting of barley and emmer-wheat. It was shown in vignettes in the Book of the Dead, in which the deceased works in the fields in the afterlife, and this fine example, although a model, was in the tomb presumably for posthumous use. Actual sickles have survived from antiquity, and they are very much of the shape of this piece. The handle is set eccentrically, as here, so that the tool could be manipulated more efficiently. The teeth of real sickles are serrated flints. This model, perhaps a ceremonial sickle, was found in the Annexe. It is made of wood, and has applied decoration in gold and electrum foil, with bands of varied designs of colored glass and calcite. The teeth are made of red and blue glass. An inscription on the gold foil gives Tutankhamun's titulary and calls him 'beloved of Hu', this deity being the embodiment of food.

BOW CASE

(CARTER 335, J.D'E. 61502;
LENGTH 153 CM)

Three composite bows of the kind introduced into Egypt from Asia about 250 years before the reign of Tutankhamun were found in this extraordinary box, which stood on its end in a corner of the Treasury. It is made of wood, covered with linen and plaster, and decorated all over with several series of scenes and designs in delicate marquetry of colored barks and green stained leather. Each end is in the form of a faience lion head, and there is a panel of gold on each side. These panels carry embossed scenes of the king in his chariot engaged in hunting with the bow. On both sides also are marquetry panels with scenes of dogs and animals in the chase, a great variety of wild life being depicted. Other panels show the king as a standing sphinx harassing Asiatic and Nubian captives. There are many zones of abstract decoration, and substantial inscriptions along the edges and between the various scenes, giving the king's titulary and vaunting his prowess as a king of action.

STICK WITH FINE DECORATION

(CARTER 50JJ, J.D'E. 61673;
LENGTH 116 CM)

Among the sticks found in the Antechamber there were several distinguished by exceptional decoration. This stick in particular is embellished with remarkable bands of geometrical and natural motifs, interspersed by lines of inscription carried out in very fine granulation. The motifs, in gold, include floral and insect elements and a variety of geometrical designs. The short texts encircling the stick contain conventional royal titles and the prenomen and nomen cartouches of the king. The long text which runs down the length of the stick announces 'the appearance by the king himself to take firm action with his forces'.

STICK WITH GILDED HANDLE

(CARTER 98, J.D'E. 61730;
LENGTH 56.2 CM)

This fairly ordinary wooden throw-stick has little to distinguish it until the handle is examined closely. It is of gold plate, embellished with texts, abstract designs and small scenes, all carried out in granulation, some being of exceptional delicacy. Even the hieroglyphs and cartouches in the two bands of inscription are worked in granulation. There are two wide zones of lozenge decoration and two narrow zones of rosettes. Most remarkable are the two zones below the upper line of text, and above the lower line of text. Both contain desert scenes with animals and plants: chases involving tiny hares, ostriches, dogs and antelopes, all worked in the finest granulation. This was not a throw-away throw-stick.

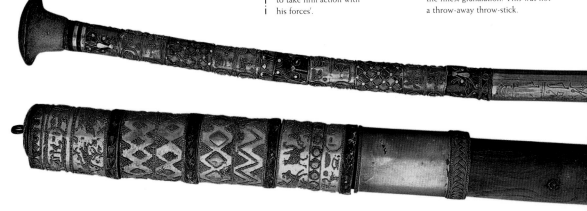

IRON DAGGER AND SHEATH

(CARTER 256K, J.D'E. 61585;
LENGTH OF DAGGER 34.2 CM)

Two daggers were included among the bandages of Tutankhamun's mummy. This iron example may not be quite so striking artistically as the gold one, but culturally it has great significance. Many centuries were to pass before Egypt would enter the Iron Age, but here is a weapon of a metal that was already being used by some Asiatic peoples like the Hittites. In the tomb it was clearly as highly regarded as the gold dagger.

It was found lying along the mummy's right thigh; the metal was black, with only a few small touches of rust. The blade is not decorated, but the handle is embellished with zones of gold granulation arranged in chevron and diamond designs, separated by bands of cloisonné inlays of glass and semiprecious stones. The pommel is made of rock-crystal, carefully shaped but not turned, as Carter suggested. The gold sheath has a feather pattern on one side with the head of a desert fox at the tip. The reverse side has a repeated design of open lily flowers contained within a rope border.

BRONZE *KHEPESH*

(CARTER 582A, J.D'E. 61588;
LENGTH 59.7 CM)

The serious involvement of the Egyptians with their Asiatic neighbors in what is called the Hyksos Period, just before the Eighteenth Dynasty, introduced them to many new weapons, methods of warfare and techniques of metal-working. Weapons of this kind were undoubtedly of Asiatic origin, but they were readily adopted by the Egyptians, and advanced processes in the production of cast bronze were employed for their manufacture.

This kind of sword was called *khepesh* in Egyptian, often translated as 'scimitar'. The scimitar, however, was a slashing, cutting weapon, while the *khepesh*, never apparently forged with a sharp edge, was used as an efficient clubbing weapon. Kings in the New Kingdom are often shown wielding the *khepesh*.

This fine example, which is cast as a single piece, is modestly decorated with sunk lines along the blade and a lily flower below the handle, which is inlaid with ebony.

GOLD DAGGER AND SHEATH

(CARTER 256DD, J.D'E. 61584;
LENGTH OF DAGGER 31.9 CM)

This gold dagger was found tucked under a girdle at the mummy's waist. It is brilliant, and could be classified more as a jewel than an offensive weapon. The blade is of hardened gold, decorated simply with a palmette design and two chased lines. The handle has areas of elaborate decoration, of the standard of the finest goldsmiths. The inlays are of semiprecious stones and glass, and geometrical designs in gold granulation. The flaring pommel carries figures of falcons, and on its top is a design of lily flowers enclosing the two cartouches of Tutankhamun. The sheath is decorated on both sides differently: on one side, probably the front, a feather or *rishi*-design is carried out in repoussé work with glass and semiprecious stone inlays; at the bottom is the head of a desert fox or fennic, and there is a line of lilies at the top. The reverse side has scenes principally of the desert hunt: dogs and lions attack ibex, calves, bulls and antelope, the figures being in repoussé work.

Boots

282–283 A fully rigged sailing boat from the Treasury of the tomb. It has a central cabin and two kiosks at the stern and prow, and two steering oars. Its sail is lowered but not properly furled.

In describing the many boats found in the Treasury and the Annexe of Tutankhamun's tomb, Carter made a good and reasoned attempt to describe the construction of the actual boats of which models had been found. Nothing, however, provides better evidence than the real thing, and no boat has been more informative than the great river craft found by the pyramid of Cheops in 1954. Here was a real boat, made of real cedar planks, fastened with ropes and ties, one which had been used in the lifetime of Cheops, and which could be used by him in his afterlife.

Tutankhamun and his celestial court were to have no shortage of craft for the many journeys to be undertaken after death. Egypt lived by the Nile, and most activities involving travel made use of boats. Of the thirty-five boats from the tomb, eighteen were in the Treasury, and were clearly seen to be 'wanted on voyage' to the afterlife. To that end, they were all pointing to the West – the direction in which the blessed dead were to travel. The rest of the boats were retrieved from the Annexe, where they were jumbled up along with a great miscellany of objects, and not in the best of condition.

As model boats held little attraction for tomb robbers, none were probably taken, and it may be thought that a complete flotilla of royal craft was recovered. There were boats for all occasions in the Treasury: one papyrus skiff for recreational trips among the reed beds of the Delta; two boats with in-turned papyrus-formed prows and sterns, for night-time lunar travel; four solar barks for day-time journeys with the sun-god Re, with up-turned lotus-flower prows and sterns, a gilded throne for the king, and two steering posts; eight barges with no sails, but with steering oars, large stepped cabins with doors and windows, and small cabins or shelters fore and aft, all gaily painted. Most impressive were three sailing boats found complete with rigging and sails. These also had large central cabins with steps for loading cargo, and small open kiosks fore and aft in which the king or the captain could sit.

All the craft are made of solid wood covered with gesso-plaster and painted according to function with simple or elaborate patterns.

283

TRANSPORT BARGE

(CARTER 309, J.D'E. 61335;
LENGTH 110 CM)

A royal progression by river would have needed a very substantial flotilla of boats, many of which would be used by the Court officials and other staff, and for the transport of materials necessary for the comfort of all. Among the boats of Tutankhamun's fleet were seven craft usually called barges, with no sails but with double steering oars. This example, found in the Treasury, and pointing West, is characteristic of the group. Its principal feature is a double roofed central cabin with three windows on each side and a door at the back end. Both roof tops have cavetto-cornices, simply painted. The whole of the cabin is otherwise decorated with checker patterns which may represent textile hangings or the painted woven wicker superstructures of actual barges. At prow and stern there are smaller cabins or kiosks which probably served as shelters for members of the crew. The hull is also painted with checker and chevron patterns. It has been noted that some of the yellow decoration is carried out with orpiment, an arsenical natural material sometimes used in ancient Egypt.

SOLAR BARK

(CARTER 311, J.D'E. 61344;
LENGTH 155 CM)

The king's destiny in the afterlife was closely bound up with two deities, Osiris and Re. The former was the personification of the dead, and his role in the posthumous future of the king was one which post-dated that of the sun-god Re. The king's expectations were clear as far as Re was concerned, but quite distinct from what could be expected by non-royal persons. One of the principal expectations for the king was to join Re in the heavens, and to accompany him on his daily journey across the sky. The bark in which he travelled was of specific shape for the daytime; it had a raised prow and an elegantly re-curved stern. The form, like those of so many Egyptian boats, is derived from primitive craft made of papyrus for travelling about the marshes, and even on the Nile itself. This boat is one of several solar boats found in the Treasury with its bow pointing to the West. It is of wood, with some gilding at both ends, and painted decoration along its length. Texts on the bulkheads, fore and aft, give the two cartouches of Tutankhamun with standard epithets.

SOLAR BARK

(CARTER 307, J.D'E. 61346;
LENGTH 148 CM)

The destiny of the king in the solar bark with Re is one of the oldest royal beliefs of Egypt. An utterance in the Pyramid Texts states: 'The reed-floats of the sky are set down for Re so that he may cross on them to the horizon, to the place where the gods were born, and where he was born with them. The reed-floats of the sky are set down for this king so that he may cross on them to the horizon, to the place where the gods were born, and where he was born with them'. In an extract from the Book of the Dead inscribed on the door of the second shrine in the Burial Chamber, the Osiris Tutankhamun is said to 'go forward in peace, sailing the barge of Re'.

This solar bark – the reed-float of the Pyramid Texts – is very similar to the one illustrated on the left. Like it, it has one throne placed in the middle. Clearly the king would be on his own in the sky 'sailing the bark of Re'. On the gilded stern and prow are inscribed Tutankhamun's names with standard titles.

Like the other boats in the Treasury, it was placed facing West.

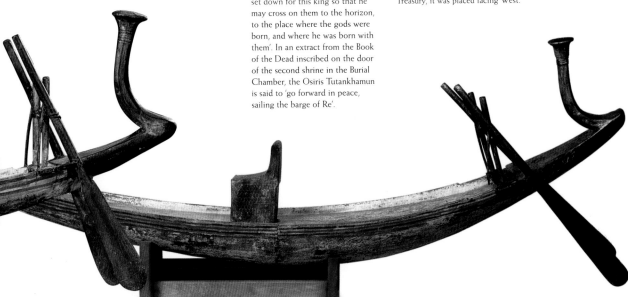

Furniture and Boxes

Culturally one can come very close to the ancient Egyptians through furniture. The best products of the ancient cabinet-makers may not quite come up to the work of the French *ébénistes* of the eighteenth century, but there is nothing primitive about them. The shapes of chairs, beds, stools and chests could all bear reproduction today.

Tutankhamun's tomb contained a great quantity of furniture, some of which would only be suitable for the very great house or palace. There were six beds, low to the ground with headboards usually decorated with figures of the household deities, Thoeris and Bes; one can be folded up, and was presumably used in travelling; its hinges are of copper. With the beds go head-rests, used to raise the head up. Of the six chairs, the Golden Throne is outstanding; but scarcely less striking in an opulent way is the ecclesiastical throne, made in the form of a grand folding chair.

The other chairs were all splendidly designed, and one is of small size and possibly used by the king in childhood. For informal sitting the Egyptians used stools, and the twelve examples from the tomb cover most of the types in use in the New Kingdom, including three-legged stools, most useful on irregular surfaces. The seats of most of the stools are coved – curved in both directions – to seat a person comfortably.

The chests and boxes from the tomb range from the painted box with remarkable miniature paintings to simple chests for domestic storage. There were more than fifty found, many containing precious objects. They provide a wonderful conspectus of the skills of the Egyptian craftsman. The techniques of joinery are precise, and even modest materials could be transformed by the application of veneers of ivory and ebony, of gilding, of inlays of faience, glass and semi-precious stones, and of simple or masterful painting.

286 A vignette from the Gilded Shrine showing Tutankhamun seated on a throne. It has a low back, a cushion, and sides decorated with a scaled or rishi pattern.

287 Gilded wooden casket placed in the Antechamber. It is richly decorated with colored faience inlays. The sloping lid could be secured with two violet faience knobs and a sealed cord.

THE GOLDEN THRONE

(CARTER 91, J.D'E. 62028;
HEIGHT 104 CM, WIDTH 53 CM,
DEPTH 65 CM)

For many people this throne, along with Tutankhamun's golden mask, typifies the beauty and opulence of the tomb. And yet its presence in the tomb raises questions which have no obvious answers. For example, why was it tucked away, covered with a piece of old linen, beneath the Thoeris couch in the Antechamber? It was as if it had been slipped surreptitiously into the tomb. But many other fine pieces were similarly stuffed into odd corners, and given little honor in their placings. One special reason provides part of the answer for why it seems to have been smuggled into the tomb.

The clue lies in the great scene on the back of the throne.

What is depicted there is not something to be associated with the court in Thebes or Memphis, but something that belongs to El-Amarna and the later years of the reign of Akhenaten. The king sits on a throne within a kiosk with floral side pillars and a cornice of *uraei* and flowers; he is being anointed by his queen with perfumed ointment. He wears an elaborate form of the *atef*-crown, and she a feathered headdress with an *uraeus* circlet and lyre-shaped horns.

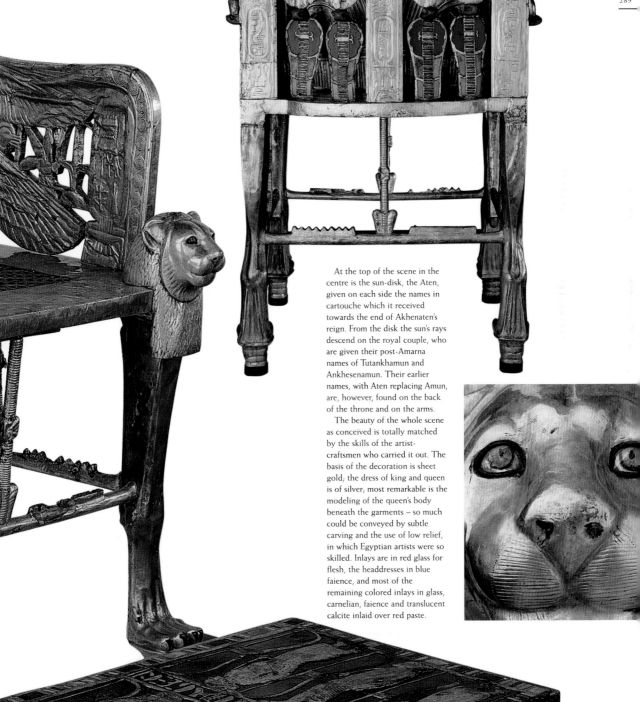

At the top of the scene in the centre is the sun-disk, the Aten, given on each side the names in cartouche which it received towards the end of Akhenaten's reign. From the disk the sun's rays descend on the royal couple, who are given their post-Amarna names of Tutankhamun and Ankhesenamun. Their earlier names, with Aten replacing Amun, are, however, found on the back of the throne and on the arms.

The beauty of the whole scene as conceived is totally matched by the skills of the artist-craftsmen who carried it out. The basis of the decoration is sheet gold; the dress of king and queen is of silver; most remarkable is the modeling of the queen's body beneath the garments – so much could be conveyed by subtle carving and the use of low relief, in which Egyptian artists were so skilled. Inlays are in red glass for flesh, the headdresses in blue faience, and most of the remaining colored inlays in glass, carnelian, faience and translucent calcite inlaid over red paste.

THE GILDED SHRINE

(CARTER 108, J.D'E, 61481; HEIGHT 50.5 CM, WIDTH 26.5 CM,
DEPTH 32 CM, LENGTH OF SLEDGE 48 CM)

In Tutankhamun's tomb there were
a number of pieces each of which on
its own might well have been
considered a good return for the
years of labour endured by Carter.
This shrine easily falls into this top
category. It contains a little gilded
stand to hold a figure, probably of
gold, and of a god. But which god?
The scenes and texts on the shrine
give no sure clue. It might be
suggested, however, that the shrine
was a private point of devotion,
placed within the king's
appartments; it was found in the
Antechamber, not in the most holy
parts of the tomb.

It is in the form of the Upper
Egyptian shrine, originally of the
vulture goddess Nekhbet; and suitably
there are fourteen forms of the
goddess with outstretched wings on
the shrine's roof. All the decoration of
the shrine – and the whole is covered
with decoration – is carried out in
gold foil fixed by gesso-plaster and
linen reinforcement to the plain
wooden shell of the shrine.

The scenes are wonderful examples of repoussé-work and chasing; they provide a mixture of semi-formal, ceremonial and private domestic scenes. On one side the king with Ankhesenamun hunts birds: above, in a papyrus skiff, below, seated on a folding stool with the queen handing him his next arrow. On the other side are intimate scenes of the queen offering gifts to the king and receiving a drink from him in her open cupped hand. On the back of the shrine the queen gently touches the king, bringing a cone of scented unguent; below, she presents him with jubilee festivals and millions of years of reign. Both leaves of the door, and the inside of one leaf, carry further scenes of the queen presenting various ritual objects to the king. The gold from the inner side of the left leaf has been lost, taken presumably in antiquity.

The doors are fastened with two silver bolts fitting into little gold staples, and the shrine stands on a wooden sledge covered with silver foil.

The Painted Box

(Carter 21, J.d'E. 61467; length 61 cm,
width 43 cm, height 44.5 cm)

One of the objects which especially caught the attention of the excavators in the Antechamber was this box, which Carter called the 'painted casket'. And this emphasis in spite of all the dazzling gold on every side! But Carter was first and foremost an artist, and it was as an artist that he looked at and appreciated the remarkable miniature paintings which embellished what was in other respects a fairly ordinary box. He could see the skill of the artist who had painted the scenes in tempera on a plaster ground, and he could appreciate the use of color and the attention to fine detail. No brushes were available to the ancient artist, apart from rushes, chewed and trimmed; and yet, as Carter wrote: 'a magnifying glass is essential to a due appreciation of the smaller details, such as the stippling of the lions' coats, or the decoration of the horses' trappings'.

The surviving contents of the box suggested that it had been used primarily to store articles of the young king's wardrobe, and it is difficult to see what relationship there was between what was in the box and what was painted on it. There are four principal scenes proclaiming the manly prowess of the king: two show him as the great conqueror in battle, and two as the fearless huntsman in the desert. On one side Tutankhamun in his chariot and with drawn bow

293

charges into a mêlée of Asiatics 'trampling on hundreds of thousands, putting them into confusion'; on the other side, in a parallel scene, the king launches himself into a tangled crowd of black enemies 'destroying this land of vile Kush'. In the former scene three registers of chariotmen support the king, and in the latter two of chariotmen and one of foot soldiers.

The two scenes on the lid show hunts in the desert: one is general, the quarry consisting of bubal-antelopes, gazelles, wild asses, ostriches and a lone hyena who is making its escape; the other is specifically a lion hunt of the kind known to have taken place in Syria in the New Kingdom.

The two ends of the box carry heraldic confrontations of the royal sphinx trampling on fallen enemies. Tutankhamun is 'the image of Re' and the 'son of Amun'.

TRAVELLING CANOPY

(Carter 123, J.d'E. 60705;
base 98.5 cm, height 201 cm)

FOOTSTOOL WITH ENEMIES

(Carter 378, J.d'E. 62045;
length 58.7 cm, width 31.7 cm)

In Egypt the sun is a blessing and a curse. It brings life to the land, and in antiquity was the omnipotent deity Re, and in the Amarna Period the Aten disk. It also made life uncomfortable, and for general living the Egyptian house had no large windows.

Associated with, and probably belonging to, the 'ecclesiastical throne' was this footstool. It is made of a very ordinary wood but with a top surface rich in decoration and full of significance. There are nine figures of captives, the conventional enemies of Pharaoh, depicted as distinctive racial types – but general rather than particular. Four are of black peoples and five of Asiatics and Libyans. Eight wear long garments, each with somewhat different arrangements of folds and pleatings. One, however, wears what appears to be a loose cloak which leaves some of the body exposed. Their hands are bound together and their necks are linked by a cord. The text on the dividing bar in the centre is quite explicit: 'all lands and all mountainous countries, and the great ones of Retjenu (Syria) are together as one beneath your feet, like Re for ever'. The bodies are gilded, and exposed flesh is of ebony or cedar; the background is made of plaques of blue faience.

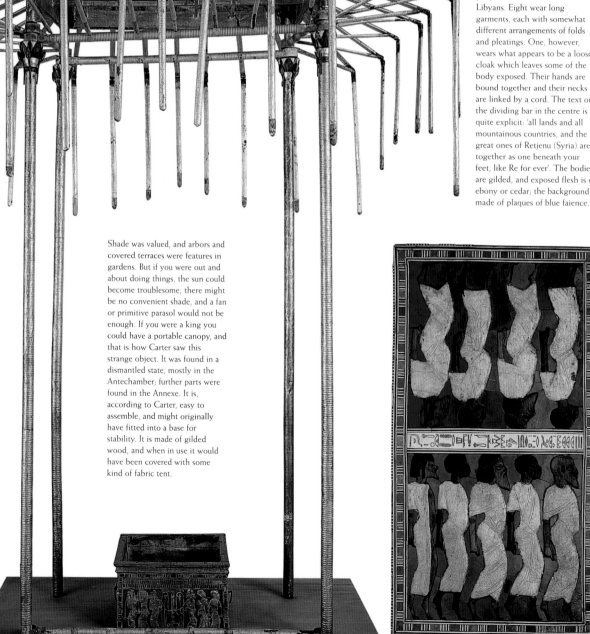

Shade was valued, and arbors and covered terraces were features in gardens. But if you were out and about doing things, the sun could become troublesome, there might be no convenient shade, and a fan or primitive parasol would not be enough. If you were a king you could have a portable canopy, and that is how Carter saw this strange object. It was found in a dismantled state, mostly in the Antechamber; further parts were found in the Annexe. It is, according to Carter, easy to assemble, and might originally have fitted into a base for stability. It is made of gilded wood, and when in use it would have been covered with some kind of fabric tent.

CEREMONIAL THRONE

(CARTER 351, J.D'E. 62030;
HEIGHT 102 CM, WIDTH 70 CM,
DEPTH 44 CM)

This highly decorated throne was found dumped unceremoniously in the Annexe of the tomb – poor treatment for such an important object. It is in the form of a folding stool with a back added, and is richly elaborate. Carter compared it with the faldstool used by bishops in cathedrals, and it has often been called the 'ecclesiastical throne'. The carved seat is marked with inlays to represent a leopard's skin. The legs terminate in duck heads, and between the legs the open-work design representing the union of the Two Lands has been partly broken away by robbers, for the gold covering.

The glory of this piece is its back: wood covered with gold plate and inlaid with semiprecious stones and colored glass. In the long inscriptions running vertically down the back, Tutankhamun is named as such, but above, on either side of the vulture's spread wings, he is Tutankhaten. The sun-disk in the middle of the frieze of *uraei* is given the names of the Aten in their later forms. It is a throne made early in the reign, and then modified with later forms of the royal name.

FALSE FOLDING STOOL

(CARTER 83, J.D'E. 62035;
LENGTH 47 CM, WIDTH 31.7 CM,
HEIGHT 34.3 CM)

Stools were the most common seats in Egyptian houses. In the New Kingdom folding stools were much used, the tops consisting of leather or animal fur.

In typical Egyptian manner, the real was reproduced in imitation, and false folding stools were made with fixed seats decorated like animal skins.

This superior example from the Antechamber is made of ebony, and the seat, which is double coved, imitates a leopard skin, with the markings made of

CHAIR WITH THE GOD HEH

(CARTER 87, J.D'E. 62029;
HEIGHT 96 CM, WIDTH 47.6 CM, DEPTH 50.8 CM)

In many respects this is the most aesthetically satisfying chair from the tomb. It may lack the splendor of the Golden Throne, and the intricate decoration of the ceremonial throne, but it has elegance, style and the distinction of restrained decoration. It is a typical chair of the New Kingdom, with coved seat, sloping back and lion legs. It is made of a fine-grained hard wood, possibly cedar, and embellished tastefully with some gilding. Between the legs there was originally gilded fretted decoration in the form of the heraldic

representation of the union of the Two Lands, but most of the gilded wood was torn away by thieves in antiquity. The back of the chair has a figure of the god Heh kneeling on the sign for 'gold'. He holds notched palm-branches in his hands, the usual divine indication of long reign for the ruling king. A large *ankh*-sign of 'life' hangs on his right arm. Most beautifully carved texts around Heh and on the frame of the chair contain Tutankhamun's titulary and proclaim his divine origins. It was found carelessly tumbled in the Antechamber.

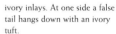

ivory inlays. At one side a false tail hangs down with an ivory tuft.

It is also possible that at each corner a paw hung down, but that these were torn away in the robbery because the claws were of gold. The legs terminate in duck heads inlaid with ivory, their beaks with pink-stained tongues clasped on the cross bars, which are embellished with gold. The foot-stool shown here was not found with the stool. It is of simple design with some ivory inlay.

CHILD'S CHAIR

(CARTER 39, J.D'E. 62033;
HEIGHT 71.1 CM, WIDTH 36.8 CM,
DEPTH 39.4 CM)

This robust little chair is very much an everyday piece of furniture, even if the everyday was that of a young member of the royal family. It was found in the Antechamber, and Carter reasonably suggested that it was used by Tutankhamun when he was a child. It is made of ebony inlaid with ivory, and embellished with gold panels in the arms carrying embossed representations of ibexes and desert plants. The joints are pinned with copper rivets capped with gold.

In form the chair illustrates the most common construction of chair found in Egypt. The back is curved, and slopes slightly backwards, supported by three vertical slats. The seat is made of five slats, curved in both directions and fastened to the main frame with mortise and tenon joints. The legs are lion inspired and end in lion paws with ivory claws, under which are gold capped drums marked with concentric circles. A lattice-work of struts holds the legs firmly together.

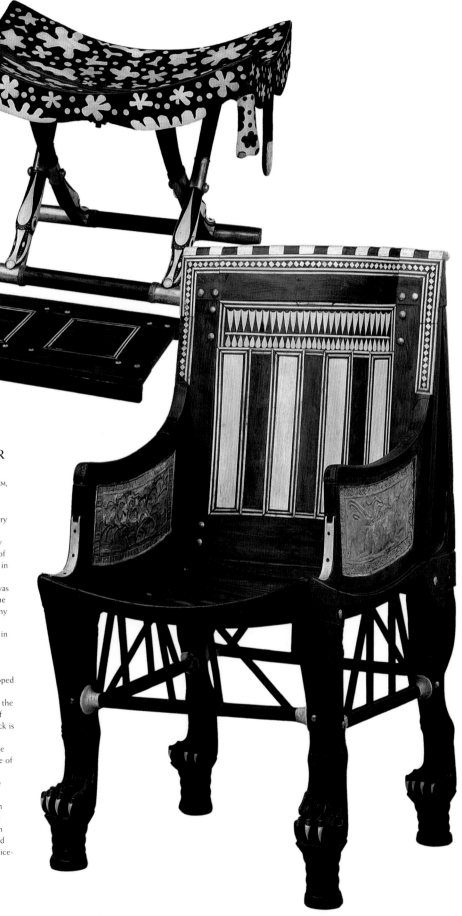

BED WITH LION HEADS

(CARTER 497; LENGTH 177 CM, WIDTH 103 CM, HEIGHT 37 CM)

Among the jumble in the Annexe were four beds. This one was in poor condition, and its footboard had been wrenched away from it.

The footboards of Egyptian beds are often incorrectly called headboards. In ancient times in Egypt, however, you slept with your head-rest at the open end and with your feet pointing towards the footboard.

It is characteristic of Egyptian beds that they were made with curves to hold the body in the bed, and the cross trusses underneath are bowed to take the sag of the mattress when a body is lying on it.

This bed is gessoed and gilded all over. It is low to the ground, and the legs are leonine, stumpy and thick. The two legs at the head end are continued through above the frame to show lion heads – almost finials – which would protect the sleeping occupant of the bed. The lions' eyes are inlaid with quartz and colored glass.

BED WITH FLORAL FOOTBOARD

(CARTER 466, J.D'E. 62014; LENGTH 175 CM, HEIGHT 68.6 CM)

Carter considered this bed to have the best proportions of all the non-ritual beds found in the tomb. It stands relatively high on its lion legs, and it is elegantly bowed from front to back. The so-called drums underneath the lion paws here and on much other furniture were designed to facilitate the stabilization of the bed on uneven floors.

The whole bed, including the mattress, is gilded. When in use it would have been lavishly piled with linen to soften the surface. The footboard is divided into panels of decoration embossed in the gold foil. In the centre is the conventional heraldic design of the union of the Two Lands of Upper and Lower Egypt. On either side are two panels, one showing a clump of papyrus, the other, narrower, a trophy bouquet of papyrus and lotus flowers. In these designs Carter claimed to see the influence of Amarna naturalistic art.

BED WITH OPENWORK FIGURED FOOTBOARD

(CARTER 47, J.D'E. 62016; LENGTH 185 CM, WIDTH 90.1 CM, HEIGHT 74.9 CM)

Of the six beds found in Tutankhamun's tomb, this one may have been a truly functional piece of domestic furniture. There was also a folding bed which could have been used on travel or campaign, but not at home and certainly not in the palace. This bed, from the Antechamber, has the characteristic bowed shape, with a mattress of woven string between the main frame. It is made of ebony and has lion legs and feet. Its most notable feature is the footboard: it has three panels, each containing three figures in openwork – centrally the god Bes, a leonine dwarf with a lotus headdress, a domestic deity charged to protect the home; he is flanked by two rampant lions with similar headdresses, their front paws resting on *sa*-signs signifying 'protection'. These finely carved figures are embellished in part with gold leaf, and all have tongues of pink-stained ivory. Here is powerful protection for whoever slept on this bed.

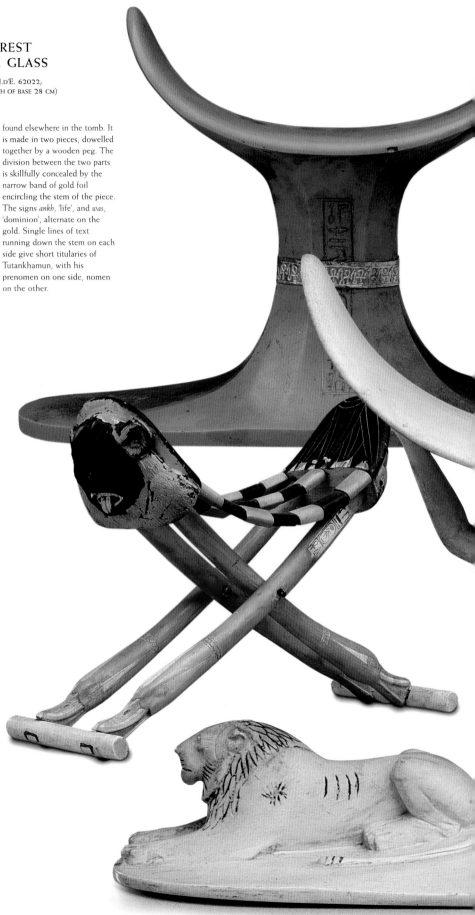

HEADREST OF BLUE GLASS

(CARTER 403A, J.D'E. 62022;
HEIGHT 18 CM, WIDTH OF BASE 28 CM)

All four of the headrests illustrated here were found in the cabinet on tall legs. Carter did not think that they were originally intended for this cabinet, but were stored there after the robberies. They form a remarkable group, put together no doubt fortuitously by the Necropolis guards.

This example is made of turquoise-blue glass, an unusually large piece for this material, although outclassed by another headrest in violet glass found elsewhere in the tomb. It is made in two pieces, dowelled together by a wooden peg. The division between the two parts is skillfully concealed by the narrow band of gold foil encircling the stem of the piece. The signs *ankh*, 'life', and *was*, 'dominion', alternate on the gold. Single lines of text running down the stem on each side give short titularies of Tutankhamun, with his prenomen on one side, nomen on the other.

HEADREST AS A FOLDING STOOL

(CARTER 403D, J.D'E. 62023;
HEIGHT 20 CM, WIDTH 26 CM)

This headrest is almost a joke-piece. The shape is that of the folding stool common in the Eighteenth Dynasty. It is made almost entirely of ivory, stained to great effect; it cannot be folded, but at the cross points where the legs would have folded small bronze pins are inserted. The legs terminate in duck heads, the beaks being dowelled to the white-painted wooden batons which form the stands. The object is outstanding for the two heads of Bes which ornament the ends of the actual rest. The faces are stained green, like some of the segments of the rest. Bes, as ever, sticks out his tongue – a vulgar gesture to warn off demons, snakes, scorpions and other harmful agents which could damage the sleeping person. Bes was, in spite of his grotesque appearance, a much loved domestic deity: by terror he turned terror away. The backs of the Bes heads are marked with lotus flowers. Tutankhamun's prenomen is inscribed at the top of one leg.

BLUE FAIENCE HEADREST

(CARTER 403B, J.D'E. 62021;
HEIGHT 19 CM, WIDTH 27 CM)

The best Egyptian ceramic craftsmen were highly skilled in producing flawless objects. Their technical processes are still not fully understood, but completed examples like this headrest and the glass example shown opposite demonstrate their remarkable control over materials prone to misbehave in the kilns.

This faience piece is a supreme example of this control in form and in the regularity of the color of the glaze. It is made in two parts, dowelled together, with the join again concealed by a gold foil band, decorated with a lozenge pattern inlaid with blue, red and green. Pale green glass is used for the king's cartouches on either sides of the stem, in each case flanked by *uraei* wearing the crown of Upper and Lower Egypt, all over the sign for 'gold'.

Tutankhamun was well served with headrests, to fulfil the invocation in the Book of the Dead: 'your head shall not be taken from you afterwards; your head shall not be taken from you for ever'.

IVORY HEADREST WITH SHU

(CARTER 403C, J.D'E. 62020; HEIGHT 17.5 CM, WIDTH 29.2 CM)

Wooden headrests, undecorated, of simple form and essentially practical, are found in many Egyptian burials from the time of the Old Kingdom, but there is no reason to believe that they were only used after death. The future comfort of a deceased person, however, would require the provision of a headrest among the tomb equipment, and specially made examples could be elaborately designed and decorated. This very imaginative example incorporates the idea of the head being lifted up to heaven on the hands of Shu, the god of the atmosphere, who separated Earth (Geb) from Sky (Nut). It is made of ivory, in two pieces, held together by a wooden peg, which is further secured by two gold rivets on each side of the body. Shu is shown as a man wearing a kilt and a tripartite wig. On each side of the base are two lions, representing the mountains of the eastern and western horizons.

A short titulary of Tutankhamun is incised on the back pillar of Shu; the king is described as 'son of Amun'.

CARTOUCHE-SHAPED BOX

(CARTER 269, J.D'E. 61490;
LENGTH 64.5 CM, WIDTH 29.8 CM, HEIGHT 31.7 CM)

This unusually shaped box, found in the Treasury, contained many pieces of jewelry, including the sets of earrings illustrated earlier. The reddish wood of which it is made is probably coniferous; there are ebony bands to embellish and strengthen the construction. The cartouche-shaped lid carries the name of Tutankhamun, executed in the most handsome hieroglyphs, made up of ebony and stained ivory. Less grand, but still elegantly formed, hieroglyphs are used for the many texts which are incised and filled with blue paint on the upper rim of the lid, surrounding the cartouche, and in three bands on the body of the box. They all include extended titularies of the king with a wealth of epithets establishing his authority at home and his power over foreign lands. The panel on the end of the box contains the king's two cartouches and his Horus name, beneath an extended sky-sign. It is thought that this box may have been used on state occasions to store changes of jewels.

CHEST WITH MARQUETRY PANELS

(CARTER 267, J.D'E. 61462;
LENGTH 44.45 CM, WIDTH 29.8 CM,
HEIGHT 27.9 CM)

A hieratic text on the lid of this box notes: 'Gold: jewelry of [or for] the funeral procession, made in the bed-chamber of Nebkheperure'. Jewels were found in it when the Treasury was cleared, but probably not those for which it was intended. But who can say? The chest, like so many in the tomb, and indeed in Egypt generally, was made of a fairly ordinary wood, and then embellished to give it a fine, finished, appearance. Good wood for joinery was not easily available in Egypt, and by this form of construction a fine external form could be made on a simple base. In this case the fine external form consists of strips of ivory veneer on the box and the domed lid, and then panels outlined in thin strips of ebony and ivory, containing bone patterned marquetry. Carter estimated that there were about 47,000 separate pieces of tiny inlay of ebony and other woods, each individually placed, stuck in position and subsequently polished. The knobs are made of pink-stained ivory.

ORNATE CHEST

(CARTER 551 (BOX), 540 (LID), J.d'E. 61477;
LENGTH 72 CM, WIDTH 40.6 CM, HEIGHT 63.5 CM)

The scenes on this masterpiece
of Egyptian decorative art are
focused on the domestic life of the
king and queen, rather than the
warlike activities given such
prominence in the tomb. The
chest found in the Annexe
separated from its humped lid is
made of an ordinary soft wood
veneered and embellished with
ebony and ivory, much of it
stained in muted colors; there are
also colored faience inlays and
gilding on the cornice. The
principal scene on the end of the
chest shows the royal couple
seated in a garden; the king shoots
his bow at birds and, it would
seem, fish in the ornamental pool.
The whole field is packed with
flowers, some growing and others
in trophies and bouquets. The
other sides of the chest have
further floral arrangements and
friezes of animals in a hunting
context, as found elsewhere in the
tomb. The domestic theme is
continued on the lid of the box,
which shows the king and queen
in a garden; she hands him
bouquets.

CHEST WITH OPENWORK DESIGN

(CARTER 271, J.d'E. 61344; HEIGHT 42.5 CM,
LENGTH 48.2 CM, WIDTH 44.4 CM)

Like all the boxes in the tomb
this chest from the Treasury was
rifled and repacked. Inside it is
divided into sixteen compartments,
thought to have contained objects
of precious metal. On discovery it
held the king's personal writing
equipment and a few other objects
not originally intended for it.
It is made of a softish plain
wood, richly embellished with
ivory veneer and gilded wood. Its
most noticeable decorative feature
consists in the repeated groups of
four gilded hieroglyphs: two *was*-
scepters flanking an *ankh*, all placed
above a basket signifying 'all', the
group meaning 'all life and
dominion'. This motif makes up
the decoration on all the sides and
also the top of the box. The feet of
the box are shod with bronze, and
the knobs used to secure the box
with sealed cord are of pink-
stained ivory. The extensive texts
which fill all the available surfaces
contain the royal titulary, repeated
many times with variants of the
epithets. In a few places the name
Ankhesenamun is also included.

303

Vessels and Other Objects of Calcite

The material used in Egypt from Predynastic times for the production of the majority of stone vessels has traditionally been called alabaster, but it is more correctly called calcite. It is a crystalline form of calcium carbonate, is white to yellow in color, translucent, and often very attractively banded or zoned. Up until the New Kingdom most Egyptian 'alabaster' was quarried at Hatnub, about twenty kilometers from El-Amarna.

This stone is relatively easy to work, and, as can be seen from the vessels and other objects found in Tutankhamun's tomb, it could be carved with great virtuosity. The largest and most important calcite object from the tomb is the Canopic Chest. More humble are the sixty or so vessels of traditional, simple forms, receptacles for oils, unguents and other materials for the use of the dead king in the afterlife. Some were made and inscribed in earlier reigns and had clearly been taken from storerooms for convenience. In addition, there were about twenty others, some of which were also used for precious materials, but were carved in fantastic and extravagant shapes which displayed remarkable craftsmanship but not always a taste that can still be appreciated. A common design element is the heraldic device signifying the union of Upper and Lower Egypt; it consists of a central sign with the meaning 'unite', on each side of which are tied lilies and papyrus stems and flowers, representing the Two Lands.

Some of the vessels are lamps, and some copy forms which might otherwise be made of less durable materials, like the chest and the most attractive ointment pot with a lion on its lid. Many of these intricate pieces were carelessly strewn around the tomb, possibly by the ancient robbers, and it is remarkable that a piece like the standing lion unguent vessel has survived virtually intact. One of the most elegant of the vessels is the so-called wishing cup which carries a good-will text on its rim. Some, like the ornate boat in a tank, have no obvious purpose; they were, perhaps, simply ornamental.

304 Bulbous calcite perfume vessel flanked by clumps of papyrus plants and the notched palm branches which were used symbolically to represent the long life of the king, terminating in tadpoles and shen-signs.

305 Elaborately designed perfume vase of calcite. It is jug-shaped, with the stems and flowers of lily and papyrus on either side. The whole is supported by an unidentified male figure with a lotus chalice on its head.

PERFUME VESSEL WITH NILE GODS

(CARTER 210, J.D'E. 62114;
HEIGHT 70 CM, WIDTH 36.8 CM)

Complicated vessels like this container were among the objects from the tomb which for many years were rejected by puritanical connoisseurs and austere designers as being outrageously vulgar. It is now easier to observe something as intricate as this without condemning it out of hand, while at the same time wondering why so much effort had to be put into the making of a simple bottle for scented oil. Who could easily pour a few drops of the precious liquid from something as unwieldy as this?

Symbolism here takes precedence over functionalism. The rebus of the main design represents the union of the Two Lands, spelled out in a wealth of symbols. The body of the vessel itself represents the *sma*-sign of unity; on its left stands a plump Nile god wearing a clump of papyrus on his head and catching hold of the fret of papyrus plants tied to the *sma*-sign. This all stands for Lower Egypt, the Delta, and this point is emphasized by the *uraeus* wearing the red crown of Lower Egypt perched on a scepter set behind the papyrus plants. On the right is Upper Egypt, with another

Nile god with a lily clump on his head, and grasping lilies tied to the *sma*-sign; here the *uraeus* wears the white crown of Upper Egypt. Overseeing the whole is a vulture with outstretched protective wings perched on the lip of the vessel. It wears an *atef*-crown and should be Nekhbet. The text on the neck of the vessel proclaims of the king: 'you have united Upper and Lower Egypt under your sandals; you will be on the throne of Horus like Re for ever'. Both Tutankhamun and Ankhesenamun are named on the body of the vessel. The fretted base shows the royal prenomen supported by two figures of Horus, all resting on signs for 'gold'.

This extravagant piece is made out of four pieces of calcite cemented together. The principal elements are highlighted with gilding and inlays of colored paste or faience. A fine detail is the gilding of the bodies of the two *uraei*, which curl down the lengths of the scepters on which they perch.

This vessel stood in front of the doors of the second shrine in the Burial Chamber.

LAMP WITH PAINTED SCENE

(CARTER 173, J.D'E. 62111;
HEIGHT 51.4 CM, WIDTH 28.8 CM)

During the New Kingdom most domestic lamps were in the form of simple open pottery saucers in which oil – probably sesame or castor – was burned with a floating wick of linen. The lighting arrangements in great houses would be expected to be more elaborate, and two pieces from Tutankhamun's tomb confirm this supposition.

The triple lamp is an elegant piece, fit to grace an ancient drawing room. The lamp shown here, however, is more formal,

grander, and unique in its decoration. The lamp itself is in the shape of a lotus chalice which is flanked by fretted side pieces which incorporate figures of the god Heh, supporting cartouches with the king's name (left) and prenomen (right) placed on signs for gold, and accompanied by *ankh*-signs of life. The figures of Heh kneel on baskets supported by clumps of papyrus. The outer edges of the side pieces are formed of notched palm branches, indicating the long life offered to

the king by Heh. The lamp with the side pieces is cemented to a calcite base in the form of a low table with fretted trellis-work.

The promised long reign of Tutankhamun is the theme of the design of this lamp, and it is taken up again in the most unusual painting, which can only be seen properly when the lamp is lit. The scene is painted on the inner side of a thinly shaped calcite insert which fits closely in the bell of the lamp itself. The fit is well-nigh perfect, and this precision says

much for ancient craftsmanship. The scene which shines through the translucent calcite shows the king, wearing the blue crown, seated casually on a throne, and in front of him stands Ankhesenamun holding out two notched palm branches: she is presenting him with the symbols of a long reign. On the other side of the lamp can be seen, again through the calcite, the names of the king who is 'the good god, lord of the Two Lands, lord of achievement' and 'son of Re, his beloved, lord of diadems'.

CALCITE PERFUME VASE

(CARTER 57, J.D'E. 62116;
HEIGHT 52.9 CM)

The variant forms used by
Egyptian stone-vessel designers
seem to have been infinite, even
when the basic theme was
conventional. This perfume or
unguent vase is no exception. It
was found along with other fine
examples in the Antechamber,
leaning against the wall between
two of the great ritual couches. It
had been opened and its contents
removed by the ancient robbers.
The container for the precious
material has a long neck and
bulbous body, and it is enclosed by
the design representing the union
of the Two Lands of Upper and
Lower Egypt. The container here
itself stands for the sign for union,
and the plants of the two parts of
the country are entwined around it
– the papyrus of Lower Egypt on
the right and the lily of Upper
Egypt on the left. On the outside
on each side is the notched palm
branch ending in the tadpole and
shen-sign, standing for a royal reign
of millions of years. This upper
part is cemented to a base shaped
like a table with struts. The
inscription gives the two names of
Tutankhamun in cartouches.

PERFUME VASE WITH PAPYRUS COLUMNS

(CARTER 61, J.D'E. 62117;
HEIGHT 61 CM)

This is one of the group of
perfume vases which were stacked
between two of the ritual couches
in the Antechamber. The theme in
the upper part is the union of the
Two Lands. In detail, however,
these vases differ from each other.
For example, a more complicated
knot unites the various stems
around the neck of this vase. Along
the base of the upper part the
environments of the two plants are
suggested: on the left the bases of

papyrus plants springing from a
marshy bed, on the right a checkered
pattern, probably representing a
system of irrigated plots for the
growing of lilies. The lower part (not
shown here) takes a novel form. The
central stand, flaring out widely at
the base, is flanked by papyrus-
capital columns, linked to the central
stand higher up by extraordinary
spirals carved out of the calcite. The
royal cartouches are inscribed on the
body of the vase.

THE LOTUS CHALICE

(CARTER 14, J.D'E. 67465; HEIGHT 18.3 CM)

When the excavators entered the tomb they found this vessel lying on the floor. It is a stemmed cup in the form of an open lotus flower with two elaborate handles. These take the form of a lotus flower and buds, on top of which is a basket supporting a kneeling figure of Heh, the god of a million years, who holds in each hand a notched palm branch which ends at the bottom with a tadpole and the *shen*-sign – the whole group indicating an eternity of reign for the king. A text on the side, inlaid with blue paint, gives the king's two cartouches and describes him as 'beloved of Amon-Re, lord of the thrones of the two lands, lord of heaven'. One half of the text running around the rim gives the king's titulary; the other half contains a wish: 'May your *ka* live, may you pass millions of years, you who love Thebes, sitting with your face towards the north wind, your two eyes seeing happiness'. Hence it has been called the 'wishing cup'. The lotus represented in this cup is the white variety which in ancient Egypt seems especially to have been used as the model for fine drinking cups. There is a fragment of a plaque in the collection of Eton College which actually shows Tutankhamun drinking from a lotus cup.

PERFUME VASE WITH HATHOR HEAD

(CARTER 60, J.D'E. 62118; HEIGHT 50 CM)

A somewhat more elaborate variant of the idea of the union of the Two Lands forms the main design in this vase. One may speculate about the significance to be placed on the use of this design on these great vases: it may have been used just for its satisfactory appearance and its ability to be varied, rather than for any subtle political or funerary significance.

In this case, however, there is an additional religious reference in the design associating it and its contents with the cult of Hathor, a goddess of many aspects. Here her head is shown like a mask on the neck of the vessel, with a broad collar underneath; there are also two swellings below the decorated base of the neck which have been interpreted as breasts.

The base of the piece, made separately, includes two amuletic groups in which a central *ankh*-sign holds two flanking *was*-signs. The multiplicity of religious and amuletic references that may be found in the decoration of elaborate pieces like these perfume vessels suggests that there may have been no careful supervision over their designers, who were allowed to incorporate symbols almost at will.

PHOTOGRAPHIC CREDITS AND AKNOWLEDGEMENTS

All the photographs of the book are by **Araldo De Luca/Archivio White Star**, except for the following:
Antonio Attini/Archivio White Star: pages 96-97
The British Museum: page 48
Giovanni Dagli Orti: page 39 bottom
Elisabeth Daynes, National Geographic Image Collection: page 42 right
Kenneth Garrett/National Geographic Image Collection: pages 42-43, 43
Griffith Institute, Ashmolean Museum Oxford: pages 47, 49, 50, 51, 52, 53, 54, 55, 58, 59, 60, 61, 62, 63, 64, 65, 66, 67, 68, 69, 70 left bottom, 70 right, 70-71, 71 bottom, 72, 73, 74, 75
Suzanne Held: page 38 top left
Andrea Jemolo: page 86 bottom
NGM Art, National Geographic Image Collection: page 42 left
News International Associated Services: page 70 top left and center
Photobank: page 38 top right
Alberto Siliotti: pagees 38 left, 38-39, 39 top
Henri Stierlin: pages 91, 198 right

The Author and Publisher would particularly like to thank: Dr Jaromir Malek, Dr Diana Magee and Elizabeth Miles of the Griffith Institute, Oxford.

The Editor would like to thank:
H.E. Farouk Hosny – Minister of Culture, Egypt;
Gaballah Ali Gaballah – Secretary General of the Supreme Council for Antiquities;
H.E. Francesco Aloisi di Larderel – Italian Ambassador to Egypt;
Ali Hassan – Former Secretary General of the Supreme Council for Antiquities;
Mohamed Saleh – Former Director of the Egyptian Museum in Cairo;
Mohammed Shimi – Director of the Egyptian Museum in Cairo;
Carla Maria Burri – Former Director of the Italian Cultural Institute in Cairo;
Samir Gharib – Artistic Counsellor for the Minister of Culture;
Nabil Osman – Chairman of the Egyptian State Information Service;
Zaki Gazi – Director of the Cairo Press Center;
Gamal Shafik of the Cairo Press Center for the organization of the photographic assignment;
The staff and the curators of the Egyptian Museum in Cairo;
Alessandro Cocconi – photography assistant.